P9-CFC-245

THE ORTHODOX CHURCH AND INDEPENDENT GREECE 1821–1852

THE ORTHODOX CHURCH AND INDEPENDENT GREECE 1821–1852

BY

CHARLES A. FRAZEE
Associate Professor of History
Marian College, Indianapolis, Indiana

CAMBRIDGE
AT THE UNIVERSITY PRESS
1969

Published by the Syndics of the Cambridge University Press
Bentley House, 200 Euston Road, London N.W.1
American Branch: 32 East 57th Street, New York, N.Y. 10022

Library of Congress Catalogue Card Number: 69 10488
Standard Book Number: 521 07247 6

Printed in Great Britain
at the University Printing House, Cambridge
(Brooke Crutchley, University Printer)

CONTENTS

PREFACE

WHILE the ancient and medieval periods of the Byzantine church usually receive a great amount of attention from western scholars, ecclesiastical history after the Turkish conquest tends to be neglected. There is a prevalent feeling that not much of importance happened during these centuries of isolation, and yet it was during this time that the Orthodox church as it presently exists in Greece and Constantinople was formed.

The purpose of this study is to trace the history of the church as it emerged from the Ottoman period in independent Greece from the opening of the Revolution in 1821 until 1852. These thirty-one years cover the period when relations were severed between the church in Greece and the patriarchate of Constantinople. Then in 1852 the two churches were reunited with the reception of the Patriarchal Synodal Tomos by the government in Athens, and a new period of history begins.

The sources for this study have been the published works concerning this period, contemporary government publications and newspaper accounts, and the diplomatic correspondence between the western embassies in Athens and Constantinople and their governments. Unfortunately, it was not possible to consult the archives of the Foreign Ministry in Athens since these have not been rehabilitated following the events of World War II. The two standard histories of this period, written in Greek, are the books by Konstantinos Oekonomos and Metropolitan Chrysostomos Papadopoulos. Both can be recommended and were very helpful in the preparation of this work.

In the spelling of Greek names, I have attempted to remain as faithful to the original as possible. As a general rule, the dates given are those of the Julian calendar, which was in use in Greece during the period which this study covers. The one exception is the dating of the dispatches of the western ambassadors in Greece. In the nineteenth century the Old Style calendar was twelve days behind the Gregorian.

C.A.F.

ACKNOWLEDGEMENTS

I SHOULD LIKE to acknowledge the many people who assisted me in the preparation of this book. First I must mention Professors Charles and Barbara Jelavich of the History Department of Indiana University, whose suggestions and corrections were of great importance. Professor Wadie Jwaideh, Director of the Near Eastern Studies Program at Indiana University, reviewed those subjects dealing with the Ottomans. The idea for the study originated with the late Professor George Soulis, of the University of California at Berkeley. His encouragement was a major factor in the completion of the work.

I am most grateful to the directors of the British Museum and the Public Record Office, their counterparts in Paris at the Bibliothèque Nationale and the Archives du Ministère des Affaires Etrangères, and in Vatican City at the Archivio Segreto Vaticano and the Archivio della S. Congregazione di Propaganda, and at Munich in the Geheimes Staatsarchiv. In Athens my work was done mainly at the Gennadion Library and my thanks go to all who work there, especially Miss Eurydice Demetracopoulou. I am also grateful to the directors of the National, the Benaki, and Parliamentary Libraries in Athens.

Correcting the manuscript and suggesting stylistic revisions was done by my colleague, Gilbert Tutungi, who contributed a great deal of time and effort to this task.

The research for the study was possible owing to the generosity of the Foreign Area Fellowship Program, which provided a grant enabling me to spend a year in Europe. To the directors of this Program and to all others who have helped me in so many ways I sincerely want to offer my thanks.

C.A.F.

CHAPTER I

THE PATRIARCHATE AND THE CHURCH UNDER THE OTTOMANS

IN the early morning hours of 29 May 1453 the Turkish army of Mehmed II forced its way through the walls of Constantinople near the St Romanos gate after a six weeks' siege. Vainly trying to hold back the Janissary attack, the last emperor of Byzantium, Constantine XI Palaeologos, died in battle. For three days, the palaces, homes and churches of the city were at the mercy of the Ottoman army.

The sultan then ordered a halt to the looting and the work of restoration began, since Mehmed wanted this to be the new Ottoman capital. As soon as it was practicable the Greek survivors were moved into the area bordering the Golden Horn, known as the Phanar, and other Christians from the districts about Constantinople were commanded to reside within the city.[1]

Of immediate interest to Mehmed was the organization of these Christians into the Ottoman political and social structure. Islamic law and tradition provided his guide. The Christians would be grouped into a *millet*, a 'nation', under the religious and civil authority of their own church leaders. In this way the Ottoman officials could count on using the services of the natural leadership of the Christian communities throughout their domain for their own purposes. The Christian hierarchy thus became, paradoxically, a very important arm of the Ottoman political administration.

Obviously, the choice of a man to lead the Christian *millet* was of great importance to Mehmed. Since he still feared the possibility of western intervention against his conquest, the first requirement

[1] The best and most recent account of the conquest of the city is the volume by Steven Runciman, *The Fall of Constantinople, 1453* (Cambridge, 1965).

for the highest Christian official of the church of Constantinople had to be a strong anti-western, anti-papal bias. He found his man in Georgios Scholarios, known as Gennadios since becoming a monk in 1430, a man of proven ability and noted for his extreme opposition to the Latin church. Gennadios was summoned from a village near Adrianople where he had been taken as a captive after the capture of the city. An assembly of clergy and laity was organized as an electoral body, and Gennadios was chosen to be patriarch without a dissenting vote.[1]

The sultan invested the newly-elected patriarch, just as in the past this office had been performed by the Byzantine emperor, with the words, 'Be patriarch with all good fortune. You have our favor in all that you desire, possessing all the privileges which are necessary for your patriarchate. You may also have the Church of the Holy Apostles for your residence.'[2] In addition, the patriarch and all of the Orthodox clergy were exempted from paying the *kharadj*, the annual tax levied by Muslim rulers on subject Christians.

Thus the status of the patriarch of Constantinople, through the action of the sultan, was actually enhanced by the conquest. Not only was he the religious leader of millions of Orthodox, but he was also *millet-bashi*, 'head of the nation'—the person responsible before the sultan for the Christian population. His situation, however, was a precarious one, for what the sultan could do he could also undo.

Gennadios and his successors were painfully aware that they held office only so long as they retained the good will of their Muslim rulers. Gennadios' first term in the patriarchate ended after only two years; named a second time around 1462 he resigned a year later, while a third period as patriarch, in the summer of 1464, lasted but a few months due to the difficult relations which came to exist between the sultan and himself.[3] A pattern was set by Gennadios and

[1] There was no patriarch present in the city at the time of the conquest—the last incumbent, Gregorios III Mammas, unpopular because of his pro-Latin sentiments, had left for Rome in 1451. He died there eight years later.

[2] 'Ιστορία Πολιτικὴ Κωνσταντινουπόλεως [The political history of Constantinople], in *Turcograeciae*, ed. Martin Crusius (Basel, 1584), I, p. 43.

[3] The chronology follows R. Janin, 'Constantinople, le Patriarcat Grec', *Dictionnaire d'Histoire et de Géographie Ecclésiastique*, XIII, 674. George G. Arnakis summarizes

Mehmed which was repeated through the following centuries. The threat of deposition constantly hung over the head of the patriarchal incumbent—resistance to the sultan's will was a practical impossibility.

Within the upper ranks of the church hierarchy, the archbishops and metropolitans who served in the patriarchal offices of the Phanar, a select few, made up the Resident Synod. Its primary function was to advise the patriarch and to serve as the highest court of appeal for the Christian subjects of the sultan. From here, too, the patriarchal candidates were almost always chosen—the Synod, in fact, could complain to the sultan and have a patriarch removed. As might be expected, ambitious and disappointed prelates frequently did not need much of an excuse to bring charges against their chief. In fact, a newly elected patriarch usually took it as a matter of course that his chances of survival were slim—for the rewards of the patriarchate were great and often the temptation too strong and nature too slow for sultan and Synod to avoid terminating the length of service of any patriarch.

Contributing to the instability of the patriarchate was a practice commenced in the late fifteenth century when the Patriarch Markos II Chylokarabis gave the sultan a monetary gift at the time of his nomination. Thus a custom was begun which plagued the church throughout the Ottoman period, for what was once given came to be demanded. Occasionally the patriarchate simply went to the highest bidder. The sultans naturally found this arrangement to their advantage—the more often the patriarchate changed hands, the more 'gifts' came to the imperial treasury. This practice was not limited to the patriarchal office alone; its corrupting influence filtered through the whole of the church hierarchy. In time an annual contribution to the Ottoman treasury was also required—a sum which was continually being set at a higher level.[1]

the rights of the Christians as follows, (1) no Christian was to be converted to Islam against his will, (2) the administration of the church was to be free of Ottoman control, (3) church property was left intact and the church retained jurisdiction over marriage and divorce ('The Greek Church of Constantinople and the Ottoman Empire', *Journal of Modern History*, XXIV, Sept. 1952, p. 242).

[1] In 1672 Paul Rycaut noted that the patriarchate was in debt seven hundred purses, a sum which was so large that not even the interest could be met easily. It had also

The officials, lay and clerical, who staffed the church offices were almost exclusively drawn from the Greek community of the capital, the Phanar. Having acquired wealth from commerce and industry certain families here formed a privileged class in the Ottoman capital. Many had come from the island of Chios or from the cities of Asia Minor, some were ethnically Italian, all realized quickly that there were great opportunities in commerce and in the Ottoman bureaucracy, especially as translators. Others chose service in the church as their career. Beginning with the sixteenth century the power of the Phanariotes grew until it was all-powerful in the eighteenth.[1]

The policy of a church run by the Phanariotes was obviously one which reflected the attitudes of the aristocratic class from which the higher clergy were drawn; in practice this meant that nothing should be done to disturb the isolation imposed upon the Orthodox population. A strong anti-western sentiment was encouraged. For good reason, the Orthodox prelates were alarmed at the inroads of the Latin church in the Ottoman empire as the result of missionaries sent from Rome and the strong influence wielded by the French embassy at Constantinople. A counter-force was the result of Protestant moves towards the East. Both western churches made strong efforts to form parties favorable to them among the Orthodox churchmen. This only added to an already complex situation at the Phanar.[2]

Another development within the church during the Ottoman period was the increasing Hellenization of the Orthodox church in the Balkans. The most striking example of this was in the Danubian Principalities, which were filled with Greek tradesmen and officials in the seventeenth century; in their train came Greek churchmen.

become customary for the newly chosen patriarch to seize the property of his predecessor to help his own financial condition (Paul Rycaut, *The Present State of the Greek and Armenian Churches*, London, 1679, p. 98).

[1] A French visitor who visited Constantinople in the 1690s noted that the Phanariote laity held all the important positions of the patriarchate save four liturgical offices (Sieur de la Croix, *Etat présent des nations et églises Grecque, Arménienne et Maronite en Turquie*, Paris, 1695, pp. 20, 93, 116).

[2] For the best general summary in English of the problems between Orthodox and Catholic in a fair presentation to both sides, see Timothy Ware, *Eustratios Argenti, A Study of the Greek Church under Turkish Rule* (Oxford, 1964), pp. 1–33.

By 1721 the native Rumanian boyars had all been removed and Greek Phanariotes were appointed *hospodars*, or princes of the area. Large amounts of land came to be owned by the church, especially by monasteries, which were more numerous here than in any other Balkan land.[1]

The Serbs and Bulgarians were also made aware of the centralization and Hellenization policies of the Phanar in the eighteenth century. For some time, the church of Constantinople had claimed the right to intervene in those churches—a privilege which, in theory, was a part of ancient Byzantine practice. Thus the patriarch was called 'ecumenical', i.e. extending over the Balkans, Russia, and the areas of the Middle East where the Byzantine liturgical rite was followed. This universal jurisdiction was first challenged in the Balkans during the tenth century.

The Bulgarian church evangelized by Greek clergy from Constantinople for a time had hesitated between the Roman pope and the Greek patriarch. As part of the contest, the pope agreed to recognize the head of the Bulgarian church as a patriarch independent of Constantinople in 927. Eventually, the Bulgarian patriarch settled at Ochrid, where he retained his title until the Byzantine conquest of that city in 1020. The patriarchate had then been reduced to a simple archbishopric. The Latin occupation of Constantinople in 1204 enabled the Bulgarians to set up a new patriarchate—this time with the see city at Tirnovo—which lasted until the Turkish conquest of Bulgaria in 1393.

The same Latin conquest of Constantinople allowed the Serbians to assert their nationality while the patriarchate was in foreign hands. Thus, Stephen II established a Serbian metropolitanate in the thirteenth century which was raised to the dignity of a patriarchal see at Peć in 1346 by the great Stephen Dushan. At first the patriarch of Constantinople had reacted to this move by excommunicating the Serbians for their temerity, but after some twenty years, in 1375, the autonomy of the church was recognized.

[1] See Gerasimos Konidaris, Ἡ Ἑλληνικὴ Ἐκκλησία ὡς πολιτιστικὴ δύναμις ἐν τῇ ἱστορίᾳ τῆς Χερσονήσου τοῦ Αἵμου [The Greek Church as a civilizing force in the history of the Balkans] (Athens, 1948), pp. 89 ff.

This brings up the interesting question of the validity of the claims of the patriarch of Constantinople to universal jurisdiction in the Balkans. In the eyes of the Byzantines and the Greek people even to the present, the patriarchate was a supranational institution—whoever occupied the see of Constantinople was not just the head of Greek Orthodox Christians, but the spiritual leader of all eastern Christians not found in the other ancient patriarchates. The Serbians and Bulgarians obviously put this claim to the test when they set up national patriarchates with one of their own race holding the position. In their view such a national patriarch would be separate from, if not equal to, the Greek patriarch of Constantinople. There is ample evidence that the claim to ecumenicity by Constantinople was heavily dependent on Byzantine political and military power; when the latter failed, as in 1204, decentralization of the church in the Balkans followed.

At any rate, the strong position of the Greeks with the Ottomans in the eighteenth century allowed them then to make the following moves during the rule of the Patriarch Samuel. In September 1766 the Serbian patriarchate of Peć was suppressed, and in January 1767 the Bulgarian church was absorbed with the forced retirement of Arsennis, archbishop of Ochrid.[1]

The Serbian church had already suffered a number of hard blows ever since the national armies had been struck down at Kosovo in 1389. The continued conflict between the Habsburgs and Turks was an ever-present reminder to the Serbs that their position might be relieved. When the Austrian armies reached Serbia in 1689, the Serbs joined them; when the Habsburg force had to retreat, 37,000 Serbian families went with it, including the patriarch, to settle around Karlowitz inside Habsburg boundaries. Peć, however, continued to have its Serbian bishop until Samuel took it over. The Bulgarian church of Ochrid had been threatened by the Greeks already in 1737 but was able to resist at that time. Once the churches were in the hands of Greek prelates, the Hellenization of these Slavic

[1] R. Janin, *Dictionnaire d'Histoire et de Géographie Ecclésiastique*, XIII, p. 681. The Serbian patriarchate had been abolished soon after 1459 and restored again in 1557 owing to the influence of the Serbian-born Grand Vizir, Mehmed Sokolovich.

peoples went on apace. Church schools made the use of the Greek language common throughout the Balkans. The Serbs and Bulgarians who sought an education in these institutions ended by considering themselves Greek. Nor was the process of Hellenization limited to the church and education. Large numbers of Greek merchants and craftsmen had emigrated to all the major cities of the Balkans setting up a Greek bourgeois society there. Thus in financial and social affairs, as well as in educational and ecclesiastical matters, the eighteenth was the Greek century.[1]

While education played the major role in keeping the Greek language alive and the people aware of their Hellenistic heritage during the whole Ottoman period, a veritable renaissance of Greek letters began anew in the eighteenth century. The patriarchate was a strong advocate of this intellectual movement. Greek schools were established in Vienna, Odessa, Corfu, Moscow, Leipzig, Bucharest and Jassy. The same was true in the Ottoman Empire; there were two colleges in Constantinople, three at Ioannina, two in Thessaloniki, and one each in Adrianople, Philippopolis, Mount Athos, Kastoria, Schatista, Maschopolis, Kozani and Serrai. Everywhere Orthodox churchmen were involved in the rebirth of the national spirit.[2]

The official policy in the eighteenth century, as dictated by the church at Constantinople, remained geared to the *status quo*, contented with educational and social progress, shying away from the more dangerous field of talk concerning political independence. Then the French Revolution broke out, and reports concerning it circulated slowly but surely into the Ottoman hinterland. The more

[1] On the Serbian church, see Charles Jelavich, 'Some aspects of Serbian religious development in the eighteenth century', *Church History*, XXIII (1954), pp. 144, 152. The church of Montenegro alone remained independent of the patriarchate. The first Greek had been appointed to the patriarchate of Peć in 1737 at the insistence of the Dragoman Alexandros Mavrokordatos on the plea that the Serbs could not be trusted. The Phanariotes began a policy which led to the exclusion of any Serbian nationals in the episcopacy. See Jean Mousset, *La Serbie et son Église, 1830–1904* (Paris, 1938), pp. 36–40.

[2] Charles Eliot, *Turkey in Europe* (London, 1906), p. 310; Charles Diehl comments, 'She (the Greek Church) has given more thought, perhaps, to Hellenism than to religion' (C. Diehl, 'The Greek Church and Hellenism' in *Greece in Evolution*, ed. G. F. Abbott, London, 1910, p. 56).

active Greeks, members of the rising merchant class, could not help but be influenced by the dramatic news and assess their own situation.

A document appeared in Constantinople in 1789 entitled *Paternal Teaching*. It was signed by Anthimos of Jerusalem but was probably the work of the later Patriarch Gregorios V. The document is a polemic against revolutionary ideas, calling on the Christians 'to note how brilliantly our Lord, infinite in mercy and all-wise, protects intact the holy and orthodox faith of the devout, and preserves all things'. It warns that the devil is constantly at work raising up evil plans; among them is the idea of liberty, which appears to be so good, but is only there to deceive the people. The document points out that political freedom is contrary to the Scriptural command to obey authority, that it results in the impoverishment of the people, in murder and robbery. The sultan is the protector of Christian life in the Ottoman Empire; to oppose him is to oppose God.[1]

The church authorities in the capital had an opportunity to prove their devotion to the Sultan Selim III when the English fleet under Admiral Duckworth appeared off Constantinople in 1807. The Patriarch Gregorios V himself, with pastoral staff in hand, led a thousand Greek workers to help construct fortifications against the western invaders. The Ottomans could not have failed to appreciate the loyalty of their subjects at such a moment. What they could not see in the future was that the French Revolution had opened the door to fundamental changes which their system could not survive. The waves of revolution had reached the Balkans, inspiring men to devote their lives to freedom and liberty under their own government. At the time neither the sultan nor the patriarch could fathom the meaning of this spirit.

[1] Text as in Theodore H. Papadopoullos, *Studies and Documents Relating to the History of the Greek Church and People under Turkish Domination* (Brussels, 1952), pp. 143–5. See also Dionysios Zakythinos, *Ἡ Τουρκοκρατία: Εἰσαγωγὴ εἰς τὴν Νεωτέραν Ἱστορίαν τοῦ Ἑλληνισμοῦ* [The Turkish rule: An introduction into the recent history of Hellenism] (Athens, 1957), p. 82.

CHAPTER 2

PRELUDE TO REVOLT

THE revolutionary spirit which was born in nineteenth-century Greece was not the result of any single cause, but resulted from a series of interacting forces. First, there was the example of the French Revolution and the Napoleonic Wars, which whetted the nationalism of subject people everywhere. Then there was the continued success of Russian arms against the Turks which commenced with Peter the Great. The Greeks, suffering from Turkish rule, could not help but rejoice at every victory of this strong and powerful Orthodox state against their common enemy. After the Treaty of Kuchuk Kaynarca in 1774, the Russians had received the right to intervene in the Ottoman lands on behalf of the Balkan Orthodox. Greek sailors were allowed to use the Russian flag—the bonds between the two people were constantly being drawn tighter.

Another factor promoting dissatisfaction was the increasing wealth of Greek merchants and shippers, as a result of their taking over the position of the French in the Eastern Mediterranean following the Napoleonic Wars. Economic prosperity burgeoned for them, yet politically and socially they were aware of their second-class status as Ottoman citizens—a sentiment of exasperation resulted, which made them turn to thoughts of revolution.

This economic revival among the Greeks was paralleled by an intellectual movement of major proportions. Immediately the names of Rhigas Pheraios and Adamantios Koraïs come to mind. Both were men of great talent and irrepressible national spirit. Pheraios, once secretary of the Hospodar of Wallachia, had been educated to read French, German and Italian; he was musician, poet, philosopher and military tactician. But all of the talents of this versatile man were centered on the rebirth of an independent Greece. In his travels about central Europe and the Balkans he distributed revolutionary tracts to the Greeks, formed secret societies and left the spark of nationalism burning in the hearts of those who caught his spirit. His great *War*

Hymn, dedicated to freedom, is still one of the most popular patriotic literary pieces of his countrymen in modern Greece. To a life spent in activities devoted to his country, Rhigas added his own blood, when, in 1798, he was executed by the Turks in Belgrade.

Adamantios Koraïs, equally inspired by the future of Greece, was of a different stamp. He was a scholar, not a politician, a man who looked to the intellectual heritage of Greece as the basis of a new independent nation. Living in Paris during the French Revolution, he was thrilled by its lofty declarations on the nature of man. Koraïs edited and translated the authors of ancient Greece, forming a library of twenty-six volumes which he believed demonstrated the everlasting vitality of the Hellenic spirit. He was the first to use modern Greek as a literary language. In his commentaries on the selections in his library, Koraïs incorporated the thoughts of a man imbued with the ideals of the Enlightenment. These books passed from hand to hand wherever Greeks lived and served to inspire his countrymen with thoughts of national glory. He lived in Paris until 1833, having seen his dream of an independent Greece come true.

Another who shared in the intellectual awakening of the Greeks prior to 1821 was Anthimos Gazis, the editor of *Mercure savant*, first published in Vienna in 1811. This was a literary magazine, devoted to Greek interests, which enjoyed considerable influence among Greeks all over Europe, but especially in Bucharest. Here was to be found a large community of Greeks committed to political as well as intellectual progress. The Wallachian capital contained a large Academy, a Philological Society, and was the home of two important contributors to Greek letters, Georgios Gennadios and Metropolitan Ignatios of Arta. A clear influence on the Greek spirit was the renaissance in Serbian literature led by Dimitrije Obradovich, as well as the military example given by Serbian warriors in their struggle against the Janissaries which began in 1804. A factor of real significance for the Orthodox church was that the men engaged in the literary revival—both among Greeks and Serbs—were seeking inspiration from the secular humanistic spirit of the West. Towards the church they were frequently very critical, for many of them believed it stood in the way of progress.

Contemporaneous with the activities of the Greek authors was the formation of secret societies. Most began during the Napoleonic era as nationalist reactions against French domination and were based on patterns borrowed from Freemasonry. After the Congress of Vienna had met in 1815 and failed to fulfil the aspirations of the members of these groups, most of them went underground and turned toward revolutionary activity. One of the few nationalist societies which operated in broad daylight was the Philomuse Society, sponsored by the Greek Ioannis Kapodistrias, who served in the tsar's foreign service as Russian minister at Vienna and later as foreign minister. Kapodistrias' intention was to organize a group of men who would provide funds so that Greek students might attend German and Italian universities and provide for a national revival through education.[1] At the head of the list of subscribers was Tsar Alexander I. The idea for the society had come from three Athenians some years before who sincerely believed in bettering the intellectual opportunities for Greek students. The Philomuse Society was especially successful in England where funds were generously given for this purpose. Kapodistrias also hoped that an academy might be founded at Athens and on Mount Pelion, but nothing came of this venture.

Prince Klemens Metternich of Austria was suspicious that the society, despite its respectable membership, might turn out to be revolutionary and, therefore, the Austrian police kept a close watch on its activities as long as it lasted. Its importance was that it provided education for many of the people who would later be prominent in the Revolution.

The most important of the Greek revolutionary groups was founded in Odessa in 1814. This was the 'Philike Hetairia', the Friendly Society, which gave the spark to revolutionary activities previous to the outbreak of the war. It began with a meeting of three Greek merchants, Nicholaos Skouphas, Athanasios Tsakalov and Emanuel Xanthos. These men gathered about them a group of patriots whom they initiated into the society with an elaborate ceremony in which the candidates pledged themselves to work for Greek

[1] For the early life of Kapodistrias, see *Αὐτοβιογραφία τοῦ Ἰωάννου Καποδίστρια* [Autobiography of Ioannis Kapodistrias], ed. Michael Laskaris (Athens, 1940).

freedom. Before long, branches of the society were established in many of the cities of Russia, the Principalities and Central Europe where Greek communities were to be found. Skouphas set up a branch of the Hetairia in Constantinople itself in 1818, but he died soon afterward.

The society had at its head a council of directors known as the Arkhi. Every member who was initiated promised on his knees unconditional obedience to his superiors, even if he had to kill members of his own family. This was only the first-class membership, and one might rise through increasing responsibilities until reaching the fifth level, which was made up of the sixteen members of the Arkhi. Supposedly, the emperor of Russia, Alexander I, sat at the head of this mysterious governing body. The orders coming from the Arkhi were written in code, signed with a seal bearing sixteen compartments containing sixteen sets of initials. Secret words and complicated codes were a part of every function. The messages from the Arkhi were carried out by personal contacts through well-paid agents known as Apostles.[1] These went through the Ottoman lands spreading the 'Gospel' which encouraged the Greeks to prepare to rise. Many of the leading Greek laity were enlisted as were the more independent bishops and priests.[2] Other Orthodox Christians in Slavic areas and even some dissatisfied Muslims were contacted and enrolled. The leader of the Serbs, Karadjordje, was initiated and contacts were also made with the Turkish governor of Epirus, Ali Pasha.

The leaders of the movement tried to persuade Kapodistrias to lead the organization, but despite all efforts he refused, feeling that armed revolt would be premature until there was a Greek educated class to provide leadership. His response was also dictated by his knowledge of the tsar's distaste for revolution, and he promised, 'If I can do nothing now, your chiefs can employ other means, and I

[1] On the Hetairia, see Ioannis Philimon, *Δοκίμιον Ἱστορικὸν περὶ τῆς Φιλικῆς Ἑταιρείας* [Historical treatise on the Philike Hetairia] (Nauplion, 1834), pp. 127 ff.; Spyridon Trikoupis, *Ἱστορία τῆς Ἑλληνικῆς Ἐπαναστάσεως* [History of the Greek Revolution] (London, 1853–7), I, pp. 21 ff. and the article by A. Otetea 'L'Hétairie d'il y a cent cinquante ans', *Balkan Studies* VI, no. 2 (1965), pp. 249–64.

[2] Among the clergy enlisted were the bishops of Methoni and of Argos-Nauplion (Valerios Mexas, *Οἱ Φιλικοί* [The Friendly Society], Athens, 1937, pp. 23, 54, and 167).

shall ask God to give them success'.[1] Kapodistrias would go no further than quiet membership. Efforts were also made to get the exiled Patriarch Gregorios, then on Mount Athos, to join. He was approached by the Apostle, Ioannis Pharmakis, but Gregorios refused to take an oath which would bind him to absolute obedience to a mysterious leader. He did not become a member but did nothing to discourage the society's activities.[2]

In Russia, the Greek Phanariote Katakazis succeeded in getting a number of prelates and military officials involved. Among these was Alexandros Ypsilantis, a Greek officer in the Russian army. In a matter of time Ypsilantis took over the direction with the title Ephor and Procurator General. He sincerely believed that the tsar would support an armed uprising, interpreting Alexander's off-hand remarks as firm promises of aid. The idea was fostered by the Arkhi that the tsar would furnish arms and money to the insurrection. In the Peloponnesus, the agents of the society were successful in enlisting the archbishop of Old Patras, Germanos, as well as a large number of other prelates and clergy who were initiated in 1819 and 1820. The society was much concerned to obtain Petrobey Mavromichalis, the chieftain of Mani, as a member. Petrobey was in close contact with the Patriarch Gregorios, and when the latter, while he was still patriarch, wrote encouraging him to found schools, the Greek chieftain supposed it to be a hint he should prepare for the Revolution, although the patriarch intended no such hidden meaning. In the islands and on the mainland the Russian consuls were the great promoters of the insurrection, laboring among the people to inspire them with patriotism. The consulate at Patras handled the correspondence of the Hetairia for the agents of the society in the Peloponnesus and served as their liaison with the Russian party.[3]

[1] Edouard Driault and Michel l'Héritier, *Histoire diplomatique de la Grèce* (Paris, 1925), I, pp. 125–6.

[2] Notis Botzaris, *Visions Balkaniques dans la préparation de la Révolution Grecque* (Paris, 1962), p. 96.

[3] Robert Walsh, *A Residence in Constantinople*, II, p. 183; George Finlay, *History of Greece*, ed. H. F. Tozer (Oxford, 1877), VI, p. 141; Germanos of Old Patras, Ὑπομνήματα περὶ τῆς Ἐπαναστάσεως τῆς Ἑλλάδος [Recollections of the Greek Revolution] (Athens, 1837), pp. 3–4.

Certainly there was no general agreement on when the blow would be struck, but the more active members did not want to wait too long. In 1821 the Ottomans were having difficulties with Persia and Ali Pasha was in revolt against the sultan in Epirus. It looked to many in the Hetairia that the opportune moment had come. Alexandros Ypsilantis was one, so he and his lieutenants planned a rising in the Peloponnesus to coincide with an invasion of the Principalities. With a handful of armed Greeks he crossed the Pruth River, the boundary between Russia and the Principalities, in March 1821, calling on all Greeks in the Ottoman Empire to rise against the Sultan Mahmud. The Revolution had begun.

CHAPTER 3

THE YEAR OF REVOLUTION—1821

WHEN Alexandros Ypsilantis crossed the Ottoman border with his small force of Greeks, he expected first that a Russian army would soon follow and second that his move would result in a general uprising in the Danubian Principalities. His goal was to shake off the fragile bonds which the Sultan Mahmud II still retained over these Greek-governed lands, while his brother Demetrios was commissioned to organize the rebellion in the Peloponnesus.

Alexandros came from one of the distinguished Phanariote families that had provided many officials in the Principalities. During the Serbian revolt of the early nineteenth century, his father, a former Hospodar of Wallachia, had been suspected by the Turks of aiding the insurgents. He had been seized, tortured and put to death. Alexandros and his brothers then had fled to Russia where he took service in the tsar's army, losing an arm at the battle of Dresden. Eventually he reached the rank of general and served on Tsar Alexander's personal staff.

Ypsilantis had been in contact with the then reigning Hospodar of Moldavia, Michael Soutzos. He too was a member of the Hetairia and was eager for revolt against the Porte. Both men believed that the native Rumanians would join the insurrection, forgetting that the instruments of Turkish rule in the Principalities were Greeks. Although the Orthodox church was common to both, it was hardly a sufficiently unifying factor.

A proclamation issued by Ypsilantis in Jassy called on the Moldavians to keep calm and invited them to throw off the yoke of the tyrant and recover their liberty. It concluded with an appeal signed by the Greek leader, 'I can assure you that Divine Providence has given you the prince Michael Soutzos, who governs you, to be a defender of the rights of your country, to be a father and a benefactor. He merits all these titles, unite yourselves to him, therefore, to defend the public good. If any desperate Turks make an incursion into your territory, fear nothing, for a great power is ready to punish their insolence.'[1] This confidence was based on Ypsilantis' fond hopes for help from the tsar, which proved to be all in vain. Upon hearing the news of the insurrection in some of the cities, Greeks began killing their Turkish neighbors and setting fire to their property. The students of Georgios Gennadios in Bucharest burned their books—it was time for action—formed a 'Sacred Battalion' and marched off to join Ypsilantis. In one village 300 Turks were killed, but, during the next few weeks, Ypsilantis saw his hard-pressed soldiers fight a losing battle. The invasion, far from stirring up the Rumanian peasants to join the Greeks, actually had the effect of rousing them against the Phanariote landowners and their own boyars. The Patriarch Gregorios condemned them, Tsar Alexander repudiated them, Soutzos left for Russia, and the Sacred Battalion was destroyed by a strong Turkish army at Dragashani. Ypsilantis fled to Habsburg territory where he was jailed by the authorities. As far as the Greek Revolution was concerned, the four months' expedition into the Principalities was a total failure.[2]

The news of the Greek incursion into the Principalities had important repercussions in two other parts of the world, in Laibach where the members of the Holy Alliance with representatives of Britain and France were consulting on revolutions in Italy and Spain, and in Constantinople where the Sultan Mahmud and the Patriarch Gregorios both heard the disturbing news of this threat to Ottoman stability.

Ypsilantis' move into the Ottoman Empire seems to have caught both the tsar and Kapodistrias by surprise. When the first announcement came to Laibach, the tsar is quoted as exclaiming 'Oh, the

[1] Quoted in *Annuaire historique universel pour 1821*, ed. Charles-Louis Lesur (Paris, 1822), p. 381.

[2] Paul Karolidis, *Ἱστορία τῆς Ἑλλάδος ἀπὸ τῆς ὑπὸ τῶν Ὀθωμανῶν Ἁλώσεως τῆς Κωνσταντινουπόλεως μέχρι Βασιλείας Γεωργίου τοῦ Α'* [History of Greece from the Ottoman conquest of Constantinople until the reign of George I] (Athens, 1925), pp. 656–65; Spyridon Trikoupis, *Ἱστορία τῆς Ἑλληνικῆς Ἐπαναστάσεως* [History of the Greek Revolution] (London, 1853–7), I, pp. 47 ff.; C. M. Woodhouse, *The Greek War of Independence* (London, 1952), pp. 50–1.

brave boy', while the Greek foreign minister took the more sober view, 'So, a premature revolution for Greece that is going to destroy all my efforts for a happy future'.[1]

A few days later the tsar was given a letter from Ypsilantis:

Do not disregard, Sire, the prayers of ten million Christians who, faithful to our divine Redeemer, are at the same time stirred by hatred for their tyrants. Save us, Sire, save religion from its persecutors; restore our churches and our altars that from the great nation which you govern the divine light of the Gospel may shine forth. Deliver us, Sire, purge Europe from the bloody monsters and deign to add to all the great titles which Europe already gives you that of Liberator of Greece.[2]

Whatever may have been the tsar's initial feelings, he was incensed to think that Ypsilantis had acted as if he had his support. He ordered Kapodistrias to reply to Ypsilantis informing him that Russia intended no intervention, and that he himself was no longer an officer in the Russian army. When the news of the tsar's reaction reached Jassy, there was utter dismay and then fear and resentment at Ypsilantis for having led people to believe Russia would support the revolution.

Kapodistrias did succeed in quietening the delegates at Laibach so that no official condemnation was issued by the Alliance. Metternich was nevertheless convinced it was just one more evidence of the influence of the Carbonari, already seeking to overthrow legitimate sovereigns in Italy and Spain.[3]

In the same month that the force of Ypsilantis invaded the Principalities, the Greeks in the Peloponnesus began their struggle for free-

[1] Edouard Driault and M. l'Héritier, *Histoire diplomatique de la Grèce* (Paris, 1925), I, p. 132; André Papadopoulo-Vrétos, *Mémoires sur le Président Jean Capo d'Istria* (Paris, 1837–8), I, p. 63.

[2] E. Driault and l'Héritier, *op. cit.* I, p. 132; Anton von Prokesch-Osten, *Geschichte des Abfalls der Griechen vom Türkischen Reiche in Jahre 1821 und der Gründung des Hellenischen Königreiches* (Vienna, 1867), III, p. 61.

[3] Stamatios Laskaris, *Διπλωματικὴ Ἱστορία τῆς Ἑλλάδος* [Diplomatic history of Greece, 1821–1914] (Athens, 1947), p. 8; see also *Αὐτοβιογραφία τοῦ Ἰωάννου Καποδίστρια* [Autobiography of Ioannis Kapodistrias], ed. Michael Laskaris (Athens, 1940), p. 105. Kapodistrias was in high favor with Tsar Alexander I but was disliked by Metternich (Charles Webster, *The Foreign Policy of Castlereagh, 1815–1822*, London, 1925, pp. 91 ff.).

dom.[1] During the winter of 1820 and 1821 the area had been tense with excitement. Acts of violence against individual Turks, the news of Ali Pasha's revolt, the intrigues of the Hetairists, all contributed to the agitation. There had been a meeting of some of the primates at Vostitsa in February, where it was agreed to send messages to Russia to sound out its intentions in case of an insurrection. Although they encouraged the monks of Megaspelaion to collect money for arms, the primates of the Peloponnesus had conflicting sentiments about a revolt. They occupied a privileged position among their countrymen; they gathered the taxes, ran the local government, and acted as mediators with the Turks, all of which would be risked by revolution. In good times the primates prospered; in bad, they might be called upon to borrow large sums in order to help the Greek peasants. In 1821, the balance was tipped for revolt, since conditions were poor and they were hard pressed by debts to the Turkish government so that 'a revolution seemed the readiest way of wiping out their accounts, and not only restoring, but strengthening their ascendency in the districts they inhabited'.[2] The higher clergy were sympathetic to this view. Then, in March, the Turkish authorities invited the Greek leaders, religious and lay, to come to Tripolis to discuss the measures to be taken in the Peloponnesus as a result of Ali Pasha's revolt.

The summons from the Turkish governor, Kemal Bey, to appear in Tripolis frightened the Greeks. There was still no word from the Hetairist agents sent to Russia. Some of the primates and bishops decided to go; others believed it best to find some excuse not to attend. The latter were guided by Bishop Germanos of Old Patras, who started out with his reluctant delegation on 18 March. Germanos and his party stopped at Kalavrita, where the archbishop claimed he was ill. A letter then arrived which purported to be from a Turk, but which was really a forgery, 'I am a Turk, but your friend and

[1] The population of the Peloponnesus in 1821 is estimated at 400,000, of whom 40,000 were Muslims (Thomas Gordon, *History of the Greek Revolution*, London, 1832, I, p. 54).

[2] George Finlay, *History of Greece*, ed. H. F. Tozer (Oxford, 1877), VI, p. 143. See also D. A. Zakythinos, 'Η *Τουρκοκρατία* [The Turkish Rule] (Athens, 1957), p. 33.

I fear God. I exhort you, do not accept the invitation of the Bey, because you and your colleagues will all be massacred...'[1] This bit of news gave the Greeks an excuse to delay, and a messenger was forwarded with the letter to Tripolis. Meanwhile, one of the primates, Andreas Zaimis, attacked the Turks. The news spread that the moment for revolution had arrived so that, throughout the peninsula, the Greeks fell upon their Turkish neighbors. At Kalavrita the standard of the cross was raised; near Kalamai 5,000 Greeks rallied on 5 April. Here twenty-four priests assisted at the Liturgy, 'Never was a solemn service of the Orthodox church celebrated with greater fervor, never did hearts overflow with sincerer devotion to Heaven, nor with warmer gratitude to their church and their God'.[2] On 25 March, Germanos gave the revolution its great symbol when he raised a banner with the cross on it at the monastery of Ayia Lavra.[3]

When he returned to Patras he was leading a band of a thousand armed peasants. Preceding the army, the clergy and monks marched singing psalms and promising the crown of a martyr to anyone losing his life in battle against the Turks. All over the Peloponnesus the Christians rose as well as in Attica and Boeotia. The towns of Salona, Levadhia and Talenti in eastern Greece fell within the month, and the islands of Poros, Idhra and Spetsai joined the revolt with their great resources of ships and sailors.

The bishops who had gone to Tripolis were seized by the Turks and imprisoned. They were eight in number: Kyrillos of Corinth, Chrysanthos of Monemvasia, Philotheos of Dhimitsana, Gregorios of Nauplion, Germanos of Christianoupolis, Philaretos of Olenos, Joseph of Androusa and Daniel of Tripolis. Of these five died while in prison; the others, Kyrillos, Joseph and Daniel, were freed when Tripolis was delivered by the Greeks in September 1821. Germanos' caution proved him right.

[1] Count Philippe Jourdain, 'La situation militaire et politique de la Grèce', 30 June 1821, Grèce, II, Paris, Archives du Ministère des Affaires Etrangères, Correspondance politique.

[2] G. Finlay, *op. cit.* V, p. 150.

[3] Metropolitan Germanos of Old Patras, Ὑπομνήματα περὶ τῆς Ἐπαναστάσεως τῆς Ἑλλάδος [Recollections of the Greek revolution] (Athens, 1837), pp. 12–15. Some historians now question the historicity of the events at Ayia Lavra.

The metropolitan of Old Patras was the most important leader of the Revolution in the Peloponnesus. He had been born in Dhimitsana in 1771 of poor parents, attended school in Argos; then ordained a deacon, he went to Smyrna, and later to Constantinople. Germanos had spent some time on Mount Athos, then returned to Constantinople to be consecrated archbishop of Old Patras in 1806. For two subsequent years, however, 1815 to 1817, he had stayed in the capital, where he was in close contact with the Patriarch Gregorios V. Back in the Peloponnesus, he threw himself into the work of the Hetairia with great enthusiasm.[1] Germanos was assisted by another cleric in his work for Greek independence; this was the Archimandrite Gregorios Dikaios, also called Papa Phlesas, known as an extreme and reckless person, not always too honest in his personal activities and constantly making promises of Russian aid.[2]

The role which devotion to the Greek church was to play in the Revolution is evidenced at once by Germanos' seizing the initiative and his direction of operations in Patras. The Turks had wisely withdrawn into the citadel above the city when news of the insurrection reached them. The British consul reported in a letter of 6 April, 'At present there may be about 3,000 Greeks in the town, who are employed in firing their small arms at the fortress. They have no cannon, but say they are expecting a large supply of ammunition daily. The arrival of Archbishop Germanos is anxiously looked for; he having been named in this emergency to the chief command.'[3] When Germanos arrived he offered the Liturgy, and all the Greeks swore an oath to deliver their country or die in the attempt, while the archbishop gave a general blessing to the army. The French consul, Pouqueville, noted that an ikon of Christ was raised in the square of Ayios Georgios and a cross put above the Turkish mosques. The priests baptized some Turkish children as a reprisal for the Turks having circumcised some Greek boys. At night the monks of Megas-

[1] For Germanos' life see Demetrios Kabouroglos, *Μελέτη περὶ τοῦ βίου καὶ τῆς δράσεως τοῦ Παλαιῶν Πατρῶν Γερμανοῦ* [A study of the life and work of Germanos of Old Patras] (Athens, 1912). His early life is contained in pp. 1–25.

[2] C. M. Woodhouse, *op. cit.* pp. 56–7; G. Finlay, *op. cit.* VI, p. 142.

[3] Quoted in W. Alison Phillips, *The Greek War of Independence* (London, 1897), p. 12.

pelaion led the army in the hymn of the Trisayion. The Revolution had become a Holy War.[1]

In the first year of conflict in the Peloponnesus, the bishops were often called upon to take the lead both in military and civil affairs. The various declarations issued by the revolutionists and the governments formed by them nearly always contained the names of at least one or two bishops and a number of clergy. The outstanding prelates of the Peloponnesus were Joseph of Androusa, Kyrillos of Corinth, Neophytos of Karystos, and, of course, Germanos of Old Patras. The church of the Peloponnesus had unanimously gone over to the side of the Revolution.[2]

The news that the Christian subjects of the Porte were in arms against him angered the Sultan Mahmud II and caused grave developments for the Orthodox church of Constantinople and its patriarch. Since his coming to the Ottoman throne in 1808, Mahmud had first settled the lingering Serbian conflict by appointing a native, Milosh Obrenovich, to be governor, but keeping the nation as a part of the Ottoman domain. Turkish garrisons remained in Serbia and the annual tribute to the Porte was continued. Mahmud then began a policy to reduce the nearly independent governors of the provinces of Anatolia and Egypt which met, however, with only partial success.

Ali Pasha of Epirus continued to act independently of the sultan's authority and even dared to send assassins to Constantinople to attempt to murder one of Mahmud's own officials. These agents of Ali were apprehended and the sultan determined to move against his unruly vassal. A *fetva*, a legal decision approving the sultan's action issued by the Muslim authority of the Ottoman Empire, the shaykh al-Islam, was obtained which declared Ali an outlaw and called upon all believers to join in the attack against him. One of the deciding factors for the Greeks in launching the revolt in the

[1] François-C. Pouqueville, *Histoire de la régénération de la Grèce* (2nd ed. Paris, 1825), II, pp. 333–4; Germanos, *op. cit.* pp. 17 ff.

[2] Maxime Raybaud, *Mémoires sur la Grèce* (Paris, 1824–5), II, p. 464. See also, for an account of the role of the church in the Revolution, Gerasimos Konidaris, '‘Ἑλλάς’ [Greece] in *Θρησκευτικὴ καὶ Χριστιανικὴ Ἐγκυκλοπαιδεία* [Religious and Christian Encyclopedia] (Athens, 1940), III, pp. 351 ff.

Peloponnesus had been the hope that the Ottoman army would be too occupied in Epirus to launch an all out attack against the Greek rebels.

Mahmud and the Porte officials had not expected the uprising in the spring of 1821. They no doubt were aware of the Hetairist agents but discounted them as a real threat. Moreover, the influence of Mahmud's most important counsellor, Halet Effendi, was such that no real preparations for defense were made. Halet Effendi had supreme confidence in the loyalty of the hospodars in the Principalities.

The invasion of Ypsilantis brought with it a flock of rumors. One report had it that this was only the beginning of an uprising by the *rayah* all over the Balkans against the Turks. The Porte was convinced of Russian support for the insurgents because the army of Ypsilantis had been organized on Russian soil, and this was sufficient evidence of the tsar's complicity. Ypsilantis dispatched a courier with compromising letters to the Hetairists of Constantinople, to the Russian ambassador, Baron Alexis Stroganov, and to the secretary of Patriarch Gregorios, which put the addressees in a very uncomfortable position. In order to allay Ottoman fears, Baron Stroganov circulated a memorandum to Russians living in Ottoman territories to stay away from the Greek revolutionists and turned the letters of Ypsilantis over to the officials of the Porte.[1] The Ottomans still were not convinced that the Russians were innocent.

Mahmud's suspicions were also centered on the patriarch, the man whose office made him responsible for Christian behavior in the Ottoman Empire. This was Gregorios V, now holding the patriarchate for the third time. The patriarch had been born in Dhimitsana (making him a fellow-townsman of Germanos of Old Patras) around 1750. At ten years of age he had been sent to Athens to study. In 1767 he began his theological studies and left there to follow the monastic life in the Ionian Islands at the monastery of Strophades, near Zante. Eventually he moved on to Patmos until he was invited by Prokopios, the Archbishop of Smyrna, to come to his see

[1] Robert Walsh, *A Residence in Constantinople* (London, 1836), I, p. 310; A. Otetea, 'L'Hétairie d'il y a cent cinquante ans', *Balkan Studies*, VI, no. 2 (1965), pp. 26 ff.

as archdeacon. When Prokopios was elected patriarch in 1785, Gregorios became bishop of Smyrna; in 1797 he was elected patriarch himself. It was a difficult time, for Napoleon had invaded Egypt, and Gregorios was accused of favoring the French. After eighteen months he was ousted and banished to Mount Athos.[1]

His stay on the Holy Mountain was ended when he was re-elected to the patriarchate in September 1806, where he was noted for his efforts to restore clerical discipline. It was during this term of office that the Sultan Selim III had been persuaded by Napoleon's envoy to Constantinople to enter the war with France against Russia and Britain in hopes of restoring Ottoman fortunes in the Black Sea area. While the Turkish and Russian armies were engaged in the Balkans, the British decided upon a naval expedition through the Dardanelles to threaten Constantinople. In charge of the fleet was Vice-Admiral Sir John Duckworth, but sharing his authority was a diplomatic envoy, Charles Arbuthnot. When the British navy appeared off the Ottoman capital in February 1807 it caused great alarm. The city was not prepared for an attack. It was at this moment of crisis that Gregorios supported his Turkish rulers, assisting in the strengthening of the city's defenses while Arbuthnot negotiated with the officials at the Porte. The delay caused by the talks was sufficient to enable the Turks to take the offensive and Duckworth had to withdraw.

Gregorios survived the deposition of Selim by the Janissaries later that year and continued in office under the new Sultan Mustafa IV. He was not so fortunate, however, when a counter-revolution led by Mustafa Pasha Bayrakdar, governor of Silistria, was successful in July 1808. Under Bayrakdar's direction, Mahmud, the brother of the now murdered Selim, became sultan. Shortly before his own assassination in the final weeks of 1808, Bayrakdar dismissed Gregorios who went into exile on Mount Athos.

After ten years of forced retirement Gregorios was re-elected patriarch of Constantinople for the third time in December 1818.

[1] Takis Kandiloros, *Ἱστορία τοῦ Ἐθνομάρτυρος Γρηγορίου τοῦ Ε′* [History of the national martyr Gregorios V] (Athens, 1909), gives a long account of Gregorios' life. See also Jules Blancard, *Etudes sur la Grèce contemporaine* (Montpellier, 1886), II, p. 116.

When he took up his duties again, he found the patriarchate was in debt almost 1,500,000 piastres, not counting the diocesan debts. Still Gregorios brought new ideas to his office. He had a printing press set up so that devotional literature might be distributed; some of his own works, as well as Scripture, were printed.

During this final period of his life, Gregorios also had to make some decisions concerning his relations to the Hetairia. He persevered in his original resolution to avoid joining it himself—the risks were too great—but quietly he permitted the work of the revolutionists to go on among clergy and people. He did not agree, however, either to the form of the oath of the Hetairia or the swearing of obedience to unknown authorities.[1]

The chaplain to the British Embassy in Constantinople, Robert Walsh, saw Gregorios during this time and describes a visit he made to see the patriarch. The Phanar, he noted, was an area surrounded by a wall and battlement, and consisted of a number of very narrow, dirty streets bounded by the harbor on one side and a considerable hill on the other. On the gate to the Phanar were hung the batons and insignia of the Janissaries whose job it was to guard the patriarchate. The church of Ayios Georgios, patriarchal church since 1712, was 'low and little dignified'; its one important relic was a portion of the pillar on which Christ supposedly had been scourged. The building in which the patriarch lived was entered by going up a long flight of stairs, then the visitor passed through large antechambers, 'splendidly furnished', until he finally was conducted into the patriarch's private apartments. 'In one corner was a post bed... and in the other was a divan on which he sat, with paper and materials for writing beside him. He was thin, pale, very aged, apparently past eighty years, with a venerable white beard; his dress was a robe of simple crape, which covered his head.' Walsh was much impressed by his simplicity—as a gift the patriarch gave him some Easter eggs.[2] Into the life of this aged prelate on a March day in 1821 came the disturbing news that a Greek army had invaded the Principalities announcing to all Christians that the moment of deliverance had come.

[1] T. Kandiloros, *op. cit.* pp. 123–34.

[2] R. Walsh, *op. cit.* pp. 240–4.

The failure to obtain correct information concerning the invasion only caused the size and extent of the rebellion to be magnified at the Porte. The letters of the staff of the British mission at the Ottoman capital trace these developments during the fateful spring of 1821. F. Chabert, a dragoman, or interpreter, at the English mission, wrote to Lord Strangford, the British ambassador, on 17 March, that when he arrived at the Porte, after the news of the Hospodar Michael Soutzos' defection had become known, he and the dragomans from the other foreign missions hesitated to approach the Ottoman officials, 'in the supposition that they would be found in extremely bad humor as a consequence of the flight of the agents of the Prince of Moldavia, and of the information which has come concerning the departure of the Prince himself'. He consulted Kiahya Bey, who held the position of Reis Effendi in the Imperial *Divan*, however, and learned that the Turks lacked definite news from the Principalities except for the information concerning the agents of the prince.[1]

Two days later, Chabert was writing to Strangford, 'it is believed that war against the Russians is decided upon'. But the Turks were still hesitant to accuse the tsar of complicity, since Baron Stroganov professed that his nation was not involved. In speaking to Kiahya Bey, Chabert found the Turk questioning the sincerity of the Russian and making the wild surmise, 'it seems that the motivator and the instigator of all these disorders is the famous Capo d'Istria'. The next report of Chabert to the British minister carried the information from the Reis Effendi that the papers of Soutzos and of Ypsilantis had been intercepted and that Kapodistrias was, in fact, giving them instructions. Such an interpretation was bound to be given to Ypsilantis' letters. The plan, he said, is to have an independent Greece, but he doubted their project could succeed without help from outside.[2]

The information received by Strangford was duly reported to the

[1] F. Chabert to Lord Strangford, Pera, 17 March 1821, Strangford MSS, 1, no. 29, British Museum Additional MSS 36299, hereafter Strangford MSS.

[2] Chabert to Lord Strangford, 19, 21 and 23 March 1821, Strangford MSS, 1, nos. 34, 36 and 39.

British foreign minister, Lord Castlereagh, in London in a letter dated 24 March 1821, including the Reis Effendi's suspicions about Russia and Kapodistrias master-minding the affair. The Turks had also said that the British-held Ionian Islands were to be included in the general uprising, and that 'although Russia might find it convenient to disavow these proceedings which had broken out sooner than she had wished, it was not the less true that she was at the bottom of them'.[1] In his further weekly dispatches during March to the foreign minister, Lord Strangford emphasized the fear that the Turks expected a general uprising of all the Greeks; that they 'had determined to strike terror into the Greek population by executing people, the members of whose families had fled the city'.[2] On 31 March an order was issued ordering every Turk to procure arms and keep them in his home lest the Ottomans be surprised by an insurrection—this was done on the pretext of Ypsilantis' instructions to the Hetairists to burn the Turkish capital. At the barracks of the Aga of the Janissaries, a depot of arms was set up to equip 12,000 to 15,000 men.[3]

April saw more random attacks against Christians—a reign of terror instituted against prominent Greeks by the Janissaries. Strangford was writing to London on 10 April: 'in the minds of the Turks, the highest degree of fury and exasperation has been produced.'[4] Churches came under attack, mobs roamed the streets looking for Christians. Walsh gives an eye-witness report:

A yong man, splendidly dressed, was dragged down the street where he stood. His robes were torn and covered with mud, his turban and slippers cast off in the struggle and his head and feet left bare. When arrived at the corner of the street, and suffered for a moment to take breath, he seemed endeavouring to expostulate; but he was forced upon his knees by two Turks pressing on his shoulders, and in that position a third came behind him with his kinshal... With a single horizontal stroke he severed

[1] Lord Strangford to Lord Castlereagh, Constantinople, 24 March 1821, F.O. 78, Turkey, vol. 98, no. 8, London Public Record Office, hereafter PRO.

[2] Strangford to Castlereagh, 24 and 31 March 1821, F.O. 78, Turkey, vol. 98, nos. 11 and 15, PRO.

[3] Chabert to Strangford, Pera, 31 March 1821, Strangford MSS, I, no. 59.

[4] Strangford to Castlereagh, 10 April 1821, F.O. 78, Turkey, vol. 98, no. 16, PRO.

his head from his neck; his body was thrown into the puddle in the middle of the street for passengers to trample on, and his head was laid contemptuously between his thighs. The executioners then hastily passed on, leaving both to be torn by the dogs who were gathering round.[1]

The news that Turkish citizens had been massacred by Greeks at Galatz and Jassy caused the Grand Vizir, Ali Benderley, to arrest seven Greek bishops, but this was only the beginning. On the evening of 2 April a messenger dispatched to Lord Strangford reached Constantinople from the British consul at Patras. He brought the report that all of the Peloponnesus had risen against the Turks. The British ambassador relayed the information to the Porte.[2]

These developments resulted in a hasty summons being sent by the Grand Vizir to the Patriarch and Dragoman of the Porte, Konstantinos Mourousi, to come to his apartments. There the two Greek representatives were accused of having knowledge of the revolt and of conniving with Petrobey Mavromichalis. Both pleaded innocence. Meanwhile, the sultan, thoroughly alarmed by the information about the uprising in the Peloponnesus, requested a *fetva* from the shaykh al-Islam announcing a Holy War against the Greek infidels. While the shaykh pondered over his decision, the patriarch met with him and successfully convinced him that only a few Greeks were involved. In a show of courage, the shaykh proceeded to reject Mahmud's request for the *fetva*. For his efforts, he was eventually exiled and killed, while a more obliging candidate was installed.[3]

The sultan's *divan* was convinced that Gregorios was at least in part to blame for the insurrection. The fact that many members of the Greek community in Constantinople were making hasty departures from the capital served to confirm their suspicions, although,

[1] R. Walsh, *op. cit.* I, p. 306.

[2] Chabert to Strangford, 16 April 1821, Strangford MSS, I, no. 88; also Memos from F. Pisani, 16 and 18 April 1821, Strangford MSS, III, no. 4.

[3] Chrysostomos Papadopoulos, "Ἡ Ἐκκλησία Κωνσταντινουπόλεως καὶ ἡ Μεγάλη Ἐπανάστασις τοῦ 1821' [The church of Constantinople and the great Revolution of 1821], Θεολογία, XXI (1950), p. 480; J. Blancard, *op. cit.* II, pp. 119–20. Three months later this newly chosen shaykh, while travelling by sea on a pilgrimage to Mecca, was seized by a Greek ship. He was killed by the sailors when his identity became known.

in fact, only a small minority of the Phanariotes really supported the Revolution.[1]

Gregorios called a meeting of the Greek leaders and people to discuss their common peril that same day after he had met with the sultan. Mahmud had demanded that the patriarch and Synod excommunicate those responsible for the uprising and those who had killed innocent Turks. At the patriarchate, therefore, the patriarch of Jerusalem, Polykarpos, four synodal archbishops, Karolos Kallimachi, Hospodar of Wallachia, the Dragoman of the Porte, Konstantinos Mourousi, and the Grand Logothete, Stephanos Mavroyeni, gathered to decide on their next step. A number of other Greeks were also in attendance 'of every class and condition'. Gregorios and Mourousi presided. The assembled Greeks were all exhorted 'to carefully guard against any move or action contrary to their allegiance and fidelity to their Sovereign'.[2] A letter was drafted which incorporated the sultan's suggestion and was sent off to be printed at the patriarchal press. The patriarch then urged that the Greeks prepare to leave the city quickly, promising that he would stay: 'As for me, I believe that my end is approaching, but I must stay at my post to die, and if I remain, then the Turks will not be given a plausible pretext to massacre the Christians of the capital.'[3]

The letter of excommunication against the revolutionaries appeared on Palm Sunday, 4 April, in all the Greek churches of the capital signed by the patriarch, Polykarpos of Jerusalem, and twenty-one other prelates. In part, the document stated:

Gratitude to our benefactors is the first of virtues and ingratitude is severely condemned by the Holy Scriptures and declared unpardonable by Jesus Christ; Judas the ungrateful traitor offers a terrible example of it; but it is most strongly evidenced by those who rise against their common protector and lawful sovereign, and against Christ, who has said there is no rule or power but comes from God. It was against this principle that Michael Soutzos and Alexandros Ypsilantis, son of a fugitive, have

[1] F.-C. Pouqueville, *op. cit.* II, p. 404; S. Trikoupis, *op. cit.* I, p. 95; T. Gordon, *op. cit.* I, p. 186.

[2] Chabert to Strangford, Pera, 23 March 1821, Strangford MSS, I, no. 39.

[3] C. Papadopoulos, *op. cit.* p. 482; G. Finlay, *op. cit.* VI, p. 184.

sinned with an audacity beyond example, and have sent emissaries to seduce others, and to conduct them to the abyss of perdition; many have been so tempted to join an unlawful hetairia and thought themselves bound by their oath to continue members, but an oath to commit a sin was itself a sin, and not binding—like that of Herod, who, that he might not break a wicked obligation committed a great wickedness by the death of John the Baptist.

The text ended by solemnly condemning and excommunicating Soutzos and Ypsilantis, having been signed on the altar itself.[1] The patriarchal letter was the final blow to strike Ypsilantis' fading expedition in the Principalities.[2]

A story is told that the patriarch and the bishops later repented of their deed, and at a midnight meeting at the patriarchate renounced what they had done and began preparing themselves for martyrdom. It is extremely unlikely that this happened. Kandiloros, the biographer of Gregorios, doubts it, noting that the patriarch was appointed by the Porte and responsible before it for its Christian subjects. 'As the representative of Christ it cannot be believed that the patriarch signed such a letter. But as the head of a threatened people, he had to take measures, as well as he could, to save his powerless and hard-pressed population from being massacred.'[3]

Despite the efforts of the Greek leaders to profess their loyalty, the sultan remained unconvinced. On the same Sunday the patriarchal letter was issued, he ordered the Dragoman of the Porte, Konstantinos Mourousi, to be executed. The Turks told the story that, when given some papers which had been captured from the Greek insurgents in the Principalities to translate, Mourousi had omitted parts which would have implicated the Russians. The sultan had asked someone

[1] The text as found in R. Walsh, *op. cit.* I, p. 311; T. Kandiloros, *op. cit.* pp. 214–19; *Sacrorum Conciliorum nova et amplissima collectio*, ed. Joannes Mansi (Graz, 1961), XL, pp. 151–4.

[2] Iakovos Rizo-Neroulos comments, 'A million Vlachs and Moldavians regarded the Greeks as criminals of state, condemned by the Christian powers, pursued by the Sultan and excommunicated by the Patriarch' in *Histoire moderne de la Grèce depuis la chute de l'empire d'orient* (Geneva, 1828), p. 297.

[3] Kandiloros, *op. cit.* p. 219; C. Papadopoulos, *op. cit.* p. 483, says that the letter was the result of 'unavoidable necessity'.

else to translate them, and learned of the omission. Mourousi was at the house of the Reis Effendi when all of a sudden he was seized and carried under an apartment of the sultan's palace where he was executed in his official dress. On his body, which was displayed in public, a sign was hung accusing him of giving information to the rebels, of having knowledge of their plans and not divulging it. His family was placed under the patriarch's protection, and he was to be responsible for them. With or without the patriarch's permission, they fled the city for Russia, as had also four Serbian deputies being held as hostages, leaving Gregorios to take the blame. The decision was then finally made by the sultan and his advisers that Gregorios must pay the penalty for the rebellion of his subjects.[1]

On Saturday afternoon, 10 April 1821, the patriarch officiated at the Divine Liturgy preparatory to the Easter vigil. The church of Ayios Georgios was filled with people praying on this occasion in great agitation. While the services were in progress around five o'clock, the Ottoman police surrounded the building, and, at its conclusion, pushed their way with difficulty through the crowd.

They seized the patriarch and the officiating bishops, pushed them outside to the courtyard, and there put ropes around their necks. The janissary whose job it was to protect the patriarch intervened only to be struck by the sword of an arresting officer. The aged patriarch was then dragged to the gate of the Phanar, the rope passed through the staple that fastened the folding doors, and he was hanged in his robes of office before a multitude of his people. Because he was so thin, the weight of his body was not sufficient to cause instant death. 'He continued for a long time in pain, which no friendly hand dared to abridge, and the darkness of night came on before his last convulsions were over.'[2] Two of his chaplains were hanged at other doorways, and in other parts of the city the bishop of Nicomedia, Athanasios, was executed, as were the bishops of Ephesus and Anchialos.

On the bodies of the executed, the Turkish officials hung signs

[1] Memo from Pisani, 22 April 1821, Strangford MSS, III, no. 4.

[2] This account of the patriarch's death follows that of R. Walsh, *op. cit.* I, p. 315, who was an eyewitness.

listing the offenses of the dead persons. On the patriarch's body, the charge read as follows:

Since it is the precise duty of all the Chiefs and Directors of each nation, whichever it may be, to keep watch day and night over the individuals under their direction and to be informed on all their actions and to communicate to the Government all that they come across of evil, the Patriarchs have thus been installed as Chiefs and Directors of the subjects who live peacefully in the shadow of the Imperial Power, they must first of all be without reproach, sincere and faithful...But this perfidious Patriarch who apparently was loyal, actually knew about the revolt, encouraged it. He has been the cause of it. Being from Morea, he has also had his hand seducing the people there. It is he himself who will be the cause of their ruin and destruction, which, with the aid of God they shall be struck. Convicted then, on all sides of treason, not only to the Sublime Porte but directly towards his own nation, it was necessary that his body be taken...from the earth and that he be hung to serve as an example to others.[1]

The charge placed on the other bishops was similar. They were accused of dereliction of duty and co-operating with the conspirators. Other bishops were arrested. Those of Derkon, Thessaloniki, Tirnovo, and Adrianople were put into the prison of the Bostandje bashi. Most of these were later killed by the Turks, as was the predecessor of Gregorios, the former Patriarch Kyrillos, now over ninety years of age, who was hanged.

The body of the patriarch was left hanging at the gate for three days requiring anyone who entered to push the body aside. Then, in order further to disgrace the patriarch's body, the Government ordered four or five Jews from the neighboring section of Balata to cut down the body. They then dragged the corpse by the legs through the dirty streets down to the harbor where it was put into a boat, and, having been weighted, thrown into the sea.[2]

[1] Strangford to Castlereagh, Constantinople, April 1821, F.O. 78, Turkey, vol. 98, no. 27, PRO. G. Finlay, *op. cit.* VI, p. 187, believes the patriarch was innocent of all charges except for a warning to a few Greek families to flee on the advice of Baron Stroganov.

[2] Memo from Pisani, 25 April 1821, Strangford MSS, II, no. 5. Fredrick Pisani, a dragoman of the British consulate, commented, 'It is impossible to carry anger,

The body floated to the surface, however, and was recognized by a Greek from the patriarchal household who had taken refuge on a Russian vessel in the harbor. The captain, Marinos Sklavos, brought the body on board under the cover of darkness, and sailed for Odessa. There the patriarch was accorded all the honors of a great funeral in the Russian Orthodox church.[1]

The man chosen to deliver the sermon for the occasion was the priest Konstantinos Oekonomos, a refugee himself from the Ottoman Empire. His words were eloquent in praise of the patriarch's devotion to his calling, his faith, and now his martyrdom: 'Venerable Patriarch, you have lost none of your glory, it has in fact increased, grown, and become eternal. It is true that you no longer hold the patriarchal throne, but you are now presenting yourself with confidence before the throne of the Divine Majesty.' The fact that his body had come to Odessa is important, for 'by this extraordinary circumstance, it renews and manifests after so many centuries the indissoluble and essential unity which has always existed between the Greek and Russian Churches'. Gregorios' death had left the Greek church desolate, so now it based its hopes upon the 'Emperor Alexander, successor of St Vladimir, the august defender of the Orthodox Church'. Oekonomos pleaded that the tsar care for the Greek emigrants now seeking refuge 'under the wings of the Great Eagle of Russia'. In conclusion, he offered a prayer for the victory of the Greeks in their efforts to be rid of their oppression.[2]

The British and Russian ambassadors along with their colleagues made strong protests to the Porte about the execution of the patriarch, which was carried out in such an ignominious manner. Strangford wrote to London that the circumstances of the execution filled all the Christians of the city with consternation. 'They plainly indicate that the Councils of this Empire are now directed by a spirit of re-

indignation and cruelty to a higher pitch'. The prison of the Bostandje bashi was that of the head gardener of the sultan's palace. His duties included police work.

1 R. Walsh, *op. cit.* I, pp. 316–17; C. Papadopoulos, *op. cit.* p. 492.

2 Konstantinos Oekonomos, *Discours prononcé en Grec, à Odessa, le 29 juin, 1821, pour les funérailles du Patriarche Grégoire* (Paris, 1821), pp. 10–26. The body of Gregorios was returned to Greece in 1871.

lentless fanaticism from which the most dreadful results may be expected.'[1]

On the very day that Gregorios V was executed, the Synod met to elect a successor. Their choice fell upon a timid man, who ascended the patriarchal throne as Eugenios II. He was formerly protosynkellos of the patriarchate and later metropolitan of Pisidia. On the way to the sultan's palace to seek confirmation of his election, he had to pass through the gate from which the body of his predecessor still hung.

The patriarch's death signalled a reign of terror against the Greeks in Constantinople during the following weeks. Mobs roamed the street, broke into Greek churches and looted them. About fourteen suffered heavy damage or were destroyed. The more fanatical Turks eventually broke into the patriarchate itself. The lay officials, priests and bishops fled out through the gates and over the roofs seeking refuge until the mob should leave. The patriarchal throne was destroyed and Eugenios himself was almost killed. Finally the Turks left, but not before much of the property of the patriarchate had been lost.

Within the capital, during May, restrictions on the Greek community were increased as the result of police investigations turning up people with large quantities of arsenic, and merchants who had combustible material thought to be intended for setting the capital afire. Christian churches continued to be assaulted. On 19 May Eugenios, the new patriarch, had been summoned by Kiahya Bey. Questions were put to the Greek churchman which he answered so well that he made a great impression upon the Ottoman officials. They promised, in turn, to prevent further executions and the destruction of churches. The patriarch took it upon himself to announce to his Greek subjects in the capital that every five families would pledge security for one another. If any individual within the families should leave the city without a passport, the heads of all the families would suffer.[2]

[1] Strangford to Castlereagh, Constantinople, 25 April 1821, F.O. 78, Turkey, vol. 98, no. 25, PRO.

[2] G. Finlay, *op. cit.* VI, p. 189.

On 24 May, the patriarch presented a memorial to the Porte written in Turkish, which begged the Ottomans to be merciful towards the Greek church and nationals. He offered to make restitution for those who had risen against the sultan, and promised unbounded fidelity and allegiance for the future. He begged the Ottomans to see that only a few Greeks were involved, not the nation as a whole. He noted that the guilt lay elsewhere, 'It is the work of those who have contrived and set them upon plans which have ended in their ruin'.[1]

There were further conferences between the patriarch and the Porte officials. In June the Reis Effendi told Frederick Pisani, another British dragoman, of a memorandum presented by the patriarch, but, after reading it, he was not pleased, asserting that what the Turks wanted 'was not words but actual facts...The Porte wants to know from him the *true source* and the name of the *original author* and of his *associates* in the Plot formed against the Ottoman Crown, which was answered by the patriarch's saying *he did not know*'.[2] The Porte in August also demanded that the patriarch issue a further condemnation of the Greek revolt. The unhappy Eugenios was thus forced into the same position as his predecessor, that of condemning the Christian armies of Greece.

In this letter, the patriarch addressed himself to all the Orthodox who lived within the Ottoman empire, urging each one to examine 'the basis on which this powerful and invincible government is founded...and he will acknowledge the inexhaustible ocean of its clemency and how vast the immensity of its unequalled humanity...' The sultan had given the Greeks the same rights as the Muslims, in fact had shown so many favors that it 'seemed incompatible with our situation as subjects'. The Greeks should be grateful to this kingdom,

> ...which rules its subjects in the strictest imitation of Divine Mercy. But alas! a great part of the Greek nation, far from evincing its due gratitude has forgotten these vast kindnesses by disavowing and even treading underfoot the ordinances of religion which command perfect submission and

[1] The inference was to Russia. The British believed them to be behind it, Strangford to Castlereagh, Constantinople, 25 May 1821, F.O. 78, Turkey, vol. 98, no. 41, PRO, and Memo of Pisani, 24 May 1821, Strangford MSS, III, no. 41.

[2] Memo of Pisani, 10 June 1821, Strangford MSS, III, no. 54.

obedience to this Heaven-protected imperial power. They have fallen into such a state of weakness and madness as even to dare to form themselves into a Hetairia, or Cabal, against this invincible Government which has ever loved and cherished all alike.

The letter continues, pointing out that the sultan has had to punish of necessity those who have been guilty, but he once more is offering pardon to all, so the Holy Synod urges that the Greeks should 'immediately lay down their arms and return to that pristine state of perfect and loyal subjection'. The Ottoman government 'will become again an affectionate Mother, ready to embrace you, ever pouring over you from the perennial source of its clemency, acts of generous kindness, and mercy, and forever burying in the most profound oblivion all those intemperate movements, which, through the influence of the miserable Devil, were so madly projected'. The church would happily lift its excommunication for those who would quit the fight.[1]

This letter to the revolutionaries was distributed in the Peloponnesus where the Greeks, 'who were less under the immediate influence of that gentle rule', responded by a unanimous rejection of the patriarchal plea. In fact, a counter-measure was drafted which was signed eventually by twenty-eight bishops and almost a thousand priests proclaiming the freedom of Greece. The patriarch himself was anathematized by the prelates of the Peloponnesus, and was called a Judas and a wolf in sheep's clothing.[2]

The sultan tried desperately to stem the revolt by harsh measures against suspect Greeks. In addition to the bishops already jailed, some more of their compatriots joined them. At Smyrna the Greek populace was ravaged by outbreaks of violence, and the same was true in Adrianople and in Crete. The continuance of the insurrection and the efforts to implicate the Russians added to the confusion during the summer of 1821 in Constantinople. The Russian am-

[1] The letter is in A. Prokesch-Osten, *op. cit.* III, p. 153 and in Strangford to Londonderry, Constantinople, 25 August 1821, F.O. 78, Turkey, vol. 100, no. 102, PRO.

[2] F.-C. Pouqueville, *op. cit.* III, p. 121; Charles Eliot, *Turkey in Europe* (London, 1906), p. 278; Nicholaos Spiliadis, *'Απομνημονεύματα διὰ νὰ χρησιμεύσωσιν εἰς τὴν νέαν ἱστορίαν τῆς* Ἑλλάδος [Memoirs to serve for a modern history of Greece] (Athens, 1851), I, pp. 49–55.

bassador, Baron Stroganov, from the very beginning had denied Russian complicity, but, at the same time, made modest protests against Muslim treatment of Orthodox Christians, which was in his rights as laid down in the Treaty of Kuchuk Kaynarca. Stroganov's protests to the Porte climaxed with the death of the patriarch. The sultan's further order that all boats through the Bosporus should be searched and that there would be a complete embargo on grain ships added to his indignation, since trade through the Straits was very important to the Russian economy. A strong note was handed to the Porte by Stroganov. He claimed that the war had become a religious one and that the Turks intended 'to strike a death blow and exterminate all who bear the name of Christian in Turkey'.[1] He told the Ottoman government he intended to leave Constantinople if necessary to impress the Turks with the seriousness of the affair. The diplomats at the Porte felt that war was imminent.[2]

Strangford preferred trusting the Porte, since it was in line with British policy to do so. When the Austrian internuncio suggested an intervention, the British envoy expressed the opinion that this was an internal matter, for the Porte had offered to show him letters from the patriarch to the clergy of the Peloponnesus which, they claimed, gave definite proof that Gregorios was involved. The British ambassador declined to look at the letters. He did have a talk with the Reis Effendi. The Ottoman official had given him the following information concerning the patriarch's death:

...the fact of the Execution having taken place on Easter Sunday was an accident and not by any means a designed insult to that Solemn Festival—that the question of the Patriarch's guilt had only been determined on the preceding day—but the nature of his punishment had not been decided on—that in the interval a fresh mass of the most convincing evidence against him had been submitted to the Sultan, who, in a fit of violent anger and indignation had ordered his immediate execution.[3]

[1] Strangford to Londonderry, Constantinople, 12 June 1821, F.O. 78, Turkey, vol. 99, no. 44, PRO.

[2] Memo of Pisani, 17 June 1821, Strangford MSS, III, no. 54; cf. also T. Gordon, *op. cit.* I, pp. 196 ff.; E. Driault and l'Héritier, *op. cit.* I, p. 150.

[3] Strangford to Londonderry, Constantinople, 12 June 1821, F.O. 78, Turkey, vol. 99, no. 47, PRO.

The news of the patriarch's death greatly affected Tsar Alexander. As protector of the Orthodox church in the Ottoman Empire, his clear duty was to demand some satisfaction, while, on the other hand, he sincerely did not want to support revolutionary movements nor did he favor unilateral action. Britain, and to a lesser degree France, would only see, in any move, the ultimate aim of the Russians to bring down the Ottoman Empire. British policy was based on the information supplied by Strangford, who, in fact, thought the Russians were involved.

On 1 June, the dragoman Pisani reported to Strangford that the Turks had heard of the arrival of Gregorios' body in Odessa. They were much put out. 'This circumstance has made a great impression with the Turks who consider it a further proof of the uniformity of sentiments, in religious as well as political matters, prevalent between the Russians and Greeks.'[1]

In St Petersburg, a decision was made to send a stiff note to the Porte, but the thought of actual military action was not considered. The tsar insisted, in speaking to western diplomats, that Russia intended no territorial gains; that it wished only to allow the Christians of the Ottoman Empire a chance to survive, to expel those who persecuted them from Europe. Stroganov, however, hinted to the French, who relayed it to Strangford, that the emperor's note '...will infallibly lead to war'.[2] The Holy Synod of the Russian church was particularly strong in pressuring the tsar to act for their oppressed co-religionists.

The Russian note, which everyone had been awaiting, was presented to the Porte on 18 July. It was twelve pages in length, but was remarkably restrained in its demands. The tsar did no more than demand that the ill treatment of the Orthodox stop, for he accused the Turks of indiscriminately attacking all Greeks, guilty and innocent; that the churches destroyed during the rioting be repaired at the expense of the Ottomans and retribution be made for the death of the patriarch and bishops. The Porte was given eight days to

[1] Memo of Pisani, 1 June 1821, Strangford MSS, III, no. 54.

[2] Strangford to Londonderry, Constantinople, 18 June 1821, F.O. 78, Turkey, vol. 99 no. 59, PRO.

reply—if nothing was forthcoming, Stroganov was ordered to leave; presumably this was to be the final step before military hostilities commenced, but in fact it was a bluff.

The British ambassador wrote London of his opinion on the Russian note. He felt it was overstated; that the charges were not based on fact. Among other points, Strangford claimed that all the Greek churches were open now—that not since the initial days of turbulence when the Janissaries ran amok had any been injured or destroyed, 'out of a number of 76 churches and chapels in the city and neighborhood of Constantinople, but one was utterly destroyed and only 13 plundered or otherwise injured by the mob'. He deplored the death of the patriarch; still, 'I feel myself bound in conscience and in honour to declare my positive conviction, founded on grounds of evidence which cannot be suspected, that not only that unfortunate Prelate, but many, if not all the Bishops who shared his fate, were deeply involved in a Conspiracy, of which the Greek Clergy were the principal agents and promoters'. Strangford pointed out that all of the vacant sees had been filled with the canons respected. The Russians had nothing to complain about on this score.

Strangford's reports to London were based on information supplied by Pisani. He gives the following details: in the city of old Constantinople there were twenty-four churches or chapels, in the suburbs thirty-six to forty, in the Princes' Islands eleven. Of those damaged in the demonstrations, seven were in the city, the worst destruction was in Bokcekoy where one church was completely destroyed and six others pillaged. In these the extent of the damage was limited to pulpits, chairs, altars, and lamps; no damage was done to the exterior. The patriarchal church was not entered, but the patriarch's palace was. The loss here is estimated at 100,000 piastres. The robes, clothes, and 9,000 piastres in cash left by Gregorios, were taken or destroyed. The sultan has given permission for the damage to be repaired, but Eugenios has not yet acted.[1]

The eight days of Stroganov's note passed without the written reply demanded. When the Russian dragoman called at the Porte,

[1] Memo of Pisani, 23 July 1821, Strangford MSS, III, no. 87; Strangford to Londonderry, Pera, 23 July 1821, F.O. 78, Turkey, vol. 99, no. 71, PRO.

he was given an oral answer. As regards the Russian complaints, the Turks answered 'that the Patriarch was punished as an individual rebel and traitor, as the head of the nation, and not as a dignitary of the Greek church. That if any church is demolished or harmed, the Porte is far from approving the conduct of a portion of the people who have dared to commit such excesses, and as soon as calm is restored, the said churches will be reconstructed and repaired.'[1] But the oral message, when written, was refused, and Stroganov prepared to leave for Odessa, but with some embarrassment; his defiant gesture had to be postponed until 9 August due to northerly winds.

The Turkish note was sent to St Petersburg, where the tsar was able to examine it. The sultan claimed he was fighting rebellion, not the Orthodox church. He cited the example of Peter the Great's killing of a disloyal patriarch. If, the sultan asked, the tsar was sincere in his interest to stop rebellions, then let him turn over the hospodar of Moldavia, Michael Soutzos. Due to British and Austrian intervention, the embargo on Russian grain ships was lifted as a conciliatory move.

During the rest of the year 1821, the British minister tried to act as a conciliator between the Turks and the Russians. One of the projects he had was to pacify the Russians on the issue of the churches destroyed during the spring riot. In November, at the urging of Strangford, Eugenios reluctantly presented a petition that he might make repairs to his property, despite the fact that he had no funds. The costs would run from 8,000 to 10,000 piastres, and the British envoy promised to underwrite it. As late as December, however, the Porte had given no reply.[2]

To return to matters in Greece itself, the uprising in the Pelopon-

[1] Strangford to Londonderry, Pera, 6 August 1821, F.O. 78, Turkey, vol. 100, no. 81, PRO.

[2] Chabert to Strangford, 14 December 1821, Strangford MSS III, no. 158; also 12 and 13 November, nos. 38 and 42. When Tsar Alexander had an opportunity to talk to Stroganov in Russia, he cautioned him against intemperate statements about war with the Turks. Alexander wrote Nesselrode that he had informed the returned ambassador nothing should be done to endanger the alliance between the Powers. Alexander to Nesselrode, Romanchino, 12 September 1821, in *Lettres et papiers du Chancelier Comte de Nesselrode*, ed. A. de Nesselrode (Paris, 1908), VI, p. 124.

nesus sparked a similar pattern north of the Isthmus. Members of the clergy were in evidence everywhere once the uprising started. Pouqueville describes the change in the priests of Boeotia during these heady days when the Turks were put to flight:

> Separated by their oppressors, the Greeks recognized no other master than the Redeemer, henceforth no other hand on their heads but the divine. The unbloody sacrifice of the Lamb was offered by his ministers to the God of armies, and the clergy, until now the timid consolers of the oppressed, found themselves, hardly realizing it, at the head of the movement for freedom in Greece. The cross was planted at the entrance of all the passes, on the summits of the mountains...[1]

The hero of the Greeks in Eastern Roumeli was a man who had been ordained deacon, and hence was called Athanasios Diakos. In April of 1821, the Turks had been ousted from Salona (now Amphissa) and Levadhia; Athens, little more than a large village at the time, was blockaded. The Turks sent a relief column from Larisa under the command of Omer Vrioni, and so Diakos and the bishop of Salona led a force to stop the reinforcements on to the plain of Lamia, closeby to Thermopylae. There, hopelessly outnumbered, the Greek band was cut to pieces, the bishop killed, and Diakos, after a three-hour struggle, captured alive.

Before being impaled, a popular poem tells what the struggle meant to the Greek warrior.

> Then Diakos fell alive into the hands of his enemies;
> a thousand guarded him before, two thousand behind,
> and Omer Vrioni secretely questions him on the way:
> 'Will you turn Turk, my Diakos?
> Will you change faith?
> Worship at the mosque? Abandon your church?'
> And he replied and told him wrathfully:
> 'Go you and your faith, you filth, to hell with you!
> I was born a Greek, a Greek will I die.'[2]

One of the great disappointments during the first year of the war was the reaction of the monks of Mount Athos. In 1821 there were

[1] F.-C. Pouqueville, *op. cit.* II, p. 372.

[2] The poem as given in C. Woodhouse, *op. cit.* pp. 70–1.

6,000 monks living there, amply provisioned; some of the monasteries had not only muskets but even artillery which was used against pirates. The apostles of the Hetairia had worked diligently among them, realizing how important it would be to have such a ready-made army at hand, plus the moral support which the Revolution would gain from having this home of Orthodox spirituality on the side of the revolt.

At the opening of the conflict, some of the monks prepared to fight. They assisted the Greeks in the neighborhood, but then, to their surprise, the promised Russian aid did not appear. The Patriarchs Gregorios and Eugenios anathematized the insurgents, and crowds of refugees begged admittance to the peninsula, straining its resources.

The abbots of the monasteries decided on what they believed a prudent course. Contacts were made with the Ottoman official Aboulaboud Pasha. He promised an amnesty to those who had revolted on condition that a sum of 3,000 purses (150,000 piastres) was paid. A small Turkish garrison was to be put on the mountain at Karies. Despite misgivings, the terms were accepted and Mount Athos was occupied on 27 December, remaining garrisoned throughout the war. During the next few years, about half the monks left to serve in the Revolution in various ways which officially were denied them as members of the monastic community of the Holy Mountain.[1]

The gaining of the islands, especially the highly developed commercialized centers of Spetsai, Poros and Idhra, was of great importance to the Greek cause. These islands had fleets and sailors, plus a good deal of capital to outfit the necessary naval forces needed by the insurgents. The church was active here, too.

On 28 April, Idhra had proclaimed its support of the Revolution, and, on the following day, Kyrillos, bishop of Aegina, blessed the flag of the independent island. Later, the Archimandrite Theodosios addressed the clergy of the three islands; he called upon them to lead the fight against the Muslims, promising a crown of martyrdom to those who might fall in the sacred struggle.[2] The Idhriotes com-

[1] T. Gordon, *op. cit.* I, pp. 176, 287; F.-C. Pouqueville, *op. cit.* III, p. 67.

[2] F.-C. Pouqueville, *op. cit.* II, pp. 446, 501; S. Trikoupis, *op. cit.* I, p. 170.

missioned one of their admirals to head a fleet to announce the news to the other islands and urge them to join. The first stop was Tinos, and there the head of the fleet, Iakomi Tombazi, met head-on with a problem which plagued the Revolution in the islands throughout the conflict—the reluctance of the Latin Catholics to participate in the Revolution. The Orthodox bishop of Tinos announced his people's willingness to join the struggle, but the Latins declined.

The Latin Catholics of the Greek islands numbered about 16,000 in 1821. They were practically all to be found on four islands in the Aegean: Syros, Tinos, Thira, and Naxos, the remnants of the Crusaders, Venetians and Franks, and their converts, who had occupied the islands for hundreds of years. Tinos had been the last of the Venetian islands to fall to the Turks; this as late as 1714. Owing to the capitulations which the Porte had made with France, the Latin Catholics were protected by that power and were strongly under French influence. The Latin bishops were ethnically Italians.[1]

Feelings of strong hostility towards one another had arisen between Orthodox and Latin islanders by the early nineteenth century. Both sides claimed the other was persecuting members of its group. Marriage was always a difficult situation; the clergy of both camps were most intolerant, although the people were not so concerned and participated in one another's feasts. But when the news of the Revolution arrived, the Catholics felt more strongly attached to their faith than to their nationality. They feared what would happen to them in a Greek state dominated by the Orthodox; their French advisers urged them to maintain a neutral position. As a result, the Latin Catholics of Tinos continued to pay the *kharadj* to the sultan during the first years of the war despite protests from their Orthodox neighbors.[2]

At Naxos, a particularly fervent Orthodox bishop led a procession into the town with the revolutionary standard flying held by a cleric and two others flanking it with drawn swords. The faithful were harangued at the church in strong words concerning the sacred cause,

[1] Georg Hofmann, *Das Papsttum und der Griechische Freiheitskampf*, vol. 136 of *Orientalia Christiana Analecta* (Rome, 1952), pp. 19 and 47.

[2] M. Raybaud, *op. cit.* II, p. 124; S. Trikoupis, *op. cit.* I, p. 184; F.-C. Pouqueville, *op. cit.* IV, p. 186.

and, since the Latins did not participate, the bishop urged their extermination along with that of the Turks. The Catholics were forced to barricade themselves in their homes and monasteries, where some Turks also took refuge. This same bishop, according to Walsh, ordered the Turkish prisoners shot and those who protested this act he condemned, calling them *Turkolatri* (Turk worshippers), the most ignominious name that could be given at the time.[1]

On the Ionian Islands, held by Britain, the governor, Sir Thomas Maitland, issued a proclamation warning the inhabitants '...that in the event of their taking part in the present disturbances, or joining in any attack of warlike operations which may take place, they will lose all right or pretension to the interference on their behalf of the Government of these States...' In fact, however, the Ionian Islanders were actively engaged throughout the conflict on behalf of their brothers on the mainland. The Orthodox clergy of the islands were in the forefront, so much so that Governor Maitland alluded to them in a statement on the conflict. He mentioned that he knew well that there were

...pastors of religion in these States, who, in defiance of the pure principles of the Holy Gospel, which inculcate universal charity and benevolence, publicly, in the face of this Government, offered up on the present occasion, prayers for the destruction of the Ottoman Power, thus blasphemously adding even the voice of religion, to increase an unfortunate irritation, already too prevalent.[2]

In the Islands, persistent attempts were made to set up an autonomous church, independent of the patriarchate. This was encouraged by the Russians, other foreigners, and some Greeks. In 1823, the patriarch recognized a special arrangement for the Islands and ratified the existing hierarchy. Obedience was still owed to Constantinople, but the church of the Ionian Islands had a great deal of local autonomy.

For the church of Greece in the areas where the Revolution was successful during 1821, a profound change resulted in many areas

[1] R. Walsh, *op. cit.* pp. 187–9. Report of H. Hamilton, 30 July 1821, F.O. 32, Greece, vol. 3, no. 39, PRO.

[2] *Returns to an Address of the Honorable House of Commons by Sir Thomas Maitland and the Senate* (London, 1822), p. 3.

of its life. When the war broke out there were thirty-eight metropolitans, archbishops and bishops in what would later become the kingdom of Greece. Sixteen of these were in the Peloponnesus, eleven on the mainland, and eleven on the Islands. All of the bishops had been canonically appointed by the patriarch in Constantinople.

The Revolution had meant an early death for some of these (five had died at Tripolis), for others there was exile, while a few led armies, such as Germanos and Gregorios, bishop of Methoni. The number of priests in the Peloponnesus had been around 2,400—among them the percentage of those killed or exiled was even greater. The result of the Revolution, therefore, meant a great disorganization in church life due to the prolonged absence or the death of so many clergy.[1]

The confusion which resulted from the hostilities meant that local leadership had to provide the initiative. Obviously, the bishops in revolutionary Greece were no longer going to send funds to the patriarchate in Constantinople, nor were any candidates sent to the church schools there. Gregorios was considered a martyr; his anathema against the revolutionists having been wiped out by his death for the Greek cause. The same benevolence was not accorded to Eugenios or the other appointees of the Ottoman government during the course of the war. The bishops treated the patriarchate as if it were empty. In the important matter of naming the patriarch during the Liturgy, the form was changed to 'all orthodox bishops' and the patriarch's name was deliberately omitted.[2]

[1] Konstantinos Oekonomos of the Oekonomos, *Τριακονταετηρὶς ἐκκλησιαστικὴ ἤ συνταγμάτιον ἱστορικὸν τῶν ἐν τῷ βασιλείῳ τῆς* Ἑλλάδος [Thirty years of church affairs or the constitutional history of the Kingdom of Greece], in vol. II of Τὰ *σωζόμενα ἐκκλησιαστικὰ συγγράμματα* [The extant ecclesiastical writings], ed. Sophokles of the Oekonomos (Athens, 1862), p. 5. Georg von Maurer found that around eighty prelates of the Greek church were killed during the Revolution in the whole of the Ottoman Empire (*Das Griechische Volk in öffentlicher, kirchlicher und privatrechtlicher Beziehung vor und nach dem Freiheitskampfe*, Heidelberg, 1835, I, p. 468); also Aurelio Palmieri, 'La chiesa ellenica nel secolo XIX', *Bessarione*, ser. II, vol. IV (1902), pp. 74 ff.

[2] G. Konidaris, *op. cit.* p. 353; Anastasios Kyriakos, Ἐ*κκλησιαστικὴ* Ἱ*στορία* [Church history] (Athens, 1881), II, p. 339; Herrmann Schmitt, *Kritische Geschichteder neugriechischen und der russischen Kirche* (Mainz, 1854), p. 136.

In the Peloponnesus, a Senate was constituted on 7 June 1821. Its membership was made up of the leading men of the Revolution, which meant the primates and the bishops. These two classes had worked together before the Revolution; it is not surprising that they took an ascendency after it had begun. Their rivals were the military chieftains who led the armed forces in the field. These were not politically conscious nor as well fitted for administration, but the nature of the war gained popular sympathy for the latter, and the balance of power tipped to their side. The arrival of Demetrios Ypsilantis, brother of the unhappy Alexandros, in June 1821, proclaiming himself leader of the Greek cause in behalf of his brother, only served to complicate matters. Both church and state were rocked by the conflicting ambitions of local leaders and their attempts to speak for all Greece. As Finlay says, 'the Revolution, before six months had passed, seemed to have peopled Greece with a host of little Ali Pashas'.[1]

The monasteries in Greece were active in support of the Revolution and none took second place to Megaspelaion. When called upon to give aid to their Greek countrymen, the community appointed two of their members to lead a detachment of seventy monks for the relief of a town under siege. The copper of the monastery, even its door knobs, was melted down for ammunition. The monastery was especially of service as a home for refugees, who poured into it during the course of the war.[2]

North and west of the Gulf of Corinth in West Roumeli, political as well as church affairs were organized by Alexandros Mavrokordatos after his arrival on 3 August 1821. He was a descendant of the famous Phanariote family of the capital, who had given many distinguished men to the service of the Porte. Having served earlier in Wallachia, he was living in Pisa when the Revolution broke out. He avoided the difficulties between Ypsilantis, the Peloponnesian

[1] G. Finlay, *op. cit.* VI, p. 229. Both he and Gordon are extremely critical of the primates and higher clergy whom they see as simply wanting to displace the Turks in order to hold all the political power themselves and use it to their own benefit. T. Gordon, *op. cit.* I, p. 224.

[2] Letter from the monastery of Megaspelaion to General Richard Church, 2 August 1831, Church MSS, XXIV, 175, British Museum Additional MSS 36566.

Senate and the Islanders, and moved on to establish himself at Mesolonghi.

There, he called an assembly of representatives of what was roughly speaking free Western Roumeli, where a constitution was adopted giving to that area its first political body. As far as religious matters were concerned, a pro-revolutionary bishop, Porphyrios, formerly of Mount Athos, was supported in preference to Anthimos, a lukewarm revolutionist and recent appointee of the patriarchate for the metropolitanate of Naupaktos and Arta and religious head of western Greece.[1]

At about the same time, Theodoros Negris assembled at Amphissa a group of representatives from Eastern Roumeli, which he called the Areopagus. At the meeting three bishops were present, Neophytos of Talantios, Dionysios of Mendenitsis, and Ioannis of Loidorikos. In the legal arrangement which was drawn up there, some definite statements on religion were made. Nationality was to be based on religion. Article One read, 'Those inhabitants of Greece believing in Christ are Greeks'. It granted toleration to all religions but noted, '...the Eastern Church of Christ and the current language only are recognized as the authorized religion and speech of Greece'. A place of importance was guaranteed to the clergy in the administration of the area. Neophytos of Talantios was placed in charge of religious affairs.[2]

The triple-headed government of Greece was an expensive luxury in a fight between a minute part of the Ottoman Empire and all the forces which that government could command. At the initiative of Demetrios Ypsilantis, who needed support against the Peloponnesian Senate, a call went out for a National Assembly. Ypsilantis found himself outmanoeuvred by the Senate, which appointed its own delegates, but the leaders of East and West Roumeli, Mavrokordatos and Negris respectively, agreed to come with delegations.

The National Assembly, first summoned for Tripolis, moved to

[1] G. Konidaris, *op. cit.* p. 353. Porphyrios only after some delay accepted his appointment; see also Chrysostomos Papadopoulos, *Ἱστορία τῆς Ἐκκλησίας τῆς Ἑλλάδος* [History of the church of Greece] (Athens, 1920), p. 22.

[2] Andreas Z. Mamoukas, Τὰ *κατὰ τὴν Ἀναγέννησιν τῆς Ἑλλάδος* [The events concerning the rebirth of Greece] (Athens, 1839–52), I, pt. I, pp. 43 and 73.

Argos and eventually to a village near ancient Epidauros. It set about the task of unifying the country under one government. At its opening on 20 December, Bishop Neophytos of Talantios offered the Liturgy before the assembled delegates. He gave a discourse on the causes and events of the Revolution, and chose to mention the relations between Greece and Russia. 'It is publicly known, that in the eyes of the Ottoman Porte, the cause of religion and of the Greek nation has always been bound to the political and national cause of the Muscovites, that, in every war between Russia and Turkey, the Ottoman government has always identified the desires of the Hellenes with the Russians.' He concluded with a prayer for the tsar, which was not entirely a compliment, but also a petition to Alexander to do something.[1]

A Constitution, largely the work of Mavrokordatos and Negris, and which, on paper, presented a picture of a united Greek state, independent and viable, was drawn up on 1 January 1822. The administration of Greece was handed over to a five-member Executive Committee, and a popularly elected legislative Assembly of seventy. At the same time, it allowed the local Senates to continue in operation; a fact which nullified the effect of the formation of a central organ of government.

Chapter I, article 1 of the new Constitution concerned religion. It read as follows: 'The established religion of the Greek State is the Eastern Orthodox Church of Christ, the government of Greece, however, tolerates every other religion, and its services and ceremonies may be practised without interference.' Chapter II, article 2 on Public Law defined, 'All the inhabitants of Greece professing the Christian religion are Greeks, and enjoy all political rights'. Chapter II, article 20 set up eight ministries; one of these was a Ministry of Religion. Also important, as far as church matters were concerned, was Chapter VI which established an independent judiciary with the *Basilika* as its norm. This would have divested churchmen of one of their most significant pre-revolutionary functions had it been enforced.[2]

[1] F.-C. Pouqueville, *op. cit.* III, p. 341.

[2] A. Mamoukas, *op. cit.* I, pt. 2, p. 52; K. Oekonomos, *op. cit.* pp. 9–15; C. Papadopoulos, *op. cit.* p. 23; A. Prokesch-Osten, *op. cit.* III, p. 249. The *Basilika* was a code issued by the ninth-century Emperor Leo VI. It had received several modifications through the centuries.

On 15 January, Bishop Joseph of Androusa, a strong advocate of the Revolution, and one of the three survivors of the imprisonment of Tripolis, was appointed head of the Ministry of Religion. His task was not an easy one. The only solution to a growing shortage of clergy was to ask those nearby to assume a greater share of the work. Vacant bishoprics were given local protosynkelloi to maintain the ecclesiastical administration until peace was restored.[1]

But the government of Epidauros was imposing only on paper. It did not function due to the great divisions between the local governments, and the gulf between the political leaders and military chieftains. Mavrokordatos, elected the head of the Executive Commission, returned to Mesolonghi, and the Assembly was left to flounder as best it could.

This much was certain, a new spirit was abroad in Greece which looked to the west, the secular west of the American and French Revolutions, rather than to the old idea of an Orthodox community as it had functioned under the Ottomans. The emotions of the times did not let men see it; Orthodoxy and Greek nationality were still identified, but the winds were blowing against the dominant position of the church in the life of the individual and the nation. The Constitution had set up a judiciary independent of the church. The Assembly, not the church, selected Joseph of Androusa. The church did not have the people or the popular support to give guidance to the direction of the Revolution. As an organization, it was too much a part of the past. From a leading position at the very beginning of the conflict, each year of war would see its influence diminish.

[1] Joseph had been initiated into the Philike Hetairia as early as 1819 and thus was known for his interest in independence. See Konstantinos Vovolinis, *Ἡ Ἐκκλησία εἰς τὸν Ἀγῶνα τῆς Ἐλευθερίας* [The church in the struggle for freedom] (Athens, 1952), p. 144.

CHAPTER 4

THE CHURCH AND THE WAR OF INDEPENDENCE, 1822-1827

THE choice of Joseph of Androusa as head of the Ministry of Religion was a wise one, for he was one of the most able members of the Peloponnesian episcopate. Born in Tripolis in 1770, he had attended a number of monastic schools until called to succeed the bishop of Androusa in March 1808. Since then he had ably served his church and his country until events propelled him to his present position in 1822. It was now his enormous task to direct the spiritual life of a people locked in war with the Turks and bitterly divided among itself. His office placed him in charge of overseeing all churches and monasteries, administering clerical life and maintaining canon law in liberated Greece. There are only a few records extant of his administration, but all his contemporaries speak highly of his ability.[1]

One of his more serious problems concerned discipline within the church. According to the law, no bishops were to be consecrated without government approval. The bishop Chrysanthos of Lakedaemonia had proceeded, however, to consecrate another bishop without getting the necessary permission. Joseph reported him to the Executive Committee of the government, but Chrysanthos argued that he had need of an assistant because of his own ill health, and that since the man chosen bishop was only titular, the consecration did not fall under the law.[2] For cases such as this the Ministry was forced to depend on its moral authority rather than on the coercive power of the state. Sometimes this was not enough.

[1] For a biography of Joseph see Ezekiel Velandiotis, *Ἰωσὴφ ὁ Ἀνδρούσης, ὅμηρος δεσμοφόρος ἐν Τριπολίτζᾳ, μινίστρος τῆς Θρησκείας καὶ Δικαίου κατὰ τὸν Ἀγῶνα* [Joseph of Androusa, imprisoned hostage in Tripolitza, minister of religion and of justice during the war] (Athens, 1906).

[2] Chrysostomos Papadopoulos, *Ἱστορία τῆς Ἐκκλησίας τῆς Ἑλλάδος* [History of the church of Greece] (Athens, 1920), p. 23.

The question of ordination of deacons and priests was also sensitive. In theory the law gave the Ministry charge of seeing that no one would be ordained without the necessity of filling a clerical opening, without having reached the canonical age, and so on, but enforcement proved extremely difficult. One other decision made by the Ministry concerned the baptism of Turks. It was ruled by Joseph that anyone might be received into the church provided that the necessary instructions be given to adults. Marriage questions were also addressed to the Ministry which retained competence in this area.[1]

Joseph submitted a plan of church organization in March 1822 to the Assembly meeting in Corinth. Among other things, the plan envisaged placing church administration under a synod made up of six or eight bishops of free Greece. A letter was also directed to Mavrokordatos as president of the Executive Council; he responded on 27 March, urging that great attention be given to the proposal of the Ministry of Religion in the Assembly and promised he would make 'those additions and deletions which he thought necessary. Thus, will be established for the first time a supreme authority which will curb abuses and with great assurance put an end to the affairs which the Government neither desires nor approves.'[2] Regrettably nothing concrete was ever acted upon in the Assembly due to the pressure of the war.

One of the problems to which the national government addressed itself was an attempt to enlist the Greek Latin Catholics in the struggle for independence. The Latins, for their part, persisted in their claims to be under French protection and asserted they had nothing whatsoever to do with the revolt. On Syros, which was nearly all Catholic, the French flag flew above the churches. The result of the Latin non-involvement meant, of course, that the bitterness between Catholics and Orthodox was intensified. There were charges and counter-charges, assassinations, intrigues and murder, all sanctioned by a situation in which each party felt itself to have God and right exclusively on its side.

[1] Demetrios Petrakakos, ''*Ἐκκλησία καὶ δίκαιον κατὰ τὴν Ἑλληνικὴν Ἐπανάστασιν*' [Church and law during the Greek revolution], *Ἐκκλησιαστικός Φάρος*, XXXV (1936), pp. 439–41, 445–7.

[2] *Ibid.* p. 436.

In April 1822 Mavrokordatos, as president of the Executive Committee, wrote to the highest ranking Latin prelate in Greece, the archbishop of Naxos, Andreas Veggetti. The president urged him to come to Corinth, 'I invite you therefore, to take the opportunity, to come here as quickly as you can, so that we may have conversations concerning the affairs of the holy church of Christ of the West, whose highest wisdom you represent so worthily. Sir, for this Greece shall be thankful and indebted to you.' Theodoros Negris, another government official, also wrote to confirm the invitation and to urge a discussion of matters which should come up between the government and 'the Most Holy Court of Rome'.[1]

Veggetti wrote to Rome, telling of his invitation and asking for instructions. He admitted he had little information concerning what might be wanted; he included a hint that negotiations 'leading to the reunion of the Greek and Latin Churches' had been made to him. If the pope wants him to go, he will do so, but he will need a safe conduct from the Porte, secured for him by the French ambassador. He doubts that the Porte will issue it. The answer from Rome agreed with Veggetti that the Holy See did not see how he could leave Naxos. Moreover, if the Greek government was serious about talks of reunion, he was authorized to say that the decrees of the Council of Florence would be the basis of any discussion.[2] Nothing more is heard of this exchange of correspondence. Presumably the archbishop never got his safe-conduct. Catholic reluctance continued, especially when the islanders were forced to pay taxes to the 'Greek government', which they considered a foreign power.

Some other island communities were drawn into the conflict—the attack on Chios becoming the most famous—for in February of 1822 a great massacre took place there. That prosperous island of nearly 100,000 people had been occupied by some revolutionaries

[1] A. Mavrokordatos to A. Veggetti, Corinth, 14 April 1822; T. Negris to Veggetti, Corinth, 14 April 1822, quoted in Georg Hofmann, *Das Papsttum und der Griechische Freiheitskampf* in vol. 136, *Orientalia Christiana Analecta* (Rome, 1952), pp. 72–4.

[2] A. Veggetti to C. Fontana, Naxos, 7 May 1822; Sacred Congregation for the Propagation of the Faith to Veggetti, Rome, 4 July 1822 quoted in Hofmann, *op. cit.* pp. 74 and 78.

from Samos who had declared the island on the side of the Revolution. The Turks easily recaptured it and began a senseless slaughter of the inhabitants. The Orthodox bishop was among the tens of thousands of victims who were either killed or sold into slavery.

In action on the mainland, June of 1822 saw the Acropolis of Athens finally fall to the Greeks after the Turkish defenders had been without water for some time. At the head of the victors was the bishop of Athens, Dionysios, a man who was also president of the Areopagus, the civil government set up by the revolutionists. A procession came up the hill with the cross preceding. The Parthenon was purified of objects used in Muslim worship and rededicated to the Virgin Mother of God. The bishop also acted to preserve the Turkish prisoners from harm, but in this he was not successful. Three days after their capture, the Greek soldiers began to kill them.[1]

As far as matters in Constantinople were concerned, the Greek upper clergy continued to be suspect of assisting the Revolution. In the early part of January, four more bishops were jailed. Pisani's memorandum gives the key to the Ottoman position, 'it must not be forgotten, that the Turkish Cabinet hold the *Greek* clergy as being the real source of the insurrection of the Greek subjects in Turkey'.[2]

When the metropolitan of Chalcedon was arrested in late January, Lord Strangford protested to the Reis Effendi. The Ottoman official admitted, 'the bishops are not to blame...The bad effect which this can produce in Europe is a false interpretation of our sentiments, but in this regard, we must not abandon a measure of security, which it is necessary for us to take.' He requested the British ambassador to realize the arrests were made because '...security must come first —our principles and our conduct as regards religion and the Greek nation have not changed and will not change one iota'.[3] Later, the Turks claimed the imprisoned bishops had been plotting against the patriarch, so that, in fact, they had done the church a favor.

Patriarch Eugenios' rule was one beset by trials and vexations.

[1] Thomas Gordon, *History of the Greek Revolution* (London, 1832), II, p. 13. Dionysios died of the plague in May 1823.

[2] Memo of Pisani, 21 January 1822, Strangford MSS, II, no. 230, in British Museum, Additional MSS 36300.

[3] Memo of Pisani, 16 and 20 January, Strangford MSS, II, nos. 247 and 262.

Worn out by his labors he died on 27 July 1822. His final rites were attended with great honor, in contrast to the ignominy of his predecessor's. The funeral procession was escorted by 2,000 Turkish foot-soldiers as a display of the Porte's esteem. For his successor, the Synod chose the formerly imprisoned metropolitan of Chalcedon, who ascended the patriarchal throne as Anthimos III.

Robert Walsh was in Constantinople at the time, and was an eye-witness to this election. The Synod was held in a large square apartment with a divan running around it. Eight bishops and an estimated 500 delegates of the Greek community of the capital were present. The center of the room was filled with spectators, who were quite ready to participate in the proceedings themselves. Three candidates were proposed and, despite the obvious wishes of the clergy, who preferred another, the people clamored for Anthimos so strongly that he won by acclamation.

He was released from his prison by the Turkish officials and conducted to the Porte where he received the usual gifts: a white horse, a black cowl, a caftan of flowered silk and an ebony pastoral staff. So equipped, he was escorted by the Janissaries and a huge crowd to the church where his ecclesiastical investiture took place. The usual sermon was given and the patriarch responded. The contents of both speeches stressed obedience to authority, especially to the sultan. Walsh has a vivid picture of the conclusions of the affair:

The tumult which had subsided during the address began with increased clamor, every one pressed forward, climbing over each other's back, and his (the Patriarch's) hand was seized by so many at once that he was nearly dragged off of his throne. Those who could not reach it caught his robe and pulled it in different directions, till it was nearly torn to pieces. It was necessary to call in the guards to keep order. Some *chouashes* returned with large thong whips; they laid without mercy on the heads and faces of the crowd. In vain, the Patriarch intervened. He was at length compelled to make his escape from his unruly flock, which he effected with much difficulty by the aid of his Turkish guards.[1]

During the late summer of 1822 the Greeks learned of the intentions of the sovereigns of Europe to hold a meeting at Verona. They

[1] Robert Walsh, *A Residence in Constantinople* (London, 1836), II, pp. 365–8.

hoped that they might be able to present their cause before the Christian states at this conference and obtain the help they needed so badly. Unfortunately for the Greeks, the chief reason for the meeting was to prevent liberalism and revolution from spreading in Europe. It was, therefore, an unfortunate time to ask for assistance in the cause of revolution.

Attached to the project of the Greek government to send a delegation to the conference at Verona was a parallel proposal that contacts should be made with the Papacy as well. In the difficult situation in which the Greeks found themselves, government officials envisioned that Pope Pius VII might look upon their cause as a new crusade.

The government was encouraged by the Papal States' willingness to protect refugees from Greece who had found refuge there by crossing the Adriatic. As early as 18 July, President Mavrokordatos wrote to Cardinal Consalvi, the Papal Secretary of State, beginning his letter, 'The cries of a Christian nation threatened by complete extermination have the right to receive the compassion of the head of Christendom'. The fact that the Greek president could speak of the Papacy as the 'head of Christendom' represents a significant change in Orthodox thought in Greece. The letter concerned the sending of an emissary to speak to the cardinal about the Greek cause.[1]

The provisional government of Greece, now established at Argos, decided on Count Andreas Metaxas and a Mr Picolo to represent them at Verona. They were equipped with three letters, one to all the sovereigns at Verona, another special letter addressed only to the tsar and a third to be delivered to the pope. The contents of the three were basically the same; they announced that the Greeks would never again submit to the Ottomans nor would they ever surrender. They begged assistance in their struggle for Christianity against the forces of Islam.

Before the two representatives could leave, Picolo became ill and Captain Philippe Jourdain, a French Philhellene, replaced him. The latter later wrote a two-volume work on his experience in Greece, providing a first-hand account of this incident. On 30 September

[1] A. Mavrokordatos to Cardinal Consalvi, Mesolonghi, 18 July 1822, in Hofmann, *op. cit.* p. 80.

1822 Jourdain and Metaxas sailed from Idhra, arriving at Ancona in the Papal States on 24 October. They were there confined in quarantine at the lazaret, the ordinary procedure for people arriving from the Orient.[1]

The letter to Pius VII was forwarded to him along with a request for an audience and a safe-conduct to pass through the Papal States so as to reach Verona. In it the vice-president of the Executive Council, Athanasios Kanakaris, wrote of the veneration that the Greek government had towards the pope and how much it appreciated his helping the refugees.[2] The Greeks therefore presumed to ask a further favor, that he intercede for them at Verona. For four centuries the Greeks have suffered, the letter continued; now freedom was approaching, if Greece should rise again 'under the auspices of Your Holiness' it would be a wonderful day for Christendom. His word would not be ignored at Verona.[3]

The days in quarantine continued to drag on, but the delegates had no answer. On 3 November they addressed a personal appeal to Pius. The tragic history of Greece under the Muslim yoke was traced. The Turks were out to destroy all Christians in the Ottoman Empire; they noted that 'the blind obedience of the patriarch and the other prelates of Greece did not stop the fatal blow which cut off their heads'. The popes, in the past, as pastors of all the flock of Christ had always sought to deliver Christians from Islam. Now a new opportunity presented itself. The Greek revolution is not like the revolutions of other nations raised against altar and throne. Instead, it is fought in the name of religion, and '...asks to be placed under the protection of a Christian dynasty with wise and per-

[1] Philippe Jourdain, *Mémoires historiques et militaires sur les événements de la Grèce* (Paris, 1828), I, pp. 144 ff.; Spyridon Trikoupis, *Ἱστορία τῆς Ἑλληνικῆς Ἐπαναστάσεως* [History of the Greek Revolution] (London, 1853–7), III, pp. 16–23; Gustav Hertzberg, *Geschichte Griechenlands seit dem Absterben des antiken Lebens bis zur Gegenwart* (Gotha, 1878), IV, p. 275. Jourdain was a former captain in the French navy who had come to Greece shortly after the Revolution broke out. In 1825 he served as a lieutenant under General Fabvier.

[2] The refugees included a Cypriote bishop, Metropolitan Spyridon. The pope sent funds to support him and his fellow exiles.

[3] A. Kanakaris to Pius VII, Argos, 27 August 1822, in Hofmann, *op. cit.* p. 191; P. Jourdain, *op. cit.* I, pp. 157–60.

manent laws'. The pope is urged to let the delegates leave their confinement as soon as possible. Another letter was sent to Rome after one more month's delay addressed to the pope, 'the common father of the faithful and head of the Christian religion'. If the pope would but intervene with the sovereigns on their behalf, 'by this act, His Holiness will see that all Greeks by their firm resolution to maintain their rights and the religion of Our Savior, Jesus Christ, are worthy of his protection and apostolic blessing'.[1]

What the stranded delegates did not know of was the great pressure being put upon the Papacy to remain neutral. Prince Metternich, the great minister of the Habsburgs and archenemy of all revolutions, wrote to the Holy See requesting that the authorities at Ancona keep the delegates there. It would prevent them, said the Austrian, from making a 'useless journey'. Since Habsburg troops were then occupying part of the Papal States to suppress revolutionary activity, the pope felt he was in no position to act contrary to the wishes of the Austrian Minister.[2]

While Metaxas and Jourdain continued their discouraging confinement at Ancona, the Greek government decided on strengthening their hand by sending two new delegates. One of these was the famous Germanos of Old Patras, the great hero of the Revolution. The other was Georgios Mavromichalis, the son of Petrobey Mavromichalis, the respected ruler of Greece's most rugged area, the peninsula of Mani. The government gave them broad powers to discuss the affairs of Greece both with the pope and the chiefs of state at Verona. Moreover, Germanos was empowered to speak to the pope concerning the possibility of reunion between the Latin and Orthodox churches.[3]

The new ambassadors arrived in Ancona where they too were shut up in the lazaret with their predecessors. From here Germanos sent word to the Papal Representative in Ancona, Bishop Benvenuti, that he wished to see him. Benvenuti went to the lazaret and, through

[1] These letters are found in P. Jourdain, *op. cit.* I, pp. 147–8 and 160–5.

[2] K. Metternich to Cardinal Spina, Verona, 30 November 1822, quoted in Hofmann, *op. cit.* p. 116.

[3] P. Jourdain, *op. cit.* I, p. 166; Chrysostomos Papadopoulos, *op. cit.* p. 25.

an interpreter, Germanos outlined his proposal. He asked if the Roman church was interested in discussions with the Greeks. The bishop replied in the affirmative, assuring the Greek metropolitan that such a conversation would be welcome, suggesting that the decrees of the Council of Florence might serve as the basis of discussion. Germanos gave Benvenuti a letter for Cardinal Consalvi to be forwarded to the pope. It contained a protestation of the Greek nation's gratitude to the Holy See for its refugee work and was followed by a request that he be granted a private audience with the pope.[1]

Cardinal Consalvi answered Benvenuti's letter on 11 January 1823. The problems concerning the Greek mission are very serious, he noted. The heads of state at Verona are convinced the Revolution in Greece is against a legitimate sovereign. Thus '...the mission of the Archbishop of Patras becomes a very delicate and difficult matter'. He should inform Germanos that the Holy Father has seen his letter and is grateful for the archbishop's statements, but that the question of granting an audience 'would compromise the Holy See with every other government of Europe'. Moreover, such a meeting might easily result in having the Catholic subjects of the Porte become 'the victims of the fury of the Turks' if they should hear of a meeting between Germanos and Pius. Therefore Benvenuti should explain to the archbishop that the pope regretted the situation was such that prudence dictated he should not come to Rome.[2]

The Latin bishop and Germanos consequently met again to discuss Consalvi's letter. The Greek prelate was very disappointed, and hoped the decision might be reconsidered. He told Benvenuti that 'because of the disgraces suffered by the Greeks and for many other reasons he wanted to enter into a discussion concerning the union of the two churches',[3] but his offer was not accepted. Rome considered the risks too great. The Papacy, in the weakened condition

[1] Archbishop Germanos and G. Mavromichalis to Cardinal Consalvi, Ancona, 1 January 1823, quoted in Hofmann, *op. cit.* pp. 134 and 135.

[2] Cardinal Consalvi to A. Benvenuti, Rome, 11 January 1823, quoted in Hofmann, *op. cit.* pp. 140 and 141.

[3] A. Benvenuti to Cardinal Consalvi, Ancona, 9 February 1823, quoted in Hofmann, *op. cit.* p. 147; P. Jourdain, *op. cit.* I, pp. 160 ff.

in which it found itself after the Napoleonic era, with its territory occupied and in face of the opposition of the great powers, felt itself in no position to be the first state in Europe to recognize the delegates of revolutionary Greece. Its decision was not a courageous one, but was dictated by political expediency, hence regrettable and unworthy of the Papacy of better days.

Jourdain blamed Austrian influence for the pope's decision not to meet with the Greek delegation. The suspicion of revolution by Pius and Consalvi must also be taken into account. It is difficult to know what might have come from such a meeting. It is certain that Germanos' idea of possible church union would have had little support in Greece itself.

Eventually, the Greek delegation broke up. Jourdain went off to Paris to treat with the Knights of St John; Germanos lingered several months in Italy, still hoping for an opportunity to serve his nation before going home, but no results were forthcoming. The other delegates returned to Greece at once. The Papacy's position remained one of strict neutrality throughout the remaining years of the conflict.

The Greeks' best hopes for aid lay with Russia, but very little help was forthcoming from St Petersburg. Tsar Alexander was torn between his desire to avoid war with the sultan and his reluctance to leave the Greek people to their fate. Caution prevailed owing to the complexities of the diplomatic scene in Europe and his policy never went further than strong protests to the Porte. The amount of actual Russian aid to the Greek effort was negligible. George Finlay comments, 'Philhellenes from other nations arrived and fought by their side; large pecuniary contributions were made to their cause by Catholics and Protestants, but their co-religionaries of orthodox Russia failed them in the hour of trial'.[1]

The mission of Jourdain to Paris to make contacts with the Knights

[1] George Finlay, *History of Greece*, ed. H. F. Tozer (Oxford, 1877), VI, p. 2. Count Metternich noted that the Ottomans really had no complaints against Russia. The tsar had not acted on behalf of the Greeks, 'But, on the contrary, this same monarch has, since the first day of the insurrection of the Greeks, given proofs to the least penetrating of his entire disapprobation of the whole thing' (K. von Metternich to F. Ottenfels, Vienna, 21 June 1823, in *Memoirs of Prince Metternich*, ed. Richard Metternich, trans. A. Napier, New York, 1881, IV, p. 77).

of St John proved in a small way to be a success. He and Metaxas had been empowered by the Greek government to offer the Knights one of the Greek islands to be the seat of their government. The plan was then that the western powers would aid the Knights, the traditional foes of the Turks, thus avoiding an open espousal of the Greek cause. Actually the Knights themselves had fallen on hard times since the Congress of Vienna. The society had no Grand Master at the time, only a lieutenant named Anthony Busca, and its resources were nil.

Still, Jourdain proceeded to negotiate with the Knights' legal adviser. The society was to get the island of Rhodes for its base; in return, they were to carry on the fight against the Turks and allow Orthodox Christians to enter their ranks. Finally on 18 July 1823 a treaty was drafted and duly signed by the representatives of the unrecognized government of Greece and the handful of men still enrolled in the Knights of St John. The treaty was never ratified by either side, however, and the great plan of a crusade with Greek and Latin knights fighting together was not fulfilled.[1]

Another strange episode concerning the relations between the Greek and Latin churches occurred in 1825, when a Greek by the name of Kephalos appeared in Rome claiming he was an agent of the provisional government of Greece to treat about the reunion of the churches. He addressed a long letter to Pope Leo XII as 'the visible Chief of the Universal Christian Church'.

The document urged the pope to distinguish the Greek revolutionists from those who fought against legitimate monarchs. Greece, said Kephalos, desires a Christian monarch to rule it in order to protect the people and the church. 'He can also renew the bonds of communication with the Holy Pontiff, recognized by Greece as the center of unity and the supreme pastor of the universal church of Jesus Christ in East and West.' There would be no change in the Greek traditions, simply a return to the agreements of Florence. The

[1] P. Jourdain, *op. cit.* I, pp. 166–88; Edouard Driault and M. l'Héritier, *Histoire diplomatique de la Grèce* (Paris, 1925), I, pp. 209–11. The projected treaty may be found in Grèce, II, no. 8, Archives du Ministère des Affaires Etrangères, Correspondance politique, hereafter MAE.

Greek church today he described as 'a widow without pastor or chief'. Those appointed by the Porte's patriarch would never be accepted in free Greece. The Roman authorities gave Kephalos no encouragement and in the course of time discovered that he had no credentials whatsoever from the Greek government, but was in Italy on business connected with selling wine. Kephalos' ideas of re-union were actually limited to his own personal opinions.[1]

Meanwhile the war was not going too well for the Greeks in 1822. North-west Greece and Euboea had been lost, East Roumeli was in a state of anarchy and the Turks were back in the citadel of Corinth. On the positive side, the Ottoman forces which had been sent to pacify the Peloponnesus had been ambushed and forced to retreat. At the head of the Greek force who won this victory was the Greek captain, Theodoros Kolokotrones. He had also received the surrender of Nauplion and as a result gained the highest prestige of any figure in the Peloponnesus. Kolokotrones represented the best and the worst in the Greek military chieftains who led the revolution; of one thing he was sure, politicians were not to be trusted.

As a result, when the Peloponnesian Senate and the Executives of the National Government called for a new Assembly it was not allowed to meet in Nauplion owing to Kolokotrones' opposition and had to move to Astros.

This second National Assembly opened there on 29 March 1823. Representatives of nearly all factions and geographical areas of Greece attended. The clergy who appeared were Germanos, Joseph of Androusa, Gregorios of Methoni and Theodoretos of Vresthenes. The last named was elected vice-president of the Assembly. The main business of the session was to seek a foreign loan and to curtail somehow the power of Kolokotrones, but church affairs also came up for discussion owing to the initiative of Germanos and Joseph of Androusa, who proposed that something must be done to put church administration on a firmer footing. Germanos spoke to the

[1] Nicholas Kephalos to Leo XII, Rome, 29 May 1825, Archivio Segreto Vaticano, Segretario di Stato, rub. 242, busta 392, no. 5. On Kephalos, see Georg Hofmann, 'I Cattolici di Fronte all'Insurrezione Greca (1821–1829)', *La Civiltà Cattolica*, 21 June 1950, p. 5.

delegates on this subject 6 April 1823; on the next day Joseph addressed the Assembly, outlining the need for church reorganization. The members of the Assembly responded by encouraging him to present a plan and established that a committee should be set up to report to the Assembly on church affairs.

Unfortunately for the cause of ecclesiastical improvement, the pressure of political matters did not allow sufficient time and the report which was to be made by the committee appointed to perform the task was never issued. Some reforms were made, however, regarding the punishment of delinquent clergy and the severity of excommunication.[1] Joseph of Androusa remained at his post therefore, still operating under the original arrangement of the Ministry of Religion. He wrote exhortations during the spring of 1823 encouraging the people to patriotic effort but also urging them to obey the laws and to work together in assuming the burdens thrown on them by independence.[2]

The Minister of the Interior addressed a new appeal to the Latins in the summer of 1823 to join in the struggle. The appeal said that the Greek state was based on nationality, not religion: 'Only barbarous nations put religion together with nationality, so that a small religious dispute serves to divide them.' The Greek Constitution says that all Christians are Greeks, 'Therefore you, Oh Christians of the Western Church who live in Greece, are inseparable from our nation'. He urged them therefore to obey the government 'with a good heart', to pay the tenths on their produce and the other taxes. 'No longer can anyone who speaks Greek, lives on Greek soil, think he is a member of the French or Austrian nation because he happens to be a Western Christian, for a new situation has arrived.'[3]

[1] Andreas Mamoukas, Τὰ *κατὰ τὴν* Ἀ*ναγέννησιν τῆς* Ἑλλάδος [The events concerning the rebirth of Greece] (Athens, 1839–52), I, pt. 2, pp. 71 and 148; C. Papadopoulos, *op. cit.* p. 25; K. Oekonomos of the Oekonomos, Τ*ριακονταετηρὶς ἐκκλησιαστικὴ ἢ συνταγμάτιον ἱστορικὸν τῶν ἐν τῷ βασιλείῳ τῆς* Ἑλλάδος [Thirty years of church affairs or the constitutional history of the Kingdom of Greece], vol. II of Τὰ *σωζόμενα ἐκκλησιαστικὰ συγγράμματα* [The extant ecclesiastical writings], ed. Sophokles of the Oekonomos (Athens, 1862), pp. 27–9.

[2] Petrakakos, *op. cit.* XXXVI (1937), pp. 38–42.

[3] Gregorios Dikeos to Latin Greeks, Tripolis, 9 June 1823, Grèce, II, no. 6, MAE. In a letter from Veggetti in July 1824 to the Greek commissioners requesting the

The problem of clerical discipline troubled the church during these years. Since contact with Constantinople had been suspended, the question of episcopal appointments and transfers was especially difficult. Besides this, problems connected with unauthorized ordinations caused much anxiety. The government's efforts to set up regulations for the ordination of priests proved impossible to enforce.

The bishops as a whole were careful not to consecrate any other bishops while the war was in progress. The one exception after the incident of Chrysanthos of Lakedaemonia occurred in 1825 when Gabriel, metropolitan of Zarnas, and two bishops of the Peloponnesus consecrated a certain Joseph to be bishop of Mani. In later years Gabriel consecrated two other episcopal candidates. The rest of the hierarchy, however, did not recognize these consecrations as valid since the canons required the approval of the patriarch.[1] Moreover, since 1821, the bishops had received no more Holy Chrism from Constantinople and this was used as an integral part of the rite of baptism. In an effort to repair this lack in October 1824, the Ministry of Religion dispatched a priest by the name of Gerasimos to Constantinople to obtain the Holy Chrism from the partiarchate, but the authorities there refused his request. Although it was not realized then, it would be many years before any Chrism would be sent to Greece. The Ministry of Religion was further occupied with the daily problems that might be expected, such as questions of transferring clergy, church repairs, ordinations and providing clergy to replace those who died in the war or were missing.[2]

A new patriarch appeared in Constantinople when Anthimos was ousted on 9 July 1824. His successor was the former metropolitan of Serron, who ascended the patriarchal throne as Chrysanthos I. Like his predecessor, his rule would last for approximately two years.

church tax money be given to them, the archbishop told them that the Latin community as a whole had the disposition of these funds and that he had no control over it. The money was deposited in the French consulate at Naxos. Grèce, II, no. 31, MAE.

[1] C. Papadopoulos, *op. cit.* pp. 27–8; K. Oekonomos, *op. cit.* p. 18.

[2] Petrakakos, *op. cit.* XXXVI (1937), pp. 147–53, 300–31, 408–40. The patriarchate affirmed throughout the war that Holy Chrism not consecrated there was invalid, see *Sacrorum Conciliorum nova et amplissima collectio*, ed. Joannes Mansi (Graz, 1961), XL, p. 115.

The proclamation issued by the Ottoman government accused the Patriarch Anthimos as being 'every way unfit for that office'. The Greeks were exhorted to pay reverence now to Chrysanthos.[1]

The year 1825 seemed to bring one difficulty after another to the Greek cause, yet there was no desire to give up the struggle. The most important event was the invasion of the Peloponnesus by the Egyptians under Ibrahim Pasha on the request of the Sultan Mahmud. After first taking his forces to Crete, he landed at Methoni in February 1825 with the intention of marching through the Peloponnesus to Nauplion.

His well-trained troops were able to handle the various Greek forces sent against them with little trouble. By June 1825, Ibrahim was within sight of the capital. On the way he passed near the monastery of Megaspelaion, where Ibrahim sent the monks a letter suggesting they surrender. The abbot replied,

> We have received your glorious and majestic epistle, in which you inform us that if we surrender to you, we shall be found worthy of many gifts, but, if on the contrary, we do not, you will fight us. What wonderful thing would there be to conquer monks—but great would be the shame if conquered by them, for we are resolved to die upon this spot. We tell you then, go first and subdue Greece and then we shall surrender to you.[2]

Ibrahim took the abbot at his word, and marched against the monastery where 10,000 refugees crowded within the walls. Their flocks were taken, but an attack on the monastery was repulsed.

At the Mills of Lerna on the Argive plain the Greeks met Ibrahim, though outnumbered nearly ten to one. The battle was no great victory for either side, but it had the effect of turning Ibrahim's forces away from Nauplion. From there he went back to Tripolis and eventually to Methoni rather than risk a new engagement.

The spirit of the conflict is seen in a description given by the English traveller James Emerson when he visited Nauplion late in the summer of 1825. 'In the outer passes of the fortification, lay the bodies of two Arabs, putrifying under a burning sun, within

[1] Memo of Pisani, Pera, 9 August 1824, Strangford MSS, III, no. 281.

[2] Letter from the monastery of Megaspelaion to General Richard Church, 2 August 1831, Church MSS, XXIV, 175, British Museum Additional MSS 36566.

100 yards of the inhabited part of the town; the religion or prejudice of the Greeks not even permitting them to cast a little earth over the bones of their infidel enemies...'[1] He also gives some impressions of the church in 1825, speaking of the high veneration the Greeks have for their faith despite the fact that 'amongst all classes the most happy ignorance of the tenets of the creed prevails...' He was surprised to see how well the rigorous fasts of the church were observed despite the difficulties involved. The priests were occupied in many secular employments, not being able to live by the small amount of money brought in by their fees. He saw, however, that they were the ones who sparked the Revolution and noted how many who served in the army had suffered. The Turks were aware of their influence so that a priest made prisoner 'is sure to be put to death with greater refinements of cruelty than his companions'.[2]

No sooner had Ibrahim's forces departed from Argos than a call went forth to have a new National Assembly. The place chosen was Epidauros, the time April 1826. Three of the bishops were in attendance, Kyrillos of Corinth, Germanos of Old Patras and Porphyrios of Arta. The major result of this gathering was to form a single governing body made up of the members of the old Assembly and Executive Committee. It also chose a commission to deal with the diplomatic side of the struggle. In its instructions to this group which was to represent Greece abroad the Assembly listed three minimal conditions for a cessation of hostilities with the Ottomans. The first required the Turkish population to leave Greece, the second required the evacuation of all fortresses in Greece, and the third stated: 'It cannot be admitted that the Ottoman Porte can have any part or influence, direct or indirect, on the interior administration be it political or ecclesiastical of Greece.'[3] The interesting question here

[1] James Emerson, Count Pecchio and W. H. Humphreys, *A Picture of Greece in 1825* (London, 1826), I, p. 95.

[2] *Ibid.* I, pp. 334–7. The idea that the Revolution was a struggle for the preservation of the Christian faith is a constant one in the speeches made by the Greek commanders. See Ὁ *Φίλος τοῦ Νόμου*, Idhra, 9 July 1826, 11 February 1827, nos. 224 and 226.

[3] Instructions soumises par l'Assemblée d'Epidaure à la commission diplomatique, 12 April 1826, Grèce, III, no. 19, MAE; A. Mamoukas, *op. cit.* I, pt. 4, p. 107.

is what effect such a declaration might have as regards the relations between an independent Greece and the patriarchate. Presumably, the thought of the authors of the draft anticipated an autonomous church structure in independent Greece; if so, it is the first official declaration of such a sentiment. In the same month that the Congress met, Mesolonghi fell to the enemy and as a result the national government which then was headed by Georgios Koundouriotes fell. The Congress had to adjourn and much of its work was left unfinished.

The victories of Ibrahim and the fall of Mesolonghi may have been disasters for Greece at the time, but these same events at last stirred the European Christian powers to act in favor of Greece. Diplomatic activity between London, St Petersburg, Vienna and Paris had been a constant factor of European life since the beginning of the insurrection. Popular sentiment in all of these countries was overwhelmingly behind the Greek cause and impatient with governmental neutrality.

Changes were effected when new personnel appeared on the scene. In London, George Canning succeeded Lord Castlereagh in August 1822; in December 1825 Tsar Alexander died and the more vigorous Nicholas became the Russian chief of state. Canning believed that Russia would not sit idly by and watch the Greeks crushed and that 'if Russia once declared war, she would "gobble up Greece at one mouthful and Turkey at the next"'.[1] He decided therefore to prevent unilateral action on the part of Russia by joining with St Petersburg in putting pressure on the Turks. Kolokotrones had written to Canning in June 1825 protesting that Greece intended to fight to the end and that Britain 'will not abandon a people who have made themselves known to the world in a manner not incongruous with the lustre of their forefathers, who have already declared that they will all to a man either bury themselves beneath the ruins of their country, or crown their divine struggle by a complete victory'.[2] At that time Canning had rejected the Greek proposals; later in

[1] Quoted in Harold Temperley, *England and the Near East, the Crimea* (London, 1936), p. 53.

[2] T. Kolokotrones to G. Canning, Peloponnesus, 30 June 1825, Wellesley Papers, series II, vol. XXI, no. 146, British Museum Additional MSS 37294.

September when a Greek delegation appeared to repeat in person their hopes for British protection the foreign minister remained unmoved.

In a memorandum, he stated that Britain could not take the Greek side since this would open the door to a general conflict, 'they forget that there existed between England and Turkey Treaties of very ancient date and of uninterrupted obligation, which the Turks faithfully observed, and to the protection of which British interests of a vast amount were and are confided within the dominions of Turkey'.[1] The foreign minister was urging moderation on the part of the Turks at the same time. He wrote to Stratford Canning, who had replaced Lord Strangford as British minister in Constantinople, to warn the Ottomans not to provoke the Russians. 'A war with Russia cannot be a matter of indifference to the Porte, and yet surely the Porte must know with what difficulty, with what compulsion, and laborious perseverance the Russian Government and nation... are kept quiet and prevented from crying out for war, with their ancient and natural enemy...'[2] Canning's policy was now changed. He commissioned the Duke of Wellington to go to the Russian capital. The result of his talks was the St Petersburg Protocol of 4 April 1826. In essence the two nations offered to mediate the Turkish-Greek conflict on the basis of autonomy for Greece within the Ottoman empire.

The Greeks were agreeable to the mediation offer; the Turks were not. The next move then was for Canning to arrange for joint efforts with France and Russia again to offer mediation and if it were refused to take the necessary action. This was the content of the Treaty of London of 6 July 1827. When the Turks again refused, the Allied fleets were ordered to intercept Ibrahim's supplies; at Navarino Bay in October 1827 the Turkish-Egyptian fleet was completely destroyed due to the initiative of the British admiral's liberal interpretation of his instructions to stop supplies from reaching Ibrahim. For Greece, this encounter guaranteed its freedom.[3]

[1] Memorandum, Wellesley Papers, series II, vol. XXI, no. 149.

[2] Instructions to Stratford Canning, 12 October 1825, Wellesley Papers, series II, vol. XXI, no. 185.

[3] The British admiral in this engagement was Admiral Codrington.

Before Navarino, the representatives of free Greece met first at Hermione, then at Troezen in the winter and spring of 1827 to revise their government. Five prelates took this opportunity to address the Assembly concerning the question of church affairs. These were Kyrillos of Corinth, Joseph of Androusa, Daniel of Tripolis, Dionysios of Rheon and Theodoretos of Vresthenes, all of the most active clergy in the conflict. They addressed a memorandum to the Assembly, signed on 21 February 1827 and delivered three days later.

The memorandum recalled the great benefits which religion had bestowed upon the struggle for freedom. During the war the church had suffered a great deal; it now had many needs and problems but the bishops were unable to act. They therefore made the following request, 'Guided by the zeal which inspires our duties as pastors we beg with earnestness that the National Assembly convoke here, at this moment all the canonical bishops which they judge worthy and capable, so that we may deliberate with them and submit to the National Assembly the most fitting measures to maintain the church canons'.[1]

A week later the president of the Assembly responded to the bishops' request. No mention was made of a general convocation of bishops, but the response decreed the formation of a commission whose job it would be to prepare some general rules for administering the affairs of the church.

The commission's report was compiled during the following month and was ready to be delivered on 9 April to the Assembly, now sitting at Troezen. The important features of the plan called for the Assembly to establish a synod of prelates of three or five members to govern the church of Greece. Its title would be the Church Commission, and it would sit annually at the residence of the government; its constitution would be based on the Apostolic Canons and Holy Councils. It would also work in conjunction with the government to encourage the people to obey all civil laws in conformity with church doctrine and the canons, while avoiding political questions itself. The Commission would handle such affairs

[1] A. Mamoukas, *op. cit.* II, pt. 6, p. 108; Baron Forth-Rouen to Baron Turgot, 30 April 1852, Grèce, LVII, no. 287, MAE; C. Papadopoulos, *op. cit.* p. 31.

as providing preachers, filling vacancies, supervising monasteries, church property and the establishment of schools.

The final section of the schema, article 24, read as follows:

All of us, and especially the members of the clergy of the Eastern Church, have known no other mother besides the Great Church and no other Lord except the Patriarch of Constantinople (the great Patriarch Gregorios sacrificed himself a few years ago for our Holy Faith and for the Motherland), thus it is not up to us to cut ourselves away from the Church and desert it. The Prelates, who are in Greece united in spirit, will govern the churches entrusted to us without causing any schism or division in our spiritual and ecclesiastical community, without changing any of the rules of the Church, until God wills the good restoration of our Motherland. Then led by facts we will all consider what is to be done correctly and judiciously on this matter.[1]

The proposal was referred to the Committee on Religious Affairs but was never brought up for discussion again.

Political affairs were once again to push the pressing concerns of church matters into the background. The delegates had gathered primarily for a new attempt at trying to bring the conflicting Greek factions together and to modify the Constitution of Epidauros. No sooner had the meeting opened at Troezen on 23 March than the faction led by Kolokotrones threatened to leave. In efforts made to satisfy him, the Islanders and Koundouriotes were estranged and left the meeting. The Assembly proceeded then to modify the Constitution by making a single person the head of the government, to be known as the 'Governor of Greece' and to enjoy a term of seven years. The choice of the Assembly was Ioannis Kapodistrias, the former foreign minister of Russia and now a resident of Geneva where he had been at work quietly promoting the Greek cause. His choice was meant to please both the Russians and British, which, in fact, it did.

Since Kapodistrias would soon be at the helm of the government, the church issue was shelved until he should arrive. The Constitution which was finally adopted was quite liberal in tone. This is evident

[1] A. Mamoukas, *op. cit.* II, pt. 8, p. 150; K. Oekonomos, *op. cit.* pp. 44–7.

from the first article of the document which dealt with religion, 'Every person in Greece professes his religion freely, and its worship is given equal protection. The religion of the state is the Eastern Orthodox Church of Christ.'[1] Those who signed the document included the bishops Kyrillos of Corinth and Theodoretos of Vresthenes.

The final draft of the Constitution, however, contained an article, number Twenty-Four, banning the clergy from civil or military functions on the plea that their spiritual authority would thus be 'more pure and more venerated', which in fact was a subterfuge aimed at getting the bishops out of the government by delegates jealous of their pre-revolutionary authority. Article Seven of the proposed schema on the church had already decreed that the clergy would not be concerned with political affairs. This move was protested by the prelates in attendance, so that a decree of 1 May was carried suspending the article until Kapodistrias should come. Troezen, nevertheless, marks a significant step in whittling away the power of the church in Greece.[2]

At the close of the meeting the president of the Assembly made an appeal to all Christians stressing again the religious nature of the conflict. He listed the Turkish crimes against Christianity, 'We are fighting against the enemies of Our Lord nor shall we ever form a common society with them anywhere...Our War is not offensive but defensive—it is a war of justice against injustice, of the Christian religion against the Koran, of reason against the senselessness and ferocity of tyranny.' The message ended with a stirring call for the Christians of the world, princes and people, to assist the Greeks in their struggle.[3]

As the conflict progressed, one can see that the Greek church slowly was losing its pre-revolutionary status. During the long years of war many of its best men had been killed or wounded and much of its wealth had been spent. A certain weariness had descended upon its activities, the result of so much destruction and bloodshed. Its

[1] A. Mamoukas, *op. cit.* II, pt. 9, p. 128; George Bacopoulos, *Outline of the Greek Constitution* (Athens, 1950), p. 11.

[2] Frédéric Thiersch, *De l'Etat actuel de la Grèce* (Leipzig, 1833), II, p. 195; B. Forth-Rouen to B. Turgot, 30 April 1852, Grèce, LVII, no. 290, MAE.

[3] A. Mamoukas, *op. cit.* II, pt. 9, p. 59.

role as leader of the Revolution was under attack. The secular tradition which had grown throughout the conflict as a result of western ideology coming to the fore wanted to minimize the role of a church which it felt was too strongly attached to the old system. In the new Greece, the church would have to abandon much of its control over such things as judicial and educational matters. For the moment the confused state of wartime affairs did not permit the program of the secularists or the churchmen to be spelled out in detail—after Troezen everything was in suspension until Kapodistrias should arrive. His decisions would shape the future of Greece.

CHAPTER 5

THE GREEK CHURCH UNDER THE PRESIDENCY OF IOANNIS KAPODISTRIAS

THE selection of the former Russian foreign minister Ioannis Kapodistrias by the Assembly of Troezen as head of the government was significant as far as the diplomatic scene was concerned. Many diplomats thought it all part of a Russian plot to bring an independent Greece under St Petersburg. Actually, Kapodistrias was not particularly in favor with the Tsar Nicholas. He himself realized that he would have to tread a delicate path between the powers if he hoped to succeed. One of his first actions as nominee of the Greek presidency was to journey from Switzerland, where he had been living, to St Petersburg. He wrote to his friend J. G. Eynard from Russia that his selection by the Assembly of Troezen was looked on as a 'cross destined for me by heaven... You know that any definite decision in this affair cannot be the result of my will alone, nor only of the wishes of the Greeks; it is still necessary that the Powers do not oppose it.'[1] Only after five sessions with Tsar Nicholas did the emperor give Kapodistrias his approval, provided the other interested parties agreed to his taking the office.[2]

Kapodistrias, up to this point, had enjoyed a distinguished career in political and diplomatic affairs. He had been born in Corfu in 1776 of one of the noble families of the island. His elementary education had been enhanced by the study of medicine in Italy. Returning to his home at a time when the Ionian Islands were being tossed in the gale of the Napoleonic Wars, the Kapodistrias family remained

[1] I. Kapodistrias to J. G. Eynard, St Petersburg, 10 June 1827, quoted in *Correspondance du Comte J. Capodistrias, Président de la Grèce*, ed. E. A. Bétant (Geneva, 1839), I, p. 137.

[2] Kapodistrias to M. Stourdza, St Petersburg, 29 June 1827, quoted in Bétant, *op. cit.* I, p. 145.

partisans of the anti-French party. When the Russians occupied the island in 1803, the authorities invited him to become Secretary of State for the Republic of the Ionian Islands. He accepted this difficult position until the tsar, according to the agreement made at Tilsit, returned the islands to French control.

Kapodistrias was then forced to return to private life, but later he received a letter from a Russian official inviting him to come to St Petersburg for employment with the tsar. He arrived in the Russian capital in the first part of 1809; after some time, at his own request, he was sent to Vienna as an official in the Russian embassy there. Over the years he distinguished himself in numerous ways at this post. Eventually, Tsar Alexander chose him to be his foreign minister along with Count Charles Nesselrode. For seven years, the position was held by both men at a time when Russian influence in Europe was at its height.[1]

Then the Greek insurrection broke out. Though convinced it was premature—Kapodistrias had refused to lead or even publicly associate himself with the Hetairia—his sympathies were naturally with his countrymen. Since the war served to compromise his position in the Russian Foreign Ministry, he took a leave of absence and settled in Geneva in 1822 where he put his influence and finances at the disposal of the Revolution. Then had come the news that the Troezen Assembly had named him president of Greece.

Following his meeting with Tsar Nicholas, Kapodistrias proceeded to visit a number of other government officials in western Europe. In London, he had to dispel the notion that he would work only on behalf of his former government. This he succeeded in doing, despite some misgivings. Here he had the strong backing of General Richard Church, the English commander of the Greek army. When he finally did arrive in Greece in January 1828, a letter from General Church

[1] For Kapodistrias' early life, see Bétant, *op. cit.* I, pp. 7–63. Nesselrode had a high opinion of his colleague and his service to Tsar Alexander's goals, 'In this regard, one cannot be more Russian than he and it would be the height of ingratitude not to recognize the services that he has rendered and that he still renders daily with this in mind' (*Lettres et papiers du Chancelier Comte de Nesselrode*, ed. A. de Nesselrode, Paris, 1908, VI, pp. 115–16, letter of Nesselrode to his wife, Laybach, 28 December 1820).

was waiting, 'Be welcome then a thousand times! We may now hope that Greece will see a foundation for her prospects of Emancipation, and order established, that she will take her place amongst the Nations of Europe, and that you by your wisdom will render her respectable, and cause her to be respected... My joy is extreme for your arrival.'[1]

Not many days after Kapodistrias' return to Greece he was met by a group of bishops who sought to lay their problems before him. They spoke of the great needs of the church, and the president agreed that a commission should be established to survey its situation in Greece. This resulted in the appointment of a committee of the hierarchy in October, whose members were Joseph of Androusa, Jonas of Damalon, Neophytos of Talantios, Gerasimos of Aegina and Daniel of Tripolis.[2] The commission was divided, and one group was assigned to investigate the situation in the Peloponnesus, while the other was to survey the islands. The president wanted lists of all the property belonging to churches and monasteries; the prelates were also to insist that, in the future, parish records were to be kept, in order to stop the prevailing customs by which some churchmen made money by forging documents for marriage and ordination. The commission was also to report on the churches damaged or destroyed during the conflict. Kapodistrias ordered the civil authorities to co-operate with the bishops in repairing the war damage as much as their resources allowed.[3]

The president had to solve many immediate political problems so that action was delayed on church matters, yet there is no doubt that he was a religious man and that he deplored the situation in which he found the Greek church. He intervened frequently in church affairs himself, since his authority had even greater weight

[1] R. Church to I. Kapodistrias, Camp of Dragomestre, 13 January 1828, Church MSS XVIII, British Museum Additional MSS 36560, hereafter Church MSS.

[2] *Γενικὴ 'Εφημερίς*, Aegina, 10 October 1828, III, no. 75; K. Oekonomos of the Oekonomos, *Τριακονταετηρὶς 'Εκκλησιαστικὴ ἢ συνταγμάτιόν ἱστορικὸν τῶν ἐν τῷ βασιλείῳ τῆς 'Ελλάδος* [Thirty years of church affairs or the constitutional history of the Kingdom of Greece], vol. II of *Τὰ σωζόμενα ἐκκλησιαστικὰ συγγράμματα* [The extant ecclesiastical writings], ed. Sophokles of the Oekonomos (Athens, 1862), pp. 50–7; Karl Mendelssohn-Bartholdy, *Graf Johan Kapodistrias* (Berlin, 1864), p. 91.

[3] I. Kapodistrias to the Church Commission, Poros, 26 November 1828, quoted in Bétant, *op. cit.* II, p. 446.

than that of the hierarchy. He answered letters and complaints about bishops, appointed chaplains for the armed forces, and arranged for refugee Greek bishops to fill vacancies caused by the war. Some bishops had assumed sees without authorization, others kept changing their residence, giving rise to a situation which called for his attention. Kapodistrias admitted to some misgivings as to how far he should interfere in church affairs. In a letter to General Ypsilantis concerning the matter, he confessed, 'a bishop is not a civil employee, and it pertains to the government only to dispose of things that concern its proper affairs and not to things which are outside its competence'.[1] Still, it was left to the president to settle such disputes as who should be bishop of Athens and Thebes.

As a man concerned with forming Greece into a state on a European model, Kapodistrias saw the need of establishing a judiciary in the country which would replace the old church courts of the Ottoman period. The high church officials and primates had successfully opposed the establishment of courts during the Revolution, since a great deal of their revenue as well as prestige came from this source. Legislation passed by the various assemblies remained inactivated. Despite the objections which were bound to occur, the president set up a justice of the peace and a lower court in each of the prefectures into which the country had been divided. Later, courts of appeal were inaugurated to sit at Tripolis and Mykonos. Only cases of marriage and divorce were left to church tribunals.[2]

Kapodistrias was well aware of the need for improved education of both people and clergy in their faith. Frequently, the Liturgy was

[1] I. Kapodistrias to D. Ypsilantis, Poros, 6 December 1828, quoted in Bétant, *op. cit.* II, pp. 477–8; Frédéric Thiersch, *De l'Etat actuel de la Grèce* (Leipzig, 1833), II, 195; Herrmann Schmitt, *Kritische Geschichte der neugriechischen und der russischen Kirche* (Mainz, 1854), p. 120.

[2] George Finlay, *History of Greece*, ed. H. F. Tozer (Oxford, 1877), VII, pp. 47 and 127; K. Mendelssohn-Bartholdy, *op. cit.* pp. 131 ff.; General Pellion, *La Grèce et les Capodistrias pendant l'occupation française de 1828 à 1834* (Paris, 1855), p. 109; F. Thiersch, *op. cit.* II, p. 195, is highly critical of Kapodistrias and his relations with the church. He claims that the president used the church for his own purposes and that his exclusion of the bishops from their former judicial power was ruthless and arbitrary, 'He demanded of every ecclesiastic whatever his dignity that he conform completely to the spirit of the government.'

rushed through by priests in a mechanical way. Only a very few clergy were educated, so that the faith of the people was overlaid with superstition. Religious instruction was non-existent. To remedy this situation, Kapodistrias sought to purchase books in Venice for the Liturgy as well as collections of sermons, catechisms and the works of the Fathers. He stated to a friend in Italy that 'the first and most essential of the needs of the Greek government is that of procuring the religious instruction of the nation'.[1]

The difficulties of founding a seminary for the clergy were such that the first foundation was delayed until February 1830. Attached to the monastery of Zoödokon Pigi on Poros, the school opened with two instructors and fifteen students living on government stipends. The course of study was outlined by government decree. The institution, small as it was, meant a beginning, since students had not gone to the schools at Constantinople for years. The seminary, however, led a precarious existence during its lifetime, and disbanded before two years had passed.[2] In the light of this move, Finlay's charge that Kapodistrias was negligent in his duties towards clerical education is too strong. He contended that 'the education of the clergy was utterly neglected and a race of priests remained whose ignorance was a disgrace to the Orthodox Church, and who increased the national corruption'.[3]

The relations of the Greek church with the patriarchate in Constantinople were an obvious source of concern to the president. As a diplomat who knew the dangers of allowing the church to be governed by an appointee of the sultan, he did not believe the time for re-establishing relations between the patriarchate and the church of independent Greece had arrived. He had an opportunity to demonstrate his sentiments when, in May 1828, a delegation arrived from the patriarchate to treat with him on the relations between the Greek church and Constantinople.

[1] I. Kapodistrias to C. Mustoxidis, Bologna, 6 November 1827, quoted in Bétant, *op. cit.* I, p. 186. The tsar contributed a large sum to purchase liturgical books for the Greeks in 1829 (*ibid.* III, p. 169).

[2] Γενικὴ 'Εφημερίς, Aegina, 19 February 1830, V, no. 15; K. Mendelssohn-Bartholdy, *op. cit.* p. 150; André Papadopoulo-Vrétos, *Mémoires sur le Président Jean Capo d'Istria* (Paris, 1837–8), I, p. 139.

[3] G. Finlay, *op. cit.* VI, p. 48.

The delegation had been sent by the Patriarch Agathangelos I on the orders of the sultan. This prelate had been chosen patriarch in September 1826, and was to rule the church in Constantinople for nearly four years. He had been ordained in Moscow, and in 1815 served as metropolitan of Belgrade; then in 1825 he transferred to Chalcedon, a post he held until his selection as patriarch. He was a very learned man, conversant in Bulgarian, Russian, French and Turkish as well as Greek, but suffered from the difficulties inherent in the office he held during the Greek Revolution.[1]

The sultan ordered Agathangelos to write a synodal letter against the Revolution in May 1827. In the usual terms, the Greeks were told of their duties to their legitimate ruler, and were threatened with dire penalties should they persist in opposing him. A second letter appeared in February 1828, expressing the same sentiments. The letter reached Kapodistrias a few weeks later; now it was the delegation's purpose to deliver a copy to him in person.[2]

The delegates were four in number, respectively the metropolitans of Nicaea, Chalcedon, Larisa and Ioannina. They landed at Navarino in May of 1828, a city still occupied by the forces of Ibrahim Pasha. From him they received new instructions and then proceeded through Lakedaemonia to Tripolis. The governor here refused them permission to enter the city since they had been giving talks along the way to the crowds they met encouraging them to give up the struggle. Some of their audience may have been convinced, but by far the majority met their appeals with scorn.[3] Escorted by police, they proceeded to Nauplion where the reception they received was cool but polite. The president decided to meet them personally at his headquarters on Poros. Kapodistrias wrote to Admiral Codrington, commanding the Allied fleets, of their imminent arrival. He

[1] Manuel Gedeon, *Πατριαρχικοὶ Πίνακες* [Patriarchal lists] (Constantinople, 1890), pp. 688, 689.

[2] H. Schmitt, *op. cit.* pp. 116 ff.

[3] Ambrosios Phrantzes, *Ἐπιτομὴ τῆς Ἱστορίας τῆς Ἀναγεννηθείσης Ἑλλάδος* (1715–1835) [A summary of the history of Greece reborn] (Athens, 1839–41), III, pp. 57, 58; Baron Forth-Rouen to Baron Turgot, 30 April 1852, Grèce, LVII, nos. 299, 300, Archives du Ministère des Affaires Etrangères, Correspondance politique, hereafter MAE.

announced that he would not ignore 'any true offers of negotiation' and if anything worthwhile was proposed, this would be communicated to the Allied courts.[1]

The patriarchal delegation arrived on Poros, 21 May, and the discussion began the following day. In attendance were the officers of the naval forces of the Allied Powers. During the course of the meeting the president was duly given a copy of the patriarchal letter, whose contents had already been published and were known to the Greek government. The prelates could do nothing more than present the letter; they had nothing to propose other than what had been written there. As a result, the meeting ended in a stalemate, since it was hardly in Kapodistrias' mind to return to a situation where the Greeks should be subjects of the sultan.[2]

Kapodistrias composed a lengthy reply to the patriarch's communication.

Very Holy Father, the February letter which you addressed to the Primates, Clergy and laity of Greece has already appeared in the European publications and even in those of Greece, when at last it came to be delivered in Poros...We were filled with sorrow to find that the mission of these prelates had no purpose but to give us the letter of the month of February and exhort the Greeks to follow the counsels of the Patriarch.

He then noted that the government of Greece would indeed be pleased to accept guarantees of peace and security. These have already been given by the monarchs of Britain, France and Russia. It was too late now to speak of laying down arms; too much blood had been shed.

Besieged and attacked on the one hand by formidable armies, seduced on the other by all the forces which evil and treachery use to sway human weakness, delivered over to the counsels of inexperience, pushed often to the brink of the abyss, this people still exists, and it only exists because God has given it the grace to find in the Christian faith the strength to fight, the courage to suffer with perseverance, and the determination to

[1] I. Kapodistrias to Admiral Codrington, Aegina, 8 May 1828, quoted in Bétant, *op. cit.* II, p. 113.

[2] Γενικὴ Ἐφημερίς, Aegina, 3 May 1828, III, no. 29; I. Kapodistrias to Admiral Codrington, Poros, 23 May 1828, quoted in Bétant, *op. cit.* II, p. 144.

perish rather than submit to the yoke which subjected its fathers, but which it will never accept.

The fate of Greece is the work of Providence. Man can only respect its decrees. The Greeks are convinced, and today more than ever, that they have almost reached the end of their misfortunes, and that their wishes and hopes are going to be accomplished. This conviction is unanimous and universal...

We must, in the name of the part of the nation which has confided to us the direction of its interests, beg Your Holiness to give us your blessing, and to believe us to be firmly attached to the principles of our holy religion. We esteem ourselves blessed, at all times, that it has pleased God to put Your Holiness in a position, where it is possible to procure the fruits which must be accorded to all the sons of the holy church, of which Your Holiness is the head.

Be sure that the Archbishops who have come have fulfilled their orders as well as they could.[1]

The position of Kapodistrias in governing Greece was no doubt a difficult one; it was made even more so because his own temperament and background did not fit in well with the democratic spirit of the Greek people. He was a diplomat, not an administrator. Soon after his arrival, he had requested that the Troezen Constitution not be put in force until he could deal with the problems urgently needing solutions, a request which was agreed to by the Assembly. As his particular attention was focused on suppressing civil strife, the military chieftains were quick to feel his wrath. The Assembly's conferring of supreme power upon him allowed him to create a centralized government under his own personal direction. A secret police force was set up to keep the president informed of the mood of the population while every area of government came under his direct scrutiny.

Such actions were bound to cause resentment. Even before his coming, the Islanders had refused him allegiance; the chieftains, who for years had borne the brunt of the war, were alienated; even the British commander, General Church, who had been so enthusiastic at his coming to Greece, was writing Kapodistrias only four months

[1] Γενικὴ Ἐφημερίς, Aegina, 9 June 1828, III, no. 41; I. Kapodistrias to Patriarch Agathangelos, Poros, 28 May 1828, quoted in Bétant, *op. cit.* II, pp. 153–7.

after his assuming office, 'I had flattered myself that on your arrival in Greece all my troubles would end. How am I, in this moment then, obliged to tell you that nothing but my extreme devotion to the cause of Greece supports me under the bitterness of the daily mortifications I am obliged to undergo...Our difficulties and embarrassments have increased beyond all idea.'[1]

His advisers were frequently inefficient or corrupt, although such a charge could never have been brought against the president himself. One of his severest critics was the newspaper *Courrier de Smyrne*, which constantly found fault with him. It accused him of violating his pledge to seek the true interests of Greece, of attempting to set himself up as a king, of imprisoning people arbitrarily and forcing others to flee.[2] Frederick Thiersch claims he made use of the clergy as spies on the people and that '...no means was neglected to augment the number of these priests at the disposition of the government'.[3]

Kapodistrias could not concern himself with internal matters alone, since Greece's independence depended on the help the country could obtain from Great Britain and Russia, and, to a lesser degree, from France. The military situation for the Greeks had taken a dramatic turn for the better when the Navarino engagement took place only three months before Kapodistrias' arrival in the country. But what had been won militarily by Admiral Codrington was thrown away by the Duke of Wellington, the new British Prime Minister, who felt the incident a disaster and said so. This, naturally, had the effect of supporting the sultan in his belief that he could count on British support against the Russians. So encouraged, the sultan pursued the Greek War with increased vigor, and denounced the Convention of Akkerman, which he had agreed to with Russia. In April 1828, Russia declared war on the Ottomans. The British manoeuvring, to support Greece against Turkey and Turkey against Russia, collapsed.

The Russians had proposed a number of solutions to the Greek

[1] R. Church to I. Kapodistrias, Camp of Anatoliko, 7 May 1828, Church MSS XVIII, 36561.

[2] *Courrier de Smyrne*, Smyrna, 29 March 1829, II, no. 58; 23 August 1829, II, no. 78; 15 October 1829, III, no. 85.

[3] F. Thiersch, *op. cit.* I, p. 28.

problem. In 1827 they had submitted a plan which would have put the Greeks in the same position as the population of the Principalities: Turkey would retain sovereignty, but local autonomy would be allowed. They proposed the patriarch be named the head of the Greek state. He 'would reside in the capital and exercise the protection of the rights of his people in the same manner as the agents of the Princes of Wallachia and Moldavia'.[1]

Another alternative would have Russian troops occupy the Principalities until the Turks should agree to the Treaty of London of 1827. The British were none too happy about this. The Cabinet's reply to the tsar was clear, 'that the proposal to occupy Wallachia and Moldavia is a measure so little in accordance with the letter as well as the spirit of the Treaty of London, being a measure obviously of War, and of War not locally connected with Greece...'[2] Britain would agree to occupation only in the event of Ottoman aggression against Russia.

All of these proposals were academic now that the Russian troops were marching as a result of the nullification of Akkerman. The surprising thing at the opening of hostilities was the strong Turkish resistance which held up the Russians for months. But then the Turkish lines cracked and Adrianople fell in August 1829. The British were again disturbed and let the Russians know 'that the approach of the Russian forces to Constantinople cannot be regarded with indifference by this Country'.[3] Then Tsar Nicholas received a report from a special committee established to study the war. Their report had it that it was to Russia's interests that the Ottoman Empire be preserved. The Treaty of Adrianople had already been signed by the commanding general of the army, and happily was in accord with the Russian shift of policy.

Meanwhile, Kapodistrias had decided on calling a new National Assembly to meet at Argos. Representatives were to be chosen from all parts of Greece. The clergy played a leading role in the elections,

[1] Memorandum of March 1827, in Grèce, III, no. 125, MAE.

[2] Memorandum to Canning, n.d. 1828, Huskisson Papers XXIX, British Museum Additional MSS 38762.

[3] Memorandum of Lord Aberdeen, 6 August 1829, in Peel MSS, CCXIV, British Museum Additional MSS 40404.

for the voting was done in the local churches only after the priest had given a lecture on how the elections were to be carried out; then he read the list of all eligible to vote and each had to take an oath on the Gospels that he was following his conscience. Nearly all those chosen were partisans of Kapodistrias. On 11 June, this fourth National Assembly met. It again confirmed the suspension of the Constitution, and agreed that all power should be concentrated in the president's hands, but he was also to have a Council, the Panhellenion, to give him advice.

On 11 July, Kapodistrias spoke to the Assembly concerning church affairs. 'The Church has suffered many things because of the great calamities of the nation. We need to be furnished above all with an exact idea of its present condition. For this reason an Ecclesiastical Commission has been established and we are awaiting its report.'[1]

The Assembly passed, on 2 August 1829, measures to help improve the conditions of the church, to provide for an orphanage, and to establish schools. The government was to have complete control of these institutions.[2] Another governmental decree in September established the Ministries and the Senate. Of the six posts set up, one was for Public Education and Ecclesiastical Affairs; at its head was placed Nicholaos Chrysolegos. In a letter to the bishops of the realm, Kapodistrias was optimistic, 'the night is coming to an end, the day is approaching...In all matters, the Government will safeguard the canons.'[3] Despite high hopes, the Ministry and Commission failed to gather much support from the clergy, who objected to governmental control over their affairs.

[1] Γενικὴ Ἐφημερίς, Argos, 13 July 1829, IV, no. 49. The *Courrier de Smyrne* speculated that the president's brother Augustinos would head the commission; moreover, 'the court news has it that Count Augustinos is disposed to enter into sacred orders in order one day to become patriarch of Greece and this opinion does not seem to be devoid of foundation, when one considers how marvellously the President attends to the concentration of the highest dignities of the state in his family' (*Courrier de Smyrne*, 6 July 1829, II, no. 72).

[2] Γενικὴ Ἐφημερίς, Aegina, 14 August 1829, IV, no. 55; Georg von Maurer, *Das griechische Volk in öffentlicher, kirchlicher und privatrechtlicher Beziehung vor und nach dem Freiheitskampfe* (Heidelberg, 1835), I, pp. 480, 481.

[3] I. Kapodistrias to the bishops of Greece, Aegina, 26 October 1829, quoted in Bétant, *op. cit.* IV, p. 73.

According to the *Renseignemens*, a history of the period written anonymously, the commissions sent to report on the condition of the church went about encouraging resistance to the government: 'Dear brothers,' they said to the priests and monks, 'if we don't unite, if we don't keep our voice strong, all is finished for us; our flocks will abandon us to the mercy of atheists, and our holy church will fall.'[1] When asked to preserve church records, bishops and priests agreed that this was not the concern of the secular power.

The French Minister to the Greek government, Baron de Jucherau de St Denis, made a report in April 1829 of the situation as he saw it at that time. He believed that the influence of the clergy under the Kapodistrias regime was very little:

Although they (the Greek clergy) have served by their zealous efforts, and often by examples of courage to excite and strengthen the revolutionary ideals of the Greeks against their tyrants, their political influence on the people and on the government can be considered as almost nil. One cannot see a single Prelate nor Priest in the Panhellenion, in the Provincial Administration or in the Demagerontes (local government). It is to their poverty, as well as to their ignorance, that one must attribute the lack of consideration to which they are subjected. They do not possess any benefices; they live as under the regime of the Turks, in which they depend on the uncertain revenues derived from the charity of the people. The property of monasteries, far from being augmented, has been lessened, for according to the ancient canonical rules, they have turned over a part of their subsistence to the wounded soldiers and for the use of lodging.

St Denis did not believe Russian influence was strong. 'There would not be a priest who would want to see intimate relations established between the subjects of the Tsar and the modern Greeks.'[2]

The question of the Greek Latin Catholics also occupied the president during his tenure of office. The Latins had looked to France and the Papacy to aid them in their efforts to remain aloof from the Revolution. In attempting this posture, both Orthodox and Turks were displeased. On the Catholic islands, there were constant dif-

[1] *Renseignemens sur la Grèce et sur l'administration du Comte Capodistrias par un Grec témoin oculaire* (Paris, 1833), p. 33; K. Oekonomos, *op. cit.* pp. 59–64; William Kaldis, *John Capodistrias and the Modern Greek State* (Madison, 1963), p. 91.

[2] 'Report of Baron de St Denis', 30 April 1829, Grèce, VI, pp. 27, 28; 70, 71, MAE.

ficulties. The Latin clergy told their parishioners not to participate in the Greek government although the French consular officials now encouraged them to do so. On Chios, fifty-four Latin Catholic families petitioned the French through the clergy at Smyrna because 'their houses have been pillaged, all they possess has been taken. They are reduced to frightful misery, treated as enemies by the Greeks, whose blind fanaticism makes them consider all who do not follow their rite as such, while on the other hand they are exposed to Turkish reprisals; thus they are placed between two bitter antagonists.'[1]

Kapodistrias had first sent Count Metaxas to Syros to be the governor of the island. He and the Catholic officials were at odds over many points such as taxes and the tribunals. The Catholics eventually wrote to the pope lamenting that they had been included in the boundaries of Greece, 'we will be forced to abandon our country or change our rite in order to live with a people so intolerant'.[2] The president actually hoped to avoid incidents with the Latin Catholics. He sent them messages of reassurance and encouragement. To the commissioners who were to act as his agents, he urged prudence but firmness. Those who placed themselves under French protection cannot also expect to be Greeks, but must renounce their rights as members of the community. 'At the time when the islanders of the Roman communion find themselves honored with the confidence of their fellow-citizens and of the government, it is presumed that they will be less docile to the ephemeral seductions of foreign protection.'[3]

Conditions on Syros took a turn for the better when Nicholaos Kalergis was sent to replace Metaxas. By a scrupulous policy of honesty he brought the Catholic community into the government. They elected two delegates to the National Assembly at Argos, Georgios Russo and Georgios Marinello.

Incidents between Orthodox and Catholics continued to erupt

[1] Catholic clergy of Smyrna to Admiral de Rigny, Smyrna, 29 November 1827, Grèce, III, p. 193, MAE.

[2] Quoted in *Courrier de Smyrne*, Smyrna, 22 March 1829, II, no. 57.

[3] 'Instructions concerning Roman Catholics', 12 May 1828, in Bétant, *op. cit.* II, p. 121.

spasmodically. On Naxos, in 1830, the Catholics were forbidden to celebrate the feast of Corpus Christi which involved shooting off muskets. There was more trouble on Syros. In 1830, the Allied Powers implemented the Treaty of London so that the king of France, Charles X, renounced his right of protection over the Latin Catholics of Greece in return for certain assurances from the Greek government. The letter to Kapodistrias from the Allied Powers informed the president that all three parties had agreed that these guarantees should be given. Catholics were to have free exercise of worship, their properties kept intact, and their bishops 'maintained in the integrity of their functions, rights and privileges which they enjoyed under the protection of the Kings of France'.[1] The French mission property was to be respected, and no discrimination was to be exercised against Catholics regarding employment or in choosing men for public office.

The final decision on Greek independence had come as the result of an agreement between the Powers' representatives in London. The protocol had then been sent to Kapodistrias in February 1830. It was further announced that the Allied courts had decided to place at the head of the country Leopold of Saxe-Coburg. The Greeks had not even been consulted on their new 'Sovereign Prince of Greece'.

Kapodistrias and Leopold corresponded over the following months. The president has been accused of painting an exceptionally gloomy picture of conditions in Greece, presumably in hopes that Leopold would resign, and he might continue in power. Actually, it seems there is no substance to these charges, and the subsequent withdrawal of Leopold was due to his failure to come to an agreement with the governments of the Allied Powers over the boundaries of free Greece.[2] It is true, however, that Kapodistrias put pressure on Leopold to become Orthodox.

[1] Residents of the Allied Powers to the President of Greece, Nauplion, 27 March 1830, in Bétant, *op. cit.* IV, p. 421; Stamatios Laskaris, *Διπλωματικὴ 'Ιστορία τῆς 'Ελλάδος 1821–1914* [Diplomatic history of Greece] (Athens, 1947), p. 42; S. Laskaris, *'Η Καθολικὴ 'Εκκλησία ἐν 'Ελλάδι* [The Catholic Church in Greece] (Athens, 1924), pp. 1 ff.

[2] *The Times*, London, 26 May 1830, editorialized, 'But it is too late now to attempt to solder up the difference between the Prince of Saxe-Coburg and the Allied

In a number of questions which he proposed in a letter of 25 March 1830, the very first was, 'If Your Highness is disposed to embrace the religion of the country, it would be well to announce this. By the fact of this declaration alone, the most sacred bond will at once unite this nation to Your Highness and dynasty.'[1] In a letter some weeks later, the president was even more insistent on the religious question:

Since they (the Greeks) have constituted a national body, their representatives have declared that the religion of the state is the Greek religion, while granting tolerance at the same time to all cults. The transaction of the Congress of London made no direct mention of the Greek religion and I hope Your Highness will consider what an impression this silence has produced on the one hand, while on the other a special disposition concerning the other faiths was enacted.

It is to you, my Prince, that it is reserved to reassure Greece on this major point, by announcing that Your Royal Highness will, before all else, embrace and profess its communion.[2]

The president gave his assurance that the Catholics of Greece would enjoy all their former privileges and rights.

In the summer of 1830, the patriarchate changed hands again, when Konstantinos I assumed its duties. The new head of the church had been born in Constantinople in 1770. He had studied there and at the Academy of Kiev. Eventually, he went to the monastery of Mount Sinai, and in 1795 had been elected its archbishop, a title

Governments. His Highness' obvious indifference to the prize renders him an improper person to receive or obtain it.' In a letter to Kapodistrias from London, 1 June 1830, Leopold expressed his regrets. He said that conditions made it impossible for him to accept, but was consoled that he had faithfully and conscientiously defended the interests of Greece (Bétant, *op. cit.* IV, p. 79).

[1] I. Kapodistrias to Leopold, Nauplion, 25 March 1830, quoted in Bétant, *op. cit.* III, p. 525. Count Metternich was in agreement. When discussing potential monarchs for Greece, he remarked that 'the Head of Greece must necessarily belong to the Greek religion. Certainly no Catholic prince would change his religion, and the King of Naples is greatly deceived if he believes that the Greek people would be contented with a Prince of the United Greek faith' (K. Metternich to M. Esterhazy, Vienna, 30 April 1829, in *Memoirs of Prince Metternich*, ed. Richard Metternich, trans. A. Napier, New York, 1881, IV, p. 623).

[2] I. Kapodistrias to Leopold, Nauplion, 12 April 1830, quoted in Bétant, *op. cit.* IV, p. 10.

which he retained until his death sixty-three years later.[1] During his four-year term, he arranged to put the church on better terms with the Sultan Mahmud. Much of the old bitterness was gone, so the sultan issued a new *firman* giving guarantees of freedom to all Christians; they were allowed to repair their churches, the sultan himself taking the initiative in providing funds. As a result, twenty-nine Greek and thirty-six Armenian churches were repaired at this time.[2]

Hardly a month had gone by since his investiture before the new patriarch sent a letter to Kapodistrias. He expressed his good wishes for the government of Greece, but he announced his fears for the spiritual needs of the Greek people. Reports had reached the patriarch that the people had been listening to foreign voices; that a small book of Calvinist teaching attacking the hierarchy and the priesthood was being circulated. He urged that the government act lest the ignorant be deceived. The patriarch also announced his hopes that Greece might be brought again 'under the rays of the grace-giving orthodox patriarchal sun, that once more its inhabitants be received under the dawn of its bishop'.[3]

Kapodistrias answered with a letter of 22 September, expressing his thanks to the patriarch for his good wishes and assuring him that the government was acting in the best interest of the Greek church and people. The nation wanted to see a speedy conclusion to the war, but the enemies of Greece constantly impeded that result. He promised that the government would be on the alert for any heretical teaching in the church. He asserted that the Greek people had the divine blessing on their struggle for freedom and that a new and wonderful era was approaching for the nation.[4]

The patriarch replied to this letter with another in which he indicated he was not altogether satisfied with the president's response. He was pleased that the government was faithful to the canons; at the same time, the Greek church, he said, should be in a state of complete unity with the mother church of Constantinople, a con-

[1] Manuel Gedeon, *op. cit.* pp. 689 ff.

[2] Robert Walsh, *A Residence in Constantinople* (London, 1836), II, p. 290. A *firman* was a decree of the sultan which granted permission for some action.

[3] K. Oekonomos, *op. cit.* p. 77; K. Mendelssohn-Bartholdy, *op. cit.* p. 153.

[4] K. Oekonomos, *op. cit.* p. 80.

dition not fulfilled at the present. The metropolitan of Rheon and Prastos, Dionysios, was commissioned to go to Constantinople, but his departure was delayed so long that the project was finally cancelled. For the moment the political situation did not allow further progress towards unity.

The summer of 1830 saw conditions go from bad to worse for the president. His efforts to centralize the government, to keep all power in his own hands, alienated the most important men of independent Greece. Commerce had declined, taxes were very heavy. *The Times* printed a letter of a correspondent:

Never was there a more arbitrary and at the same time inept system; nothing has been done to improve the country, or cure the evils inflicted by the late sanguinary war—the Government having occupied itself solely in prying into the secrets of families and discovering what was said in coffee-houses for which purpose they have kept on foot whole armies of spies: these last did not fail to invent abundance of plots.[1]

In August, Alexandros Mavrokordatos, Spyridon Trikoupis and Admiral Miaulis joined Georgios Koundouriotes and others on Idhra where they declared the island independent of the government. Miaulis proceeded to seize the arsenal and fleet at Poros. Kapodistrias called on the Russian admiral, Ricord, to support his government. The Russians then recaptured Poros, and, rather than lose the Greek fleet to the Russians, Miaulis sank his own frigate, the *Hellas*, and other vessels anchored in the harbor. The Russians went further and sacked the town of Poros in retaliation for Miaulis' sabotage. The English Philhellenes and General Church especially were in despair:

If the Russians are permitted to go on making war in this country and Kapodistrias provided with money, it becomes a permanent province of Russia, of which it is at present to all purposes a dependency... The misery to which the Greeks are reduced by the late war and the delay in the settlement of their country by the Allied Powers has reduced to ruin every family in the country.[2]

[1] *The Times*, London, 4 June 1830.

[2] Extract of a letter, Nauplion, 16 August 1830, Church MSS XXIV, no. 187. It is true that interest in Western Europe concerning Greece was at a low point. France had undergone the July Revolution, George IV had died in England, Belgium had declared its independence and was threatened by the Netherlands.

Not the least of the president's problems was to secure an effective control of Mani and its powerful chieftains of the Mavromichalis family.[1] Petrobey had been appointed one of the senators in Kapodistrias' government, and the president had forbidden anyone to leave Nauplion without his permission. When Petrobey requested permission to leave, it was denied him. He left anyway, and Kapodistrias had him arrested and brought back to Nauplion, where he was jailed in the fortress. Here he languished for months until his son and brother resolved to avenge him. As Kapodistrias stepped out of church on 27 September 1831, the two men shot and killed the president of Greece.

Thus, the career of Ioannis Kapodistrias ended, leaving Greece without capable leadership for almost a year and a half. Even his enemies will admit he was a man of quality with the best of intentions, but his failure to appreciate the actual state of Greece at the time, his impossible desire to supervise all the administration of the country, and his strong reaction to any opposition were all regrettable. The people were not ready for his changes. Moreover the impression is felt that Kapodistrias either could not or would not give to church affairs the attention they deserved. He seems to have considered the church as just one more governmental agency according to the model of St Petersburg which would one day be reorganized but, until then, must shift for itself.

The condition of the church was hardly better after Kapodistrias' term of office than it had been at its beginning. The efforts made in its behalf were never followed through. The major problems: internal administration, education of the clergy, relations with the patriarch, were no nearer a solution. Obviously these difficulties were greater than any one man could solve, but Kapodistrias' efforts seem to have been very weak. To his credit, he insured that the church should not hastily join the Ottoman-controlled patriarchate without assurance that what the Revolution had gained might not be lost.

[1] In a letter to his friend Eynard, the president prefaced a comment on the situation, 'It remains for me to say a word about this eternal plague of the Mavromichalis' (Nauplion, 28 February 1830, quoted in Bétant, *op. cit.* III, p. 485), and on the Phanariotes in Greece (Mavrokordatos, Ypsilantis, Soutzos), 'There is not one (Greek) who does not detest to the depths of his soul the Greeks of the Phanar' (to Eynard, Nauplion, 10 November 1830, in Bétant, *op. cit.* IV, p. 164).

CHAPTER 6

THE REGENCY OF KING OTHO AND THE ESTABLISHMENT OF THE AUTOCEPHALOUS CHURCH OF GREECE

THE assassination of the president of Greece, Count Ioannis Kapodistrias, under tragic circumstances, only tended to perpetuate the divisions within the country. Those loyal to the dead leader grouped around his brother Augustinos, a man whose talents, however, were only a pale reflection of those possessed by the late president. The Roumeliotes or Constitutionalists, under the leadership of Ioannis Kolettis—their most vigorous personality—were no more satisfied with Augustinos than they had been with the count; while the Russians, whose fleet had played such an important role in suppressing discontent against the late president in the islands, threw their support to his brother, the British and French resident ministers in Greece favored the opposition, but only in a half-hearted manner.

Both factions agreed to meet in a National Assembly at Argos which convened in December 1831. The Kapodistrian party had more delegates, which caused the Roumeliotes to refuse to participate with them in any common deliberations—instead they formed an Assembly of their own. The Kapodistrian body proceeded to choose Augustinos as president after a discussion of three days. The newly-elected chief-of-state and his advisers then decided to oust the Roumeliotes from the city and, after two days of fighting in the streets of Argos, Kolettis and his followers were expelled.

The Kapodistrian Assembly then continued about its business which included a report from the Minister of Religion, Nicholaos Chrysolegos, on the progress made during the late president's term of office. He regretted that no final establishment had been effected:

The governor of blessed-memory, awaited the occasion which he alone knew would come, in order to carry through to its conclusion the great task, the establishment of an ecclesiastical authority along with the political settlement of the nation. This is evident from the speeches of our respected and high-minded leader; you know it further from his letters to His Beatitude the Patriarch of Constantinople and his response to them.[1]

The Assembly passed several resolutions which were meant to guide the church and strengthen it. It also selected another Minister of Religion, Iakovos Rizo-Neroulos, who announced a new drive to provide better educational facilities for the clergy.[2]

But the deterioration of the European situation left the problems of Greece in suspension at the time. Russia was concerned with the Polish revolt, revolution in the Netherlands occupied the attention of Britain and France, while the internal difficulties of Louis Phillipe in establishing himself in Paris and the attempts to pass the Reform Bill in England obviously made the governments of the Powers consider the problems of Greece secondary. Their representatives in Nauplion thought it best to support Augustinos, but this did not deter the Roumeliotes from setting up their own government in Perachora.

As the early months of 1832 passed, a state of anarchy descended upon independent Greece. Local governments were in existence wherever military chieftains could impose their will; Augustinos' authority hardly extended beyond the walls of Nauplion. The French army occupied parts of the country, other sections were totally at the mercy of brigands.[3]

[1] *''Αναφορὰ τοῦ ἀπὸ τῶν 'Εκκλησιαστικῶν κτλ., Γραμματέως πρὸς τὴν Σεβαστὴν Ε' 'Εθνικὴν τῶν 'Ελλήνων Συνέλευσιν'* [Report on ecclesiastical affairs, etc. by the Secretary to the fifth Grand National Assembly of the Greeks], in Chrysostomos Papadopoulos, *'Ιστορία τῆς 'Εκκλησίας τῆς 'Ελλάδος* [History of the church of Greece] (Athens, 1920), p. 49.

[2] *'Αθῆνα*, Nauplion, 6 August 1832, I, 42, pp. 165–7.

[3] George Finlay, *History of Greece*, ed. H. F. Tozer (Oxford, 1877), VI, pp. 102 ff.; Paul Karolidis, *Σύγχρονος 'Ιστορία τῶν 'Ελλήνων καὶ τῶν Λοιπῶν Λαῶν τῆς 'Ανατολῆς ἀπὸ 1821 μέχρι 1921* [Contemporary history of the Greeks and the other peoples of the East from 1821 until 1921] (Athens, 1922–4), I, pp. 279–322; *The Times*, London, 21 March 1832, p. 5.

The British traveler, William Greg, who was in Greece at this time, reported in a book published on his return just how bad conditions were, 'every town and village on the mainland—I do not speak hyperbolically—is in ruins: Athens, Corinth, and Tripolitza are almost utterly swept away'. Many people lived in huts of straw and mud, while the most unfortunate had to subsist in tents or with no shelter at all. The soldiers had no pay; they had to resort to pillaging the already destitute peasants. He found Athens 'one vast heap of mean and undistinguished ruins'. The population he estimated at 300; Epidauros had only twenty or thirty families left. In entering Corinth, nothing living was to be seen. '...there was nowhere any sign of human existence; here and there a wet and solitary dog prowled about the deserted streets and in no way was disturbed by our approach; the houses were all barricaded and the wooden windows closely shut...We thought we had arrived at some city of the dead.'[1]

While Greece suffered through this bleak winter, the representatives of the Powers began turning the diplomatic wheels once again to find a suitable candidate to rule the country. The search centered among the princes of the German states and narrowed down eventually to the Wittelsbach dynasty of Bavaria. The reigning King, Ludwig, had been a Philhellene from the very beginning of the conflict and his interest in the Greek cause had prompted him to contribute significantly to the Revolution. Feelers had been sent out to ascertain his sentiments on supplying a candidate for the throne of Greece from his sons even before Leopold of Saxe-Coburg had been considered as first choice. However, nothing concrete had resulted from these overtures.[2]

The ambassadors of the Powers, meeting in London, after Leopold's resignation, now informed the Bavarian envoy that they were seriously considering Ludwig's second son Otto for the Greek throne. A formal declaration to that effect arrived in Munich on 13 February

[1] William Greg, *Sketches in Greece and Turkey* (London, 1833), pp. 17–18, 61, 72, 79.

[2] *Die Berichte der französischen Gesandten*, II, p. 273, in *Gesandtschaftsberichte aus München, 1814–1848*, ed. Anton Chroust (Munich, 1935).

and the king conditionally accepted the invitation made by the ambassadors for his boy, since Otto was only sixteen years old at the time. At length, all the interested parties reached a satisfactory agreement on the conditions of Otto's accession.[1]

One of the decisions made by Ludwig and his advisers was that the young monarch should have a regency to accompany him as well as a contingent of Bavarian troops. The attention of the Powers then centered on pressuring the king to choose men favorable to their respective governments. The Russians moved first. Count Nesselrode informed the Bavarian ambassador he hoped 'his Majesty would not refuse to make the choice of Colonel Heideck to accompany Prince Otho to Greece'.[2] Heideck, in fact, was the first of three regents chosen. He was a strong Philhellene and had been sent to Greece by Ludwig, in December 1826, as the Bavarian monarch's representative and as an observer of the Revolution. He and his officers served there, giving logistical assistance to the Greek army although they had not taken any active command in the field.[3]

The second member of the Regency appointed by Ludwig was Georg von Maurer, then serving as a government official in Munich. Von Maurer's training had made him one of the outstanding men in the legal profession in Bavaria, having studied both at Paris and Heidelberg. When he returned to Munich in 1826, he had been appointed professor at the Hochschule there, where he remained for

[1] H. Howard to Lord Palmerston, Munich, 23 February 1832; T. Erskine to Palmerston, Munich, 19 May 1832, F.O. 9, Bavaria, vol. 64, no. 5, vol. 65, no. 14, London, Public Record Office, hereafter PRO; C. Nesselrode to G. Potemkin, St Petersburg, 4 March 1822, in Barbara Jelavich, *Russia and Greece during the Reign of King Othon* (Thessaloniki, 1962), pp. 37, 38; Stamatios Laskaris, *Διπλωματικὴ Ἱστορία τῆς Ἑλλάδος* [Diplomatic history of Greece] (Athens, 1947), pp. 46 ff. 'Otto' became 'Othon' in Greece and will be called by his Greek name henceforth in its Anglicized version.

[2] Baron de Lerchenfeld to Ludwig, St Petersburg, 7 March 1832, MA III, Russland, 2720, no. 17, Munich, Geheimes Staatsarchiv, hereafter GS. The Bavarian foreign minister Baron August de Gise told Lerchenfeld to inform the tsar that the regents 'will be very favorable to the interests which Russia wants protected' (Gise to Lerchenfeld, Munich, 10 March 1832, MA III, 2720, no. 18). Gise was concerned that the democratic factions in Greece be suppressed.

[3] Thomas Gordon, *History of the Greek Revolution* (London, 1832), II, p. 375; Leonard Bower and Gordon Bolitho, *Otho I, King of Greece* (London, 1939), p. 46.

three years. Thence he had transferred to the University of Göttingen, but his abilities were so highly regarded by this time that the Bavarian government made frequent demands on him for affairs of state. At length, he had to abandon the academic life to serve in various official capacities until he was chosen as a member of the Regency.[1]

The third of the regents was the liberal-minded Count Joseph von Armansperg. A man of experience and pleasant disposition, he had twice served in the Bavarian cabinet as minister of Finance and Foreign Affairs. His wife and three daughters, however, exercised a strong influence over him, which was not always for the good. More than the other two regents, he gained the confidence of the young Otho.[2]

In religious sentiments, Heideck and von Maurer were Protestants, but of the liberal variety of the early nineteenth century. The father of von Maurer, in fact, was a minister of the Evangelical church. Count Armansperg was a formal Catholic, but also a Freemason, a fact which was not known by King Ludwig.[3]

In general, the representatives of the Powers were well-pleased with the choices made. The British minister to Munich, Lord Erskine, wrote Palmerston, 'A very general sentiment of surprise prevails that so many of the most efficient and sensible Statesmen could be spared from their country at the present moment'. While his French colleague informed Paris, 'France can well be pleased with the new Greek government except for Heideck, who perhaps is inclined to the Russian side'.[4]

As for the young monarch himself, he had been born in Salzburg, 1 June 1815. His father Ludwig was a man of considerable instability bordering on the neurotic whose interests were not in his family. Otho and his brothers had been brought up by a Catholic priest, Father Oettl, as their tutor in Würzburg. There, Otho was known

[1] For Georg von Maurer's life see Karl Dickopf, *Georg Ludwig von Maurer, 1790–1872* (Kallmünz, 1960).

[2] G. Finlay, *op. cit.* VII, p. 110.

[3] K. Dickopf, *op. cit.* p. 2; Hans Rall, 'Die Anfänge des Konfessionspolitischen Ringens um die Wittelsbacher Thron in Athen', *Bayern: Staat und Kirche, Land und Reich* (Munich, 1961), p. 200.

[4] T. Erskine to Palmerston, 18 July 1832, F.O. 9, Bavaria, vol. 65, no. 44, PRO: de Sercey to Prince de Broglie, Munich, 23 October 1832, in Chroust, *op. cit.* III, p. 95.

as an indifferent student and given to outbursts of temper and depression which lasted two or even three days. Swimming and riding were his favorite sports. According to his biographers, 'Otho's education had been that of a Prince who was only to fill a minor position in the state; in fact, his father had intended that he should enter the Church and his early upbringing had been planned on those lines'.[1]

On 7 May 1832, the three Powers and Bavaria signed the final treaty which guaranteed Greece's independence and named Otho the monarch of the new nation. The regency was to extend till his twentieth year. It was further stipulated that the succession would pass to his brothers in case of the death of the king and provided further that the two crowns of Bavaria and Greece would never be united.[2] The Powers guaranteed a loan of sixty million francs, part of which would be needed to pay for 3,500 Bavarian troops to be sent to Greece as the core of a new national army.

Even before the Treaty of London was signed, Tsar Nicholas had begun a campaign to urge the Bavarian government to convince Otho he should convert to Orthodoxy. The Russian ambassador in London, Prince Christopher Lieven, received instructions from Count Nesselrode while the negotiations were in progress concerning the choice of Otho, which summed up the Russian position:

> We will not develop here the motives which press us to consider the conversion of the future Sovereign of Greece to the religion of the country as one of the most important considerations for the strengthening of his reign and the good of his subjects. These motives can be easily recognized and appreciated by all those who know the state of public opinion in this nation...more than in any other country the throne and church must mutually support one another so that there, more than anywhere else, a young sovereign and a people recently summoned to political independence, may be able to invoke the assistance of the Almighty before the same altar.[3]

[1] L. Bower and G. Bolitho, *op. cit.* p. 28.

[2] The treaty is found in F.O. 32, Greece, vol. 40, 7 May 1832, PRO. Otho's two younger brothers were Luitpold and Adalbert.

[3] C. Nesselrode to C. Lieven, St Petersburg, 17 February 1832, in B. Jelavich, *op. cit.* p. 40.

The Bavarian negotiator, Cetto, made vague statements concerning the possibilities of Otho becoming Orthodox when he was older, but Ludwig warned him to make no definite promises.

The Russian court was sincere in wanting a strong monarch established in Greece, one who would be able to resist both the internal pressure of the people of the country for a democratic form of government and the external influences of the British and French. Tsar Nicholas believed that the situation in Greece demanded the same type of autocratic rule that he exercised in Russia—anything less reminded him too much of revolutionary France and what that had meant for Europe. There can be no doubt that Nicholas was concerned, for he felt that a Catholic monarch would not be able to cope with the difficult situation, especially at a time when Greek nationalism and orthodoxy were practically identified. The Russian efforts at London mark the beginning of a religious problem which plagued the conscience of Otho throughout his reign. He did want to have the affection of the Greek people and he realized that his Catholicism was a major obstacle to obtaining it, yet he could not agree to abandon the faith in which he had been baptized and educated.

The subject of Otho's conversion became a topic for discussion in St Petersburg as well as in London during the month of April. The tsar summoned the Bavarian minister, Baron Lerchenfeld, to St Petersburg for a long conversation in which he called Otho's conversion 'indispensable'. Lerchenfeld wrote to Ludwig that he was convinced that Nicholas meant every word, for 'the Emperor spoke on this subject with such ardor and eloquence that it surpasses everything that I have ever heard from his mouth'.[1]

Ludwig's reply to Tsar Nicholas, transmitted through his ambassador, was a continuation of the Bavarian policy as enunciated in London. He stressed that Otho's religion was the result of 'conscience and conviction' and hence could not readily be changed, while at the same time he admitted the possibility of conversion to Orthodoxy when he was older. He also suggested

[1] B. Lerchenfeld to Ludwig, St Petersburg, 26 April 1832, MA III, Russland, 2720, no. 27, GS: H. Rall, *op. cit.* pp. 189 ff.

the probability that all of Otho's children would be raised in the Orthodox faith.[1]

Nesselrode reluctantly accepted Ludwig's response as did the tsar, so that the Treaty of London was signed without any religious conditions attached, although this did not mean the Russians were content. The tsar intensified his communications on the subject during the summer of 1832, at last sending a personal letter to King Ludwig. By now the Bavarians were a bit weary of 'the great perseverance of the Court of St Petersburg on the question', but they responded courteously to the tsar's letter. Once again Ludwig insisted that he could not violate the freedom of his son's conscience on the matter, but that he believed the future might bring a number of changes. The Russians must be patient.[2]

While diplomats talked and statesmen planned the future of Greece in cities hundreds of miles away, affairs in the country itself were going badly for President Augustinos Kapodistrias and his shaky regime. In early April the Roumeliote army had defeated the Government troops, and the residents of the Powers then forced Augustinos to resign and appoint a commission to govern Greece. The commissioners whom the president chose were rejected by the Roumeliote leader, Ioannis Kolletis, and a new seven-man body favorable to the Roumeliotes and the ambassadors at Nauplion emerged. In fact, the new executive organ had only scattered support throughout the country and were it not for the French army of occupation, which had taken positions in parts of the Peloponnesus as a result of the various agreements reached by the Powers, the

[1] A. Gise to Lerchenfeld, Munich, 4 May 1832, Bayer Gesandtshaft, St Petersburg, GS; Nesselrode to Potemkin, St Petersburg, 11 May 1832, in B. Jelavich, *op. cit.* pp. 44, 45.

[2] A. Gise to Lerchenfeld, Munich, 12 July 1832; Lerchenfeld to Ludwig, St Petersburg, 27 July 1832, Bayer Gesandtshaft, St Petersburg, GS. The British envoy T. Erskine wrote to Lord Palmerston, 'The answer of the King of Bavaria was that he could not undertake to bias the conscience of his son upon so highly delicate a point, but that he entertained no doubt that all the descendants (if there should be any) of the new King of Greece would be brought up in the Greek religion' (Munich, 23 August 1832, F.O. 9, Bavaria, vol. 65, no. 54, PRO). There were also rumors to the effect the tsar hoped Otho would arrange a marriage with a Russian princess.

Nauplion government would have been completely without authority.

It was this government's Assembly which ratified the choice of Otho by acclamation when the news of his election reached Greece. The delegates determined further to send a delegation made up of Admiral Miaulis and the members Botzaris and Kolliopoulos to Munich to congratulate the new sovereign on his nomination to the throne of Greece and swear their allegiance to him. The three men made their way to Munich in October, where they were received with great ceremony. For the first time some representatives of Greece were able to meet with their sovereign. In the Wittelsbach palace, the Greek delegates took the oath of allegiance to Otho on a copy of the Gospels with the archimandrite of the Orthodox church in Munich witnessing the ceremony. It was an auspicious beginning.[1]

The regents, for one reason or another, found reasons to delay their departure for Greece despite the urging of Ludwig and the various ambassadors of the Powers to Munich. It was only on 6 December that everyone was ready to leave and then amid great fanfare Otho and his advisers started on their journey to Greece. The slow-moving party journeyed south through Italy where Otho along with his elder brother Maximilian called on Pope Gregory XVI and attended Mass on Christmas Day in St Peter's. In an audience with the pope, Otho was requested to look after the fortunes of his co-religionists in Greece. Thence the regents and Otho went to Naples where they boarded a ship for Greece.[2]

[1] L. Bower and G. Bolitho, *op. cit.* p. 32; Edouard Driault and M. l'Héritier, *Histoire diplomatique de la Grèce* (Paris, 1925), II, p. 97.

[2] P. Karolidis, *op. cit.* I, pp. 514, 515. An exchange of notes between Ludwig and the pope on the occasion of Otho's visit to Rome took place in October. The Bavarian minister at Rome wrote to the Papal Secretary of State, Cardinal Bernetti, 'His Majesty the King of Bavaria does not doubt that the Holy Father will be pleased to share in the satisfaction that he feels at this event and in his high wisdom will appreciate the immense good that is promised by the occupation of the throne by a prince of a royal house which on every occasion has given proofs of its attachment to the Holy Father...' (Letter of 18 October 1832). The cardinal's reply of 22 October agreed that the pope was happy to see Otho as monarch of Greece and he hopes 'that the young monarch and the Regency which governs in his name

Otho's arrival could come none too soon. A new military coup had taken place in Nauplion which brought to power a coalition of Kolettis, Andreas Zaimis and Andreas Metaxas which announced it would govern as a 'Military Commission' until the king should arrive. Recognized as legitimate by the residents of the Powers in Nauplion, its jurisdiction was no more extensive than its predecessor's. In the other parts of liberated Greece, the military chieftains were in command. They insisted on holding on to their authority until Otho's arrival, then they would transfer their allegiance to him. In a remarkable way, the news that Greece should have a young monarch from a distant land excited their imaginations. Happily for Otho, his arrival was 'ardently desired by all parties and by every class'.[1] The people of Greece, weary of war and suffering every sort of privation, could only live in hope until their young ruler should come.

While Otho was still at sea, Greece heard once again the sound of gunfire in the streets. In preparation for the arrival of the new sovereign, the French troops occupying the Peloponnesus had been requested by the Bavarian agent of the Regency, who was in charge of arrangements for the king's arrival, to take up stations in Argos. Theodoros Kolokotrones, still as independent as ever, was holding the city and refused the French entry, even going so far as to arrest some of the officers. Some French and Greeks exchanged fire; then the French artillery opened up on Kolokotrones' position. After three hours of bombardment, the Greeks withdrew having suffered some 300 casualties. Kolokotrones and some of the other chieftains who hoped for a privileged position in the new government saw their opportunity fade after this encounter.[2]

In the field of international relations the month of January saw important developments take place owing to the revolt of the Egyptian governor, Muhammad Ali, against the sultan. Mahmud sought

will accord to the Catholic religion of Greece the freedom it has been promised' (Archivio Segreto Vaticano, Segretario di Stato, 'Questioni di Alta Diplomazia', rub. 242, busta 394).

[1] W. Greg, *op. cit.* p. 19. The population of free Greece in 1833 is estimated at something between 500,000 and 700,000 people.

[2] E. Dawkins to Palmerston, Nauplion, 26 January 1833, F.O. 32, Greece, vol. 36, nos. 3 and 4, PRO.

aid from both Britain and France but was turned down. Facing the prospect of almost certain defeat and the end of his own dynasty, he determined to ask the Russians, the ancient enemy of the Turks, for assistance rather than admit such a catastrophe. The tsar responded affirmatively and Nicholas dispatched a fleet to the Bosporus to protect Constantinople from the Egyptian force, thus sparking a new crisis with Russia's sometime allies, the British and the French. The French troops, scheduled to depart from Greece when Otho and the Regency arrived, refused to leave—with the excuse there were not enough boats—in order to be able to counter any Russian moves in the East Mediterranean. In late June, the Turks paid for the Russian help by signing the Treaty of Hunkiar Iskelesi, which guaranteed mutual aid and friendship in case of attack by a foreign power. A secret clause, however, allowed the Turks only partially to fulfil the stated terms of the Treaty for it provided that they allow Russian warships to pass through the Straits in wartime, while stopping all others from entering. There is some doubt as to whether the parties understood this clause in the same way.

The people of Greece could ignore these matters, since the nation at last saw its king arrive in the harbor at Nauplion, on 18 January, aboard the British ship *Madagascar*, accompanied by both French and Russian vessels bringing the Bavarian troops and the king's household. On the day of his official reception a week later, the ministers of the Powers went aboard the *Madagascar* for breakfast with Otho and the regents; then, amid the enthusiastic cheers of the citizens of Nauplion, the king disembarked. He was met on the quay by the members of the provisional government who turned over their powers to him. Otho made a short response, then entered the city riding down its main street, which was lined by French and Bavarian troops, to the metropolitan cathedral where Kyrillos, archbishop of Corinth, accompanied by the city's clergy, met him. The archbishop made a congratulatory speech pledging the devotion of the Greek clergy to him. Otho, in turn, promised 'the Church of Greece may be assured that on every occasion it will ever enjoy my fullest protection'. He kissed the Gospel book, entered the church and a service begging God's blessing on the monarch was celebrated. At its conclusion everyone took the oath of allegiance to the new sovereign of Greece. The rest of the day was given over to celebrating the inauguration of a new era for Greece. The one disappointment noted by many listening to Otho's speeches during the day had been his failure to mention a constitution—it had not been an oversight.[1]

On the evening of the 25th, the government proclaimed the division of the ministries between the regents. Von Armansperg held the ministries of Finance, Interior and Foreign Affairs, Colonel Heideck was naturally appointed to head the War Ministry and Georg von Maurer took up the ministries of Justice, Ecclesiastical Affairs and Public Instruction. Spyridon Trikoupis was to head the Greek members of the government with the title of President of the Council of Ministers.[2]

The Bavarian Regency began with great urgency to refashion Greece according to preconceived notions as to how the nation should be governed. None of the regents had any experience with conditions as they were, save for Colonel Heideck who had spent some time in Greece. Nevertheless, they believed that the Greeks themselves had little to recommend and proceeded to govern the country in large measure without their assistance. In a short time, large sections of the Greek nation were alienated, while the members of the Regency found it increasingly difficult to work together.

The conflict in the Regency was the result of personality clashes. Armansperg, who was the dominant figure as head of the Regency, came from an aristocratic background and proceeded to conduct the business of state with a flourish reminiscent of the Munich court, while Maurer, of bourgeois background and with a practical mind, found the count's ways most distasteful. Both Maurer and Armansperg sought to undermine one another's position so that intrigue

1 The full account of this day is given by many witnesses. The best are E. Dawkins to Palmerston, Nauplion, 3 March, F.O. 32, Greece, vol. 36, no. 13, PRO; B. Forth-Rouen to the Duke de Broglie, Nauplion, 10 February, Grèce, XVI, no. 85, Archives du Ministère des Affaires Etrangères, hereafter MAE; Otho to Ludwig, Nauplion, 6 March 1833, quoted in L. Bower and G. Bolitho, *op. cit.* p. 39 and P. Karolidis, *op. cit.* I, p. 526.

2 Tryphonos Evangelides, *Ἱστορία τοῦ Ὄθωνος, Βασιλέως τῆς Ἑλλάδος* [History of Otho, King of Greece] (Athens, 1893), pp. 44 ff.

among their own subordinates and in concert with the representatives of the Powers was the order of the day.[1]

The problems which the Regency faced were really monumental. Greece was prostrate after so many years of war and civil strife. The economy of the country was at a complete standstill, the nation's capital having been exhausted, so that everything depended on the loan made by the Powers. There were still areas of the country which the Turks had not evacuated; the chieftains, stripped of their power, were restless, while their dismissed men took to brigandage; housing was needed for large segments of the population, as were schools and public buildings. In the midst of all these problems the situation of the church in Greece also demanded immediate attention.

The condition of the church, which had improved but slightly under Kapodistrias, left much to be desired. Large numbers of priests—perhaps so many as 6,000 or 7,000, as well as a large group of bishops—had been killed during the war; almost half of the sees were unoccupied, with protosynkelli holding positions as vicars. Some bishops had incorporated other dioceses. For years there had been no organized education possible for the clergy save for the Poros seminary. Maurer estimates that only ten out of a thousand priests were able to write their name.[2]

As a result of this situation, an ecclesiastical commission was named by the government on 15 March to study the problem. Its duties were 'to ascertain the condition of the Greek Church and of the monasteries, and to propose means for improving the position of the church concerning the organization of the higher and lower clergy and the establishment of a permanent Synod for ecclesiastical affairs, to present also a detailed statement concerning its competence and its object'.[3] The Regency selected Spyridon Trikoupis to be president of the board and chose as members Ignatios, bishop of

[1] G. Finlay, *op. cit.* VII, pp. 110–15.

[2] Georg von Maurer, *Das griechische Volk in öffentlicher, kirchlicher und privatrechtlicher Beziehung vor und nach dem Frieheitskampfe* (Heidelberg, 1835), II, p. 153. C. Vovolini gives the number as between 6,000 and 10,000 clergy who were killed during the struggle ('Η 'Εκκλησία εἰς τὸν 'Αγῶνα τῆς 'Ελευθερίας [The church in the struggle for freedom], Athens, 1952, p. 120).

[3] 'Αθῆνα, Nauplion, 8 April 1833, II, 101, p. 390.

Ardamerios, Paisios, bishop of Elaias and vicar of Messenia, Panoutsos Notaras, Skarlatos Vyzantinos, Konstantinos Schinas and Theokletos Pharmakidis.[1] The commission had a great number of issues to decide, but all hinged on how the problem of the church's relationship with the patriarch of Constantinople would be settled. The essence of the problem was whether or not Greece should be independent of the patriarchate. The members of the Regency thought it should, and so did a minority of the Greek churchmen. The membership of the commission was chosen in such a way that there was little doubt as to their confirming the wishes of the regents. The steady hand of Georg von Maurer saw to that.

The question of an independent church for Greece had first been raised by the noted Greek author Adamantios Koraïs. A very prolific writer, residing in Paris, his influence extended farther than any other Greek who was his contemporary. When he wrote about the church and its clergy he found there was much to reform—most of his criticism he aimed at the monasteries. The greatest evil besetting the Orthodox church, according to Koraïs, was the fact that 'it was living under the yoke of title-bearing monks'.[2] In his commentary on Aristotle's *Politics*, published in 1821 in Paris, he broached the idea of a church in Greece whose clergy would be independent of the patriarch:

From this hour the clergy of the liberated parts of Greece no longer owe recognition to the ecclesiastical authority of the patriarch of Constantinople who remains contaminated under the throne of a lawless tyrant. Now it must be governed by a Holy Synod, freely chosen by the clergy and laity as was the custom of the ancient church and still, in part, is practiced today by the church of the believing Russians. A clergy of free and independent Greeks is most unfitting as long as it obeys the commands of a patriarch chosen by a despot and forced to bow down before a tyrant.[3]

[1] Chrysostomos Papadopoulos, *op. cit.* p. 71. Papadopoulos notes that the two bishops were both refugees from the Ottoman empire and not natives of independent Greece. He believes the commission was packed and is baffled by Maurer's statement that the commission had a 'majority of clerics' (Maurer, *op. cit.* p. 153).

[2] D. S. Balanos, '*Αἱ θρησκευτικαὶ ἰδέαι τοῦ Ἀδαμαντίου Κοραῆ*' [The religious thought of Adamantios Koraïs], *Ἀθῆναι* (1920), pp. 82 ff.

[3] Adamantios Koraïs, *Ἀριστοτέλους πολιτικῶν τὰ σωζόμενα* [The extant work of Aristotle's *Politics*] (Paris, 1821), p. 120.

Koraïs' ideas on an autonomous church for Greece were shared by his fellow countryman, Theokletos Pharmakidis, who became one of the truly great churchmen of Greece during this period. Along with Maurer he was co-author of the settlement decided upon for Greece from 1833 until 1852. It was his spirit and conviction, both within and outside the ecclesiastical commission, which was the deciding factor in the discussions on the future of the church.

Theokletos Pharmakidis was born on 25 January 1784 in a small Thessalian village, and was educated in Larisa where his great devotion to learning and to the life of the church was first noted. He received the diaconate there on Christmas Day in 1802, thence he went to Constantinople, attended the Patriarchal School for some years, and later took up residence in the Principalities, where he witnessed the Russian occupation during the Russo-Turkish War of 1806 and developed a strong dislike for the ways of the Slavic conquerors. At Bucharest in 1811 he was ordained a priest and during the next few years travelled extensively in Italy and central Europe, eventually settling in Vienna for about eight years to serve the Orthodox church there. By this time, he had learned Latin, French and German, and began to do some translating and publishing on his own.

The reputation of Pharmakidis reached the Ionian Islands so that the Governor, Lord Guilford, sought him for professor of theology at the Academy of Corcyra. It was decided that Pharmakidis should first go to the theological school at Göttingen in order to become acquainted with western theology. He enrolled at the university, therefore, in October 1819 and remained until news of the Revolution reached Germany. Then he left for Greece. During his year and a half as a university student in Germany he came into contact with German Protestant thought and Koraïs' books, which no doubt did much to influence his own thinking on the situation of the church in Greece.

He arrived on the island of Spetsai in July 1821 and offered his services to his country. He eventually joined Demetrios Ypsilantis and while in his employ began the first independent Greek newspaper, in August 1821, the *Greek Trumpet*, published in Kalamata.

The newspaper did not have a long life, and Pharmakidis during the following months served as a member of the Assembly of Epidauros and later as supervisor of schools and education. The disorganized state of affairs, however, did not allow him to make much progress here, so at last he went to Corcyra to fulfil his agreement with Lord Guilford, remaining at the Academy from November 1823 until May 1825, when he returned to Greece to launch the government newspaper in Nauplion, the *General Newspaper of Greece*. He was a member of the Troezen Assembly which invited Kapodistrias to Greece, but, on the arrival of the president, Pharmakidis gave up his position. He became an outspoken critic of the policies of Kapodistrias because of the latter's authoritarian character and dependence on Russia. For a while Pharmakidis was kept under surveillance by government officials in a monastery. Eventually, he joined the opposition party on Idhra and was there when Kapodistrias was shot. During the interim period, before Otho's arrival, he directed a school at Aegina.[1]

It was through a recommendation given by the famous scholar Georgios Gennadios to Maurer that Pharmakidis was invited to come to Nauplion to assist in matters of church affairs. Maurer was already at work drawing up a constitution for the church in the new state of Greece, and Pharmakidis' advice was to prove extremely helpful. On his role as adviser, Pharmakidis states, 'I do not know what suggestions others gave him concerning this (law) nor have I ever taken the care to learn them. I know this, however, that whenever I gave him an opinion it was completely in agreement with the principles of the Eastern Orthodox Church and demonstrated the wishes of the Greek nation and the clergy of the church of Greece.'[2] Basically, Pharmakidis' thesis was that an independent Greece demanded a break with the patriarchate of Constantinople because of the latter's dependence on the Turks and even on the Russians; that without an autonomous church the indepen-

[1] For the best account of Pharmakidis' early life, see D. S. Balanos, Θεόκλητος Φαρμακίδης, *1784–1860* [Theokletos Pharmakidis] (Athens, 1933), pp. 1–19, and his own Ἀπολογία [Apologia] (Athens, 1840), pp. 6–9.

[2] T. Pharmakidis, *op. cit.* p. 18; see also T. Haralambides, 'Die Kirchenpolitik Griechenlands', *Zeitschrift für Kirchengeschichte*, VI (1935), p. 162.

dence of the nation would be 'incomplete in an essential area'. The Russians he felt were the natural enemies of Hellenism, a people whose political goals were masked behind religious protestations.[1]

Pharmakidis worked for a month on a sketch of the proposed constitution, which was then translated into German for Maurer and became the major resource for the Bavarian lawyer, whose knowledge of the life of the Orthodox church was minimal. It is interesting that Maurer never made any acknowledgement of Pharmakidis' assistance when he later wrote about the construction of the Church Constitution.

The primary architect of the church settlement in Greece was the regent Georg von Maurer, a German Protestant heavily dependent upon a legal training obtained in Napoleonic France. In his own way he was a genius. In the space of less than a year he had drawn up not only a church constitution but also a civil code which proved its worth for many years. When Maurer arrived in Greece there was great disorder in church and state; by the time he left it he had established the legal and ecclesiastical foundation of the new Greek state.[2]

Maurer's own summary of his position on church affairs is contained in his work *Das griechische Volk in öffentlicher, kirchlicher und privatrechtlicher Beziehung vor und nach dem Freiheitskampfe*, which was published after his dismissal from Greece in 1835. He claims that when he arrived in Greece all was in confusion; he believed it his task 'to bring order now into this nearly complete chaos'. The members of the clergy were demoralized and terribly poor; they had lacked leadership ever since they were cut off from the patriarchate. Maurer believed that the church of Greece needed to be independent of a patriarch appointed by the sultan, 'it was certainly fitting that freedom should come to the Greek church as part of the struggle made for independence. Just as it sought to be free of the political relationship which bound it to Ottoman authority, in the same way Greece endeavored also to have religious autonomy, i.e. freedom from a patriarch appointed and supported by the sultan.'[3]

A second danger was seen by Maurer in the threat of Russia to

[1] D. Balanos, *op. cit.* p. 24.

[2] K. Dickopf, *op. cit.* pp. 51–82.

[3] G. von Maurer, *op. cit.* II, p. 154.

Greece. It was obvious to all, according to him, that Russia was interested in expansion at the expense of the Ottomans and that the Orthodox populations in the Balkans could be used by that country as a means to reach her goal. Many of the Greek clergy were devoted to Russia and would support Russian ambitions in this area. The tsar could easily use the patriarchal appointments as a means to control the Greek church, Maurer contended, so that the only way for the new state of Greece to withstand this pressure would be to have a synod independent of Constantinople.

Maurer looked upon the church as a department of the state and subordinate to it. The situation in his homeland was a model for him, for in Bavaria both Catholic and Protestant churches were dominated by the secular power. Catholic bishops were allowed to correspond with Rome only through the intermediary of the king. Jesuits were excluded by royal fiat from entering the country. The reformed church of Bavaria was in the paradoxical position of having the Catholic king as its 'supreme bishop'.[1]

In early April, the Regency issued decrees which spelled out the duties of the various ministries of the new state; the one which pertained to Maurer's ministry of Ecclesiastical Affairs and Public Instruction contained eleven sections. In broad terms these covered such issues as the division of power between secular and religious authorities, the care of churches and church property, the regulation of ordinations and the licensing of documents issued by the bishops and—even at this early date—spoke of the ministry's powers to summon a synod.[2]

The really important business of April, however, was the beginning of the meetings of the ecclesiastical commission which started its work on 17 April and continued until 2 May. The discussions ranged over all of the problems existing in the present state of the church in Greece. The very first session was able to agree that the

[1] A. Chroust, *op. cit.* II, pp. 275, 279. In letters from the French ambassador Rumigny to Prince Polignac the unsuccessful efforts of the papal nuncio to Munich to remove these barriers to church freedom are reported (Letters of 15 July and 18 August 1830). See also H. Rall, *op. cit.* p. 202.

[2] Ἐφημερὶς τῆς Κυβερνήσεως [The Government Newspaper], Nauplion, 10 April 1833, no. 14, p. 93. The decree was issued 3 April.

church must be autocephalous and in subsequent meetings the setting up of a synod, its composition and functions, as well as measures to be taken to better organize the clergy, were proposed. In all, there were eleven meetings and at the conclusion a statement was issued which was sent to the bishops along with a questionnaire seeking their opinion on the issue of separation from Constantinople.

The report of the commission explained the reasons for drafting a new church constitution which would make the church of Greece independent of the patriarchate. The history of the Greek church in ancient and medieval times was traced and precedents cited of other churches, such as those of Russia and Cyprus, which were united with Constantinople in faith and practice but were autonomous. All of the advantages of such a relationship were proposed, and nothing was mentioned of the problems which an independent church must face. It was hardly an objective presentation. According to Maurer, the response of all the bishops was favorable to the commission's report and urged the king to set up an autonomous synod to govern the church.[1]

There was, however, some immediate opposition to the committee's report from two or three persons. One such opponent was a monk named Prokopios Dendrinos who came from Mount Athos and preached in Nauplion against the separation. Pharmakidis mentions that the bishop of Rethimnon also spoke in opposition. Some other clerics claimed that the projected constitution was a plot to make everyone a Catholic while others saw it as a trick to support Protestantism. Though, in late April with the issue still pending, the party opposed to independence received a hearty lift when the Russian envoy to the Greek government, G. A. Katakazis, arrived, yet in the long run these were voices crying in the wilderness with little strength compared with what the government could command.

As his name shows, the Russian emissary was ethnically a Greek,

[1] C. Papadopoulos, *op. cit.* pp. 72–90; G. von Maurer, *op. cit.* II, p. 155; Konstantinos Oekonomos of the Oekonomos, *Τριακονταετηρὶς ἐκκλησιαστικὴ ἤ συνταγμάτιον ἱστορικὸν τῶν ἐν τῷ βασιλείῳ τῆς* Ἑλλάδος [Thirty years of church affairs or the constitutional history of ecclesiastical events in the Kingdom of Greece], in Τὰ *σωζόμενα ἐκκλησιαστικὰ συγγράμματα* [The extant ecclesiastical writings], ed. Sophokles of the Oekonomos (Athens, 1862), pp. 99–108.

a member of a Phanariote family who had been employed in the tsar's foreign office. His appointment to Greece had come in January of 1833 at which time Nicholas outlined his instructions. He was to let the Regency know that St Petersburg wanted it 'to exercise royal power on its own authority, in all its plenitude, and that there be no appearance of subordinating this power to the will of the nation'. The tsar also counselled Katakazis to be intent on watching over the interests of Orthodoxy and that he should offer the good offices of Russia as mediator between the church of Greece and the patriarch of Constantinople. In order to assist the church, it was stated:

We think that a Russian ecclesiastic, sent to Greece with the title of chaplain of the legation, could be the best intermediary for the distribution of gifts which his Imperial Majesty will designate for this cause. His sojourn in the country will only be temporary and in the course of his mission he shall conduct himself as a simple traveller, and without the least ostentation in the poorest districts of the Morea and Levadhia.

The emissary was to obtain exact figures on the needs of the churches and monasteries, so that aid might be sent and the Greeks convinced 'they always will have the powerful support of the Emperor and protection full of benefits'.[1]

The British ambassador to St Petersburg, John Bligh, was informed that Katakazis' main mission was to compliment King Otho on his arrival in Greece and to investigate the situation there. Bligh wrote to Palmerston that he thought it 'strange that a Mission principally of ceremony and ostensibly for the purpose of doing honor to the new Sovereign should not have been entrusted to a Russian'.[2] Katakazis also wanted to dispel any suspicion, if that could be done, concerning Russian intentions in Greece by journeying first to Munich. Here he spoke with the Bavarian foreign minister, August de Gise, and delivered a letter from Tsar Nicholas which outlined his mission. The meetings with the Russian ambassador prompted

[1] Instruction to Katakazis, January 1833, enclosure in a dispatch from Nesselrode to Gagarin, St Petersburg, 8 May 1833, quoted in Jelavich, *op. cit.* pp. 57–67.

[2] J. D. Bligh to Lord Palmerston, St Petersburg, 26 January 1833, F.O. 65, Russia, vol. 207, no. 12, PRO.

Gise to write Armansperg, 'it is essential that the Regency begin to govern, from its inauguration, and not question the bounds of its authority'.[1]

Katakazis at last arrived with the other members of his staff in Nauplion, where he soon assumed the power which had formerly been held by the Russian minister, Baron Ruckman. He met with the king and the regents, with whom his first business after the congratulations was to urge the removal of the French troops in the Peloponnesus. This earned him the appraisal from the French minister, Baron Forth-Rouen, 'Katakazis is a man of talent and spirit, but unfortunately of a character full of intrigue'.[2] Having come too late to interfere in the work of the ecclesiastical commission, it soon became Katakazis' purpose to prevent the ratification of the church establishment proposed by that body which would officially sever Greece from the patriarchate. In the Russian view the bond with Constantinople was an important link between independent Greece and the tsar because of the great influence exercised by Russia in the Ottoman Empire. Pharmakidis and Maurer were well aware of this opinion and acted precisely with it in mind.

In a number of new regulations issued by the Ministry of Ecclesiastical Affairs and Public Instruction during April and May, the department reaffirmed its position regarding several questions and broadened its control over the church. The founding of any new religion was forbidden, all proselytism was banned, as was correspondence between the clergy and any religious authorities outside of Greece (the pope was included), the clergy were required to take a loyalty oath, they were not to convoke an assembly without governmental approval, and so on. In all these decrees the church was made more subservient to secular control and granted the 'privilege' only to conduct its internal affairs without supervision. The ministry's actions were clear evidence of things to come.[3]

[1] Baron de Gise to Count Armansperg, Munich, 16 April 1833, Bayer Gesandtshaft, St Petersburg, GS.

[2] B. Forth-Rouen to the Duke de Broglie, Nauplion, 29 April, Grèce, XVI, no. 264, MAE.

[3] 'Εφημερὶς τῆς Κυβερνήσεως, Nauplion, 26 April, 4 May 1833, nos. 17 and 18, pp. 116 ff.; 'Αθῆνα, Nauplion, 10 May 1833, no. 110, p. 443.

Otho shared Maurer's opinion on church affairs. In a letter he wrote to his father, he noted:

the spiritual authority of the clergy in the country could become dangerous to the secular ruler if the upper clergy attached themselves to a party, since then the whole clergy might bring over the people to their side and against him. I think that one could overcome all these difficulties if one set up a synod under the direction of a metropolitan who would function like the president of our chambers and not actually possess power. The ruler could choose the members of this synod at certain times.[1]

Thus Otho's thought was added to the general feeling of the Regency and Pharmakidis that the church must be safely tucked under the control of the state. In order to give legitimacy to their actions concerning the church, the Regency and its ecclesiastical commission knew that the bishops themselves must be consulted. Thus it was decided to summon a synod to meet in Nauplion where the government could present its case. Letters of invitation were sent out on 3 July announcing the convocation twelve days later.[2] The recipients were not limited to bishops who actually held dioceses in Greece, but also included prelates who were refugees from the Ottoman Empire. There were, in fact, only eight canonically appointed bishops left in the Peloponnesus and not many more in northern Greece and the Islands.

On the opening day of the Nauplion synod, 15 July, there were twenty-two prelates in attendance, a number which was divided between nine native bishops and thirteen refugee prelates. In charge of the conduct of the meeting was Spyridon Trikoupis, assisted by Schinas and Vyzantinos.

Trikoupis gave the inaugural address at ten in the morning in which he outlined the purpose of the synod—the restoration of the dignity the Greek church had possessed before the Turkish conquest. He proposed that two steps be taken:

The official and definitive declaration of the already existing independence of the Greek Church from all foreign authority as far as regards its external position (preserving at the same time a perfect unity relative to

[1] Otho to Ludwig, Munich, 13 May 1832, quoted in H. Rall, *op. cit.* p. 193.

[2] The letter of invitation is reprinted in *Ἀθηνᾶ*, Nauplion, 12 July 1833, no. 128, p. 511.

the doctrines uniformly professed by all the churches of the East) and secondly the establishment of a permanent Synod, appointed by the King, which shall be considered as the supreme ecclesiastical authority, according to the example of the Russian Church.[1]

After some discussion and explanation of the several points, Trikoupis and his aides withdrew so as to allow the assembled bishops to debate the measures. According to most accounts, there was little opposition to the spirit of the proposals. Pharmakidis says only two prelates took a contrary view to the government proposition. Among the bishops, there were some who 'were strongly worked up against the expression of the second proposition "according to the example of the Russian Church", asserting that there was nothing in that country which the Greek church needed to look to for an example, either of principles of ecclesiastical order or of orthodoxy'.[2] One zealous prelate, who had appeared wearing a decoration of the Russian church, took it off and threw it away since he did not want to appear with an emblem of a foreign power.[3] At length the discussions were ended, Trikoupis was summoned and the decision was given that the consensus was favorable to the proposals but the bishops did want them reworded.

The suggested phrasing declared that the Orthodox church of the kingdom of Greece acknowledged no spiritual head but the founder of the Christian faith, Jesus Christ. On the other hand, its secular administration was vested in the person of the king of Greece, in so far as that was consonant with the sacred canons; i.e. the church was autocephalous and independent of every other authority. It professed unity with regard to all doctrines uniformly held by the other Orthodox churches. Concerning the second proposal, the bishops insisted that an amendment be added stipulating that the Synod would be composed only of bishops and that it would administer the church according to the sacred canons. The reference to the church of Russia was deleted.

The members of the ecclesiastical commission were agreeable to

[1] Ἐφημερὶς τῆς Κυβερνήσεως, Nauplion, 1 August 1833, no. 23, p. 175.

[2] B. Forth-Rouen to the Duke de Broglie, Nauplion, 31 July, Grèce, XVI, no. 362, MAE.

[3] *The Times*, London, 17 March 1834.

the amended versions of their proposals and these were duly drafted and signed by all the bishops present. By four in the afternoon all was accomplished. After eleven centuries of unity, the church of Greece had taken the momentous step of officially separating itself from the patriarchate of Constantinople in less than seven hours.[1]

On the following day, 16 July, eight more bishops added their signature, among them Joseph of Androusa, Minister of Religion during the early period of the Revolution. Five days later three more bishops affixed their names and on 26 July another three, bringing the total number of bishops who agreed to the government's resolutions to thirty-six. Actually the last prelates to sign would do so as late as October. The fact that so many of the bishops who signed the document were either not canonically appointed bishops of pre-revolutionary Greece or were refugees from the Turks has caused the validity of the Synod to be called into question.[2] No matter what figures are accepted, there can be little doubt that the government's policies succeeded in large measure because of the refugee bishops, who obviously depended on the good will of the Regency more than their established brethren. Maurer was, of course, delighted though hardly surprised at the result, and, within a few days, was ready to submit the new Church Constitution.[3]

[1] B. Forth-Rouen to the Duke de Broglie, Nauplion, 1 August 1833, Grèce, XVI, nos. 362, 363, MAE. The French minister commented, 'Thus occurred without difficulty and with the consent of the high clergy, the separation of the Greek church and that of Constantinople, to which the Regency had attached the highest importance, the principal aim of which is evidently to remove for the future powerful means of influence for Russia'; Dawkins to Lord Palmerston, Nauplion, 20 August 1833, F.O. 32, Greece, vol. 37, no. 49, PRO. Among other things, Dawkins noted that the decision ratified the separation which in fact had been the case since 1821.

[2] There is a great deal of confusion as to the number who were refugees. C. Papadopoulos, *op. cit.* p. 100, says that only ten of thirty-six were resident bishops, K. Oekonomos, *op. cit.* p. 173, says there were eighteen. Of the forty-eight dioceses of pre-war Greece nineteen were vacant and four others had bishops of questionable occupancy, which presumably means that if all the bishops of free Greece who were residents would have come, there would have been twenty-five, while in fact only ten (Papadopoulos) or eighteen (Oekonomos) did attend. My count favors Oekonomos.

[3] Maurer describes it, 'And for my part, I was convinced that this world historical document would begin a new epoch and not only for the Greek Church' (*op. cit.* II, p. 160).

This new ecclesiastical Constitution, issued on 23 July 1833, in the name of the king, brought into existence a transformed church for Greece. The major provisions of that document are as follows:

Article One. The Orthodox Eastern Apostolic Church of the Kingdom of Greece, in spiritual matters recognizes no head other than the founder of the Christian faith, Our Lord and Savior Jesus Christ, while in secular affairs it respects the authority of the King of Greece. It is autocephalous and independent of all other authority, but preserves perfect unity according to the doctrines uniformly professed by the Orthodox Eastern Churches.

Article Two. The highest ecclesiastical authority is entrusted, under the authority of the King, to a permanent Synod, entitled 'The Holy Synod of the Kingdom of Greece'. The King will determine by an organic decree of the Secretary of State who will exercise this authority and under whom, as regards this authority, the Synod will act. The Synod will hold its meetings at the seat of the Government and will have its own seal, with a cross engraved on it exactly like that on the national arms and with the inscription 'Holy Synod of Greece'.

Article Three established the Synod's membership. It would be made up of a president and at least two counsellors with two others who might, or might not, be counsellors. The government could appoint assessors instead of counsellors if it wanted. The difference was that the assessors would not have to be bishops, but chosen from among lesser clerics or monks, as was stated in Article Four. The government reserved to itself the right to make all the appointments.

The following articles dealt with changes in the membership of the Synod and how business was to be conducted—a majority vote was decisive on all questions. Article Six established a royal procurator and a secretary and the following article outlined their duties. Special importance was attached to the procurator—he had to be present at all meetings of the Synod, 'and every act in his absence shall be null and void'. The procurator had the authority to submit propositions to the Synod and these received precedence over all other business.

The Synod's power to act on its own 'internal matters' was subject to governmental control and 'no decision of the Synod could be published or carried into execution without the permission of the

Government having been obtained'. Article Ten spelled out what was considered internal affairs: doctrine, liturgy, catechetical instruction, clerical discipline and the care of church buildings. The church was told, in the following sections, to see to it that church doctrine was preserved intact, and to inform the secular authorities of anyone seeking to disturb the dogmatic belief of the church. Proselytism was forbidden. The Synod was also to see to it 'that priests do not engage in political affairs or in any way take part in them'.

The government noted that many activities are of such a nature that they have both religious and secular aspects; all of these therefore must be subject to the inspection of the state and, if found detrimental to the public interest, could be vetoed. In a truly astonishing list, these 'mixed' affairs included 'ordinances concerning external worship, the time, place and frequency of its celebration', founding monasteries, ordinations, conducting processions, clerical education, etc. In Article Sixteen the bishops were told that they were completely subject to the Synod, that the government would decide on the number of dioceses and that, with the advice of the Synod, the state officials might 'transfer, suspend or entirely depose them'. The clergy were also subject to secular courts, civil and criminal, in case of a crime. Clerics were forbidden to correspond or have any immediate contact 'with any foreign power, civil or ecclesiastical'.[1]

In all, there were twenty-five articles, each of which made the church more subservient to the state. If ever a church was legally stripped of authority and reduced to complete dependence on the state, Maurer's constitution did it to the church of Greece.

Maurer was impressed by his work—he felt that he had done much to restore the church to the position it held during the Byzantine period. He admitted that he had used the example of the Russian Synod and its relations with the state for a model. Even more pertinent is his dependence on the example of the 1818 Constitution of the Bavarian Protestant church, the Consistorium. Maurer claimed

[1] The text is published in the 'Εφημερὶς τῆς Κυβερνήσεως. Nauplion, 1 August 1833, no. 23, pp. 169–74. It is also found in K. Oekonomos, *op. cit.* pp. 177–84, and in *Sacrorum Conciliorum nova et amplissima collectio*, ed. Joannes Mansi (Graz, 1961), XL, pp. 169–78.

there were both similarities and differences—it was like comparing a rose with a carnation, they look alike but are definitely not the same. There are some exact parallels in three articles between the German and Greek documents where even the wording is identical.[1]

Opinions on the Constitution among the representatives of the Powers in Nauplion varied from British approbation to French misgivings and Russian opposition. When Dawkins wrote his report to the Foreign Office he noted many of the advantages of the new arrangement. The privileges of the clergy under the old establishment, which had been very extensive and had interfered with orderly civil administration, were now curtailed. The contributions levied by the patriarchate which eventually ended up in the sultan's treasury and had been a serious drain on the resources of Greece were halted. There would be no reforms in the church of Greece if the patriarch had his way. Dawkins further believed that the Greek people, having had no connections with Constantinople for twelve years, honestly did not want to return to this jurisdiction, especially since the patriarchate was subordinate to the sultan, the great enemy of Greek independence.[2]

Baron Forth-Rouen thought the settlement a 'considerable means of assuring political and religious independence', but regretted that it had been done so hastily. Prudence, he felt, demanded that nothing be decided intemperately on such a 'grave question'.[3]

The Russian envoy, Katakazis, for obvious reasons, looked upon the Constitution which separated the Greek church from the patriarchate as a grave error. He had arrived too late to gather enough support among the clergy to resist the change; once the Nauplion Synod had adjourned, however, he began to urge the monks and lower clergy to have nothing to do with it.

[1] Maurer, *op. cit.* II, p. 165. C. Papadopoulos, *op. cit.* pp. 105 ff., makes the comparisons: Articles X, XIV and XVIII are taken from the Bavarian documents, sections 38, 76 and 64 respectively.

[2] E. Dawkins to Lord Palmerston, Nauplion, 20 August 1833, F.O. 32, Greece, vol. 37, no. 49, PRO.

[3] B. Forth-Rouen to Duke de Broglie, Nauplion, 1 August 1833, Grèce, XVI, no. 363, MAE.

Everything seemed to be going wrong for the Russians at this time. They had many supporters in Greece, especially those who had been attached to the Kapodistrian government. These had been rapidly disenchanted by the Regency which offered them little hope of regaining the power they once enjoyed. At the head of the Russian party was Theodoros Kolokotrones. He eventually wrote to the tsar outlining his complaints about the regents and asking for Russian support, but instead of getting the tsar's blessing for an uprising against the government, Nicholas spoke vaguely about being united to Greece by the 'bonds of a common religion' and of an interest 'full of sympathy' and encouraged all Greeks to devote themselves to their young king. Thus the Russian faction was rebuffed by the tsar himself from whom it had expected strong support.[1] The Court at St Petersburg believed its interests for the moment lay in upholding the monarchy in Greece despite its faults. Over the years these could be corrected, while aiding Kolokotrones and the other chieftains might open the door to all revolutionaries and set in motion a chain of events which could never be checked.

Katakazis' dealings with the regents, his suggestions on personnel, his urging the government to request the French troops to leave the Peloponnesus, and now the separation of the Greek church from the patriarchate had all been areas in which the Russian minister had met defeat. When the day arrived to celebrate the adoption of the Church Constitution, Katakazis did not attend nor did any other Russian national, and when the tsar heard of the developments he saw to it that Prince Gagarin, Russian minister in Munich, should inform King Ludwig of his displeasure. He regretted that 'an intemperate reform has dissolved the bonds which attach the church of the new state to the patriarchal see of Constantinople'. Mr Katakazis, the tsar emphasized, worked diligently to stop this development which disturbed the 'tranquillity of the country and the consciences of many', but he failed because Count Armansperg

[1] G. Finlay, *op. cit.* VII, p. 138; Count Nesselrode to Kolokotrones, St Petersburg, 11 July 1833, Grèce, XV, no. 59, MAE. In September Kolokotrones and his companions were arrested and put on trial for treason. Convicted, they were condemned to die, but this was changed to life imprisonment and eventually they were pardoned by Otho.

would not listen. Nicholas complained that the president of the Regency took advice only from the British and French ministers and while Russia did not want to gain an ascendancy in Greece, it would not sit idly by and watch Britain and France take over. King Ludwig had better take some action.[1]

The Greek bishops themselves had hardly bargained for what they received in the Constitution. Even those willing to set up an autonomous church had not done so in expectation of being relegated to the status of office boys in the governmental bureaucracy—a position to which Maurer's document reduced them. The Regency expected Patriarch Konstantinos to ratify benignly the arrangement and the Greek minister at the Porte, Konstantinos Zographos, was to make the contact. In fact, the much more natural reaction of the patriarch was to resist the move, and this is what occurred in fact. Only the intervention of the tsar prevented the patriarch from excommunicating the whole Greek church which had been set up in total disregard of the church canons and which had established a synod subject to an heretical king.[2]

For his part, Sypridon Trikoupis, who played a significant role in the Nauplion Synod, supported the separation of the church from the patriarchate on the grounds that it had removed it from 'the hands of an infidel enemy'. He noted that it was a move 'less religious than political' and that it should bring benefits to the church.[3] Pharmakidis was the strongest supporter of separation among the Greeks of his day but only a few authorities now share his views. The two church historians of this period, Konstantinos Oekonomos and Archbishop Chrysostomos Papadopoulos, have altogether condemned the Constitution.[4]

[1] C. Nesselrode to Prince Gagarin, St Petersburg, August 1833, MA I, Russland, no. 515, GS.

[2] Information contained in a letter from Count Medem to Nesselrode, London, 6 August 1834, in B. Jelavich, *op. cit.* p. 117.

[3] S. Trikoupis, 'The Actual State of Greece', Paris, 18 February 1834, memo in Grèce, XVII, no. 296, MAE.

[4] 'The Constitution is altogether foreign to the canons of the Orthodox Church, contrary to its traditions and its historical past.' C. Papadopoulos, *op. cit.* p. 104; K. Oekonomos, *op. cit.* pp. 57–87. He calls Maurer's assertion the church had been independent since 1821 'a wintry dream' (*ibid.* p. 7).

Two days after the document was proclaimed, 25 July, the members of the governing body of the church of Greece, the Holy Synod, were announced. The president was Metropolitan Kyrillos of Corinth and his council was made up of the Metropolitans Paisios of Thebes, Zacharias of Santorin, Kyrillos, administrator of Elis, and Joseph of Androusa. The state procurator was to be Konstantinos Schinas and as secretary to the Synod, Theokletos Pharmakidis. On the 27th, the new Synod sent a letter to the various churches of Greece justifying the new situation, claiming that the church had in fact been autocephalous since 1821 and the Constitution simply regularized the position of the church. It claimed that the benefits to be gained in the future both for religion and morality were great, provided all were loyal to the church and state of Greece.[1] When Metropolitan Kyrillos dispatched a letter to the patriarch concerning the new state of affairs in Greece, it was returned to him unopened.

In order properly to celebrate the new church Constitution the Regency declared 27 July a holiday. The sound of cannons opened the day, crowds poured into the streets in a festive air, proceeding to celebrate, says Maurer, their sense of pride in their own independent church. In the cathedral the members of the new Synod took their oaths of office. Only the sulking Russians stayed at home, as has been mentioned. Two prelates were also dissenters on this day, the archbishops of Adrianople and Rethimnon. They departed from free Greece eventually to return to Constantinople where they washed their hands of the Greek establishment and professed their allegiance to Patriarch Konstantinos.[2]

Meanwhile, Otho had been enjoying his kingship. He did a great deal of riding about the country, and even made a short trip to Smyrna, despite Russian protests that such a move was likely to upset the sultan, where he was received by the Greek population with acclaim. In Nauplion he spent the mornings learning Greek and greeting visitors. Count Armansperg hovered over the young monarch, sent glowing reports to everyone about his popularity and

[1] Ἐφημερὶς τῆς Κυβερνήσεως, Nauplion, 1 August 1833, no. 23, p. 177; K. Oekonomos, *op. cit.* pp. 190–3; C. Papadopoulos, *op. cit.* p. 111.

[2] Maurer, *op. cit.* II, p. 167.

tried to marry him to one of his daughters. Sage advice came from his father, King Ludwig, 'Never be alone with one of the Armansperg girls'.[1]

While Otho was kept busy, the Regency moved on with their plans for remaking Greece according to their image. Maurer labored on law codes, both civil and criminal; efforts were made to begin schools; severe press laws were decreed to discourage opposition newspapers, while subsidies went to papers loyal to the government, thus giving it effectual control of the Press. The Regency, well aware of the influence the representatives of the Powers wielded, requested their several governments to recall them and appoint new (and perhaps less wise) ministers. This feint failed, Dawkins and Forth-Rouen only changed their titles and Katakazis was not about to leave.[2]

The diplomatic atmosphere in Nauplion was never thicker than it was after the establishment of the autocephalous church which came only two weeks after the Treaty of Hunkiar Iskelesi had been signed between Russia and Turkey. The secret clause which let the Turks out of their part of the Treaty leaked out within a matter of days. When Lord Palmerston, the British Foreign Secretary, heard of it, he was quite upset and his dissatisfaction was transferred to Greece. The air was full of suspicion and rumors of plots and counter-plots. Katakazis was treated with marked coolness by Count Armansperg, the British favorite. Moreover, the Regency president believed him to be behind the attempt of Kolokotrones to undermine confidence in Bavarian rule. The Russian minister had claimed innocence when Kolokotrones and his party were arrested in September 1833, for treason, and put on trial by the government. In every Russian move, especially after Hunkiar Iskelesi, the western Powers saw the hand of the tsar reaching towards the Straits. For his part, Count Nesselrode informed the Bavarian minister in St Petersburg

[1] Ludwig to Otho, Munich, 20 December 1833, quoted in L. Bower and G. Bolitho, *op. cit.* p. 50. Armansperg to Lerchenfeld, 'The King is adored by the nation and enjoys the greatest popularity', Nauplion, 5 June 1833, Bayer Gesandtshaft, St Petersburg, GS.

[2] E. Driault and M. l'Héritier, *op. cit.* II, pp. 106, 107; G. Finlay, *op. cit.* VI, p. 125; Henry Parish, *Diplomatic History of the Monarchy of Greece* (London, 1838), p. 234.

that he was 'exasperated with the Regency' while labelling the representatives of Britain and France 'the principal causes of the elements of discord existing in Greece'.[1]

As far as church affairs were concerned, the Regency continued its reform. With all of the weapons for control of the church in its hands, its first target was the monasteries of the country. Many of them had suffered great damage during the war, some were completely abandoned, others had only a handful of monks. The Synod therefore recommended that any monastery with less than three monks be closed, but the Regency raised the number to six, and by a decree of 25 September 1833 the government closed all the small monasteries of the country. Any establishment whose buildings were destroyed was included regardless of the number of monks who might still be attached to it. The number of dissolved monasteries totaled 412. The government, of course, would thus receive considerable land and property; the 2,000 monks of Greece were to be resettled in the remaining 148 monasteries. The lesson taught by the sixteenth-century reforming princes had not been lost on the Regency. In the beginning of 1834 the confiscation began.[2]

The remaining monasteries were made liable to taxation from both the local and national governments. The collection of these taxes was farmed out to public contractors who bid for the right to make the assessments, a situation which left the monks open to serious exploitation by unscrupulous agents. In 1838, the government acknowledged that this system was abused and decreed that

[1] Baron de Lerchenfeld to Ludwig, St Petersburg, 31 October 1833, MA III, Russland, 2721, no. 61, GS. Dawkins wrote Palmerston, 'It is indeed but too apparent that the Russian Envoy is seeking, by his language and example, to discredit those members of the Greek Regency who are disposed to conduct this Government upon independent principles...' (E. Dawkins to Lord Palmerston, Nauplion, 25 October 1833, F.O. 32, Greece, vol. 38, no. 65). Palmerston wrote Erskine, British envoy to Munich, that he should support Count Armansperg to keep the Russians from gaining 'an ascendancy over the Greek Government' (Palmerston to Erskine, London, 10 October 1833, F.O. 9, Bavaria, vol. 66, no. 8).

[2] Konstantinos Dyovouniotis, ''Η *κατὰ τὸ* 1834 *Διάλυσις τῶν Μοναστηρίων ἐν τῇ* 'Ελευθέρᾳ 'Ελλάδι' [The 1834 dissolution of the monasteries in independent Greece], 'Ιερὸς Σύνδεσμος, XII (1908), p. 4. G. Finlay, *op. cit.* VII, pp. 130, 131. G. Maurer, *op. cit.* II, pp. 178 ff. He claims there were nearly 8,000 monks in Greece, but this is much too high a figure.

henceforth the monasteries would pay a fixed sum directly to the state treasury.

The next order of business was the refashioning of the diocesan structure of the church. The Regency had divided the country for administrative purposes into ten departments or nomes with a nomarch, as governor, at the head of each. It was now determined to restructure the church boundaries along the same lines, just as it had been done by the revolutionary government of France. Maurer's experience in Paris is evident. By a decree of 20 November 1833 it was ordered that in the future there would only be ten bishops in the kingdom of Greece, one for each nome. The bishop would have his see at the capital of the nome and bear its name. Because there were actually forty bishops in independent Greece at that time —due to the influx from Ottoman territory—capable of exercising their office, for the moment each was assigned a provisional see. As the bishops would die, they would not be replaced until the number of ten was reached. Therefore each nome got several prelates: Lakonia had eight, while only two were appointed to the nome of Achaea and Aetolia. There were to be no more metropolitan dioceses, everyone was simply to be a bishop. An individual who had the title of metropolitan, however, was allowed to retain it as a personal honor. This law, as might be imagined, was most unpopular among the bishops.[1]

The Russians continued to react adversely to the steps taken by the Regency during the winter of 1833, while the British minister remained optimistic about the outcome. The Nauplion government's representative to St Petersburg, Prince Soutzos, was lectured about the church rupture which had been effected with such precipitation and lack of politeness. The Russians predicted that 'its consequences can become incalculable'. The tsar reiterated that Russia would have been happy to settle the difficulties between Greece and the patriarchate, but that instead the advice of Katakazis had been ignored.

[1] *'Εφημερὶς τῆς Κυβερνήσεως*, Nauplion, 27 November 1833, no. 38, pp. 285–8; Karolidis, *op. cit.* II, pp. 18 ff.; Maurer, *op. cit.* II, p. 175. For a list and short biography of all the bishops see Vasileios Atesis, *'Επίτομος ἐπισκοπικὴ 'Ιστορία τῆς 'Εκκλησίας τῆς 'Ελλάδος* [An abridged episcopal history of the church of Greece] (Athens, 1948).

The Russian envoy at Nauplion had spoken to Armansperg and believed the latter would make no important change without great reflection, 'Imagine the pain the Minister of Russia felt when he saw the publication of the news when he considered the project defunct...' The tsar's feelings were outlined thus: 'This arrangement must appear profoundly regrettable to His Majesty for two reasons, because it was done without any previous contact with the patriarch of Constantinople and at a time when the Greek nation does not find itself united to the person of its sovereign by the indissoluble bond of a common belief...' The tsar predicted that schism and instability would result, for either the Synod or the king would lead the church, and the people would have to choose between them.[1]

George Finlay, who witnessed the change, believed there was opposition to the Constitution from the monks, clergy, and discontented bishops but that, on the whole, the Greek people were passive to the move. He blamed the Russians for keeping the issue alive.[2] Dawkins noted the bishops' displeasure at being shifted around, 'but if the original principle of the Reformation be steadily adhered to there can be no doubt of its popularity and success'.[3]

The Latin Catholics of Greece, numbering some 14,000 in 1833, were little touched by the momentous events affecting the Orthodox church during that year. On the other hand they profited very little, if at all, from the fact that their king was a Catholic. Otho, on the advice of the regents, forbade a public ceremony of welcome by the Latin clergy at Nauplion, and his chaplain Matthew Weinzierl was kept out of public view. He quietly held services in a private chapel of the palace for Otho and on Sundays celebrated Mass for the 300 Nauplion Catholics, mostly Bavarian troops, in another place in town. The Latin bishop of Zante and Cephalonia, a citizen of the Ionian Islands whose jurisdiction covered mainland Greece,

[1] Copy of memo given to Soutzos enclosed in a dispatch from Baron de Lerchenfeld to Ludwig, St Petersburg, 1 December 1833, MA III, Russland, no. 2722, GS.

[2] G. Finlay, *op. cit.* VII, p. 129: 'Russian diplomacy echoed the outcries of these zealots and patronized the most intriguing of the discontented priests.'

[3] E. Dawkins to Palmerston, Nauplion, 22 December 1833, F.O. 32, Greece, vol. 38, no. 78, PRO.

paid his respects to Otho in March and spoke a good word for his co-religionists. He was very pleased with the advantages and the 'protection' offered the church by having a Catholic king.[1] The pope also wrote to Otho encouraging him to be steadfast in his faith immediately after his arrival in Greece.[2]

At the end of 1833 the church of Greece had gone through a great transformation. For the next nineteen years Greece would live with this situation. The Constitution had both positive and negative features, and the debate continues to this day on its significance. Those who attack it on the grounds that it was done by foreigners will also have to admit that the patriarchate itself was hardly free of external influence. The danger of Turkish and Russian interests using appointments to religious offices in Greece to further their own national ends was a real threat which the Constitution averted. It is also true that the church had in fact made moves to separate itself from Constantinople previous to 1833. Even if one allows for the breakdown in communication between Constantinople and revolutionary Greece, the omission of the patriarch's name during the liturgy signified a break in communion with the Church of Constantinople. Kapodistrias surely recognized a separation between the churches when he declined to agree with the delegation sent from the patriarchate in 1828. Rather than charge Maurer with causing the separation, one may more rightly accuse him of ratifying it.[3]

There can be little justification for the subservience which the

[1] Bishop of Zante and Cephalonia to Cardinal Redicini, Nauplion, 2 March 1833, in vol. 39, Scritture Referite nei Congressi, Archipelago, Rome, Archivio della S. Congregazione di Propaganda. See also Georg Hofmann, 'La Chiesa Cattolica in Grecia, 1600–1830', *Orientalia Christiana Periodica* (Rome, 1936), II, p. 178. There were Latin Catholic bishops on Syros, Tinos, Thira and an archbishop at Naxos.

[2] Gregory XVI to Otho, 21 January 1833, in *Acta Gregorii Papae XVI*, ed. Antonio M. Bernasconi (Rome, 1901), I, p. 221.

[3] For two divergent opinions on the matter, see Christos Androutsos, *Ἐκκλησία καὶ Πολιτεία ἐξ ἐπόψεως ὀρθοδόξου* [Church and state in the Orthodox view] (Athens, 1920), and D. S. Balanos, *Πολιτεία καὶ Ἐκκλησία* [State and church] (Athens, 1920). Androutsos argues that the church suffered great damage due to Maurer's uncanonical establishment and his incorporation of foreign ideas into Greece (pp. 67–76). Balanos believes that Pharmakidis was correct in his survey of the situation and that the establishment served the needs of the day. The state was not the enemy of the church and many of its reforms were worthwhile (pp. 10–19).

church was forced to swallow as the result of the Constitution. On paper it was divested of practically all its authority and Caesar had taken what was his and God's, but the moral authority of the church remained—it was too much a part of Greek nationalism. Obviously the church needed reformation but it also required sympathetic assistance after such a calamitous period. It also needed reorganization, but instead of helping the church to make the necessary internal improvements, Maurer's Constitution simply made it an agency of an authoritarian state and a poor one at that. On this score, Georg von Maurer stands condemned.

CHAPTER 7

THE GREEK CHURCH UNDER THE INDEPENDENT SYNOD, 1835-1850

In the very first year of its existence the Holy Synod of Greece set about its task with two goals in mind—one was to reform and reorganize church life within the nation, the other was to insure that foreign influence was kept to a minimum. Under the latter heading was included everything from Protestant English missionaries to monks from Russia and the Ottoman Empire. The results during the year 1834 were impressive.

The very first encyclical letter of the Synod was concerned with controlling the journeys of monks outside their monasteries. Frequently these men would appear in villages unannounced with holy ikons and relics, preaching and taking up collections for their establishments. The Synod now wisely laid down the rule that the local bishops must first give the monks permission to preach in their dioceses and that their own abbots should be consulted on these matters. All unnecessary trips were to stop.[1]

This was only the beginning of considerable legislation on monasteries and monks. The government was anxious to obtain some of their property and the first step had already been taken by closing down the small monasteries and confiscating their estates in September 1834. A fund was established from these confiscations to help support the larger monasteries, churches, and public education. According to Maurer, whose agents had thoroughly inspected

[1] Encyclical Letter of 4 January 1834 in Αἱ *ἀναγκαιότεραι Ἐγκύκλιοι Ἐπιστολαί, Διατάξεις, καὶ Ὁδηγίαι τῆς Ἱερᾶς Συνόδου τῆς Ἐκκλησίας τῆς Ἑλλάδος (1834–1854)* [The most important encyclical letters, decrees and directives of the Holy Synod of the church of Greece from the years 1834–1854] (Athens, 1854), pp. 1–4. Those who signed the decree were Kyrillos of Corinth, Zacharias of Thira, Kyrillos of Argolis, Joseph of Messenia and Anthimos of the Cyclades. The members of the Synod had been shifted around somewhat since the original appointments.

all of the monasteries, much of the revenue, estimated at 600,000 drachmas per year, had been going to waste or had been used to support the relatives of the monks. Now this income was to be put to 'productive' uses. The total number of monasteries was reduced eventually to eighty-two, 'one still too big for the amount of men in Greece'.[1] It was not lost on the regents that the monks were more opposed than any other group in Greece to the church settlement. They were also the most vigorous partisans of Russia and anything done to curtail their influence in the Greek church would be advantageous to the Bavarian Regency.

Throughout the year, more decrees concerning monasteries whittled away at their former privileges. The government set up rules for the election of the abbot and tried to limit the candidates to monks who were priests. The procedure for administering monasteries was outlined, requiring that they make regular reports of their property, movable and immovable, of the number of monks and their age, nationality, date of arrival, as well as the daily income and expenses of the establishment. These reports were to be certified by the chief political official of the area, the local nomarch, and then sent to the Ecclesiastical Ministry.[2] Further legislation forbade weddings and baptisms in monasteries. Toward the end of the year new directives tried to keep the monks at home and announced that surplus property of the monasteries would be taken over by the government and sold for the benefit of the church.[3] The wandering of the

[1] Georg von Maurer, *Das Griechische Volk in öffentlicher, kirchlicher und privatrechtlicher Beziehung vor und nach dem Freiheitskampfe* (Heidelberg, 1835), II, p. 182. The number of monasteries and monks is not certain; estimates vary as high as 545 establishments and 8,000 inhabitants. C. Papadopoulos estimates there were only 3,000 monks, while the newspaper *Savior* counted 1,100 in 1834. Chrysostomos Papadopoulos, *Ἱστορία τῆς Ἐκκλησίας τῆς Ἑλλάδος* [History of the church of Greece] (Athens, 1920), p. 133; *Σωτήρ*, Nauplion, 15 April 1834, no. 27, p. 111. To be honest it has always been difficult to count monks. Papadopoulos says that 151 monasteries were left after the confiscation (p. 142).

[2] *Αἱ ἀναγκαιότεραι Ἐγκύκλιοι Ἐπιστολαί*, 26 February 1834, pp. 46–9; Andreas Mamoukas, *Τὰ Μοναστηριακά* [Monastic Affairs] (Athens, 1859), pp. 2–6. This book contains a wealth of material on monastic legislation throughout this period on the church in Greece.

[3] *Αἱ ἀναγκαιότεραι Ἐγκύκλιοι Ἐπιστολαί*, 4 April 1834, pp. 30, 31; *Ἐφημερὶς τῆς Κυβερνήσεως*, Athens, 21 December 1834, XLI, pp. 290–2. Gustav Hertzberg states

monks as well as the management of monastic lands continued to occupy the Synod over the years—it was a problem which did not lend itself to an easy solution.

Despite their initial difficulties with the government and the Synod, the number of monasteries increased during this period, since they numbered 128 in 1840, containing 1,646 monks. The government still taxed them rather heavily but the payments were spread out over the year and were not too burdensome. Popular feeling was not too favorable to the monks, according to the British traveller, William Mure, who visited Greece in 1838. He asserts that, in conversation with some people in Elis, he found 'monasteries in general were pronounced to be mere hives of useless drones; the government was commended for what had been already done towards their suppression and hopes were expressed that the country would soon be rid of them altogether'.[1]

The convents of Greek nuns also felt the heavy hand of Maurer's reformation. Numbering anywhere from eighteen to forty according to various authorities, the convents' inhabitants were few and poor—in this all are in agreement. In a government decree of 25 February 1834, all of the nuns were ordered to combine into three institutions: one for the Peloponnesus, one for Attica, and one for the Islands, set up on Thira. Their properties were to be handled in the same way as the monastic lands. Each convent was required to have at least thirty nuns or it would be disbanded. The decree allowed any nun under forty years of age to be dispensed from her vows with a minimum of difficulty. Convents were to be supervised by the local bishop and nomarch, while an oeconom was to be nominated by the Holy Synod immediately to care for the temporal affairs of each convent and provide its necessities. The abbess, who was to be nominated by the nuns' submitting three names to the Holy Synod,

that one-fourth of the agricultural land of Greece still belonged to the church or monasteries in 1835 (*Geschichte Griechenlands seit dem Absterben des antiken Lebens bis zur Gegenwart*, Gotha, 1878, III, p. 82).

[1] William Mure, *Journey of a Tour in Greece* (London, 1842), II, p. 297. The statistics on monasteries are from Frederick Strong, *Greece as a Kingdom; or a Statistical Description of that Country from the Arrival of King Otho in 1833 to the Present Time* (London, 1842), p. 361.

ultimately was the choice of that body.[1] As a matter of fact, two of the convents, in Attica and on the Peloponnesus, were closed at the end of the year because they did not have the required number of sisters. Another was established at Aegina, however. Thus, within the space of a year, monastic and convent life was drastically reorganized and reformed.[2]

The Synod was also busy with many other problems of church life. It ordered that each of the new nomes should have, as assistants to the bishop, a protosynkellos and an archdeacon, the former serving as the episcopal counsellor, the latter as his secretary. The Holy Synod appointed these officials.[3] Other legislation was concerned with the troublesome problem of ordinations. The bishops were ordered to observe the canonical age of thirty years and to be certain the candidate was of good character. The person seeking ordination was required to present a written testimonial from the parish in which he would serve as to its needs. Only after documents covering these points had been received and the Holy Synod had reviewed them and given its approval, was it permitted for the bishop to ordain.[4] Other decrees forbade the ordination of men who had come to Greece from the Ionian Islands or from Ottoman territory. Subsequent legislation stated that clerics who came from outside independent Greece were not permitted to serve in the country until proof of their ordination was given and the necessary approval granted by the Holy Synod.[5] In an effort to discourage contacts with the churches outside of Greece, clerics had to apply for permission to leave the country from the Holy Synod stating the purpose of their journey.[6]

One strong decree of 1835 was aimed at rooting out simony, the Synod making the admonition, 'The right time has come to stop this evil wherever it exists.'[7] The bishops themselves were counselled

[1] G. von Maurer, *op. cit.* II, pp. 183 ff.; Ἐφημερὶς τῆς Κυβερνήσεως, Nauplion, 23 April 1834, XV, pp. 123–6.

[2] Ἐφημερὶς τῆς Κυβερνήσεως, Athens, 25 December 1834, XLIII, p. 293.

[3] Ἐφημερὶς τῆς Κυβερνήσεως, Nauplion, 29 January 1834, V, p. 46.

[4] Αἱ ἀναγκαιότεραι Ἐγκύκλιοι Ἐπιστολαί, 3 February 1834, pp. 8, 9.

[5] *Ibid.* 21 July 1834, pp. 33, 34.

[6] *Ibid.* 11 January 1835, pp. 44, 45.

[7] *Ibid.* 26 January 1835, pp. 52, 53; 21 February 1836, pp. 72, 78.

on their obligations and duties, cautioned not to use titles they did not possess and to avoid political and judicial matters.[1] They were to see to it that each parish kept a record of baptisms, weddings and funerals.[2] Probably the greatest amount of legislation by the Synod over the years concerned marriage, the area which traditionally had been of so much concern to the church.[3]

There was also concern evidenced over the construction of churches. The erection of any more private chapels was prohibited; those not in use were to be closed and the keys turned over to the bishop. The king and the Regency themselves donated funds for two churches, Ayios Georgios in Nauplion and the church of the Savior in Athens.[4]

The concern over the relationship between the independent Synod of Greece and the patriarchate continued. In the spring of 1834, Colonel Demetrios Kallergis visited the Patriarch Konstantinos and discussed the situation. The patriarch assured Kallergis that his first resolutions on the matter were to anathematize the Greek church because of its peculiar position established by the Constitution, but that the Russians had urged him to be patient. He stated he had decided not to take any action concerning the church of Greece until King Otho reached his majority and the Regency was dissolved. The Greek minister at the Porte, Konstantinos Zographos, had received instructions to talk with the patriarch and explain the situation to him. Hopes for a final settlement were to be put forward, but a suggestion that a delegation of bishops from Greece be sent to negotiate with the patriarch was vetoed by the Regency.[5]

[1] *Ibid.* 31 January 1834, pp. 5–8.

[2] *Ibid.* 7 February 1834, p. 12.

[3] *Ibid.* 30 March 1834, pp. 25, 26. On marriage laws, 7 February 1834, p. 10; 23 February 1834, pp. 18–23; 31 March 1834, pp. 27–30. No wedding was allowed to be solemnized without the permission of the local bishop. A priest who witnessed a marriage without it might be suspended for three months.

[4] *Ibid.* 7 March 1834, pp. 19–23; Ἐφημερὶς τῆς Κυβερνήσεως, Nauplion, 22 August 1834, XXX, pp. 236, 237; G. von Maurer, *op. cit.* II, pp. 177 ff. The Church of the Savior was not finished and dedicated until March 1838.

[5] Baron de Lerchenfeld to King Ludwig, St Petersburg, 3 February and 28 March 1834, MA III, Russland, 2722, nos. 8 and 15, Munich, Geheimes Staatsarchiv, hereafter GS; Baron Forth-Rouen to Duke de Broglie, Nauplion, 7 February 1834, Grèce, XVII, no. 284, Paris, Archives du Ministère des Affaires Etrangères, Correspondance politique, hereafter MAE.

The Russians continued to protest the separation of the church of Greece from Constantinople. The Greek minister to St Petersburg, Prince Soutzos, was frequently reminded of the Russian dissatisfaction, while in Greece itself the Russian representative, G. A. Katakazis, encouraged the opposition not to co-operate with the Synod. He also supported the newspaper, *The Century*, which represented the conservative view. The Russian foreign minister, Count Nesselrode, moreover, demanded that he exert every effort to question the Bavarians: 'Do the Regents have a firm desire to put an end to the schism which afflicts Greece, do they show themselves animated by a sincere desire to effect a prompt and complete reconciliation between the church of the new state and the Metropolitan See of Constantinople?'[1] The answer was no.

The British policy in 1834 was to support the church settlement and to keep Russian influence at a minimum. The Greeks were constantly warned in London and Nauplion to be on their guard against the Russians and of the use Russia might make of a Synod under patriarchal control. Their envoy to Nauplion was to inform the Regency of continued British support for its church policy, since London assumed 'that measure to be wise and judiciously calculated to render Greece independent of foreign influence...'[2] The London government believed further that a definite treaty with Greece, incorporating into a single document all of the protocols of the various conferences which dealt with Greece, would be advantageous. But the plans of the foreign secretary, Lord Palmerston, were frustrated by the growing Russian intransigence on questions concerning Greece.[3]

The conflict between the powers on the international scene was paralleled by the dissension within the Regency. The British supported Armansperg, the Russians counted on Heideck, while Maurer

[1] Count Nesselrode to Katakazis, St Petersburg, 17 August 1834, quoted in Barbara Jelavich, *Russia and Greece during the Regency of King Othon, 1832–1835* (Thessaloniki, 1962), p. 93; E. Dawkins to Lord Palmerston, Nauplion, 8 February 1834, F.O. 32, Greece, vol. 43, no. 10, London, Public Record Office, hereafter PRO.

[2] J. Backhouse to E. Dawkins, London, 1 April 1834, F.O. 32, Greece, vol. 42, no number; also Dawkins to Palmerston, Nauplion, 26 May 1834, F.O. 32, Greece, vol. 44, no. 39, PRO; *The Times*, London, 21 August 1834

[3] Edouard Driault and Michael l'Héritier, *Histoire diplomatique de la Grèce* (Paris, 1925), II, p. 109.

and Abel, who was the secretary of the Regency, joined forces with Heideck in seeking to outwit the count for their own reasons. Armansperg was closest to the king, in whose company he spent practically every evening—an influence which the other regents considered extremely bad. Moreover, the count depended on the advice of the British minister Edward Dawkins for major decisions, a point which added to the estrangement of the other regents. The first move of the opposition was to remove the treasury from Armansperg's hands. After this Maurer wrote to Henry Parish, a British official who held an unfavorable view of Armansperg and his own superior, Dawkins, 'Count d'Armansperg is now no longer dangerous, he is the fifth wheel of the waggon, but he must now stay with us till the 1st June, 1835. Chained three living to a fourth dead man, it is a point of honor with us that we should all still hold together, but the Count's power is quite gone.'[1]

Otho himself seems to have been little aware of the intrigue going on around him. He had, in fact, begun to lose interest in public affairs according to reports sent to King Ludwig by the regents. They blamed this partly on the influence of his chaplain Father Matthew Weinzierl who encouraged him to devote too much time to his religious practices. The regents demanded that Weinzierl be recalled. Another aspect of this situation appears from the hint that Armansperg was trying to get Otho to change his religion—a move which the Catholic chaplain strongly resisted.[2]

Maurer and Abel plotted to get completely rid of Armansperg by a well-documented complaint sent to King Ludwig, but Armansperg and his friend, the British minister, having heard of their plan, sent a letter to Ludwig which reached him before that of Maurer and Abel. The king was convinced by the first letter and ordered the recall of Maurer and Abel at once; thus, in late June, Georg von

[1] G. Maurer to Henry Parish, Nauplion, 31 March 1834, MA 1, Russland, no. 521, GS; Dawkins to Palmerston, Nauplion, 31 March 1834, F.O. 32, Greece, vol. 43, no. 24, PRO.

[2] Prince Vaudreuil to Prince de Rigny, Munich, 14 April 1834, in *Die Berichte der französischen Gesandten*, Part 1 of *Gesandtschaftsberichte aus München, 1814–1848*, ed. Anton Chroust (Munich, 1935), III, p. 180; Leonard Bower and Gordon Bolitho, *Otho I, King of Greece* (London, 1939), pp. 59–67.

Maurer, architect of the independent church of Greece, left for Munich.[1] There were no objections from the Russians or the British. Maurer's replacement, Egid von Kobell, arrived in July. His orders were to support Armansperg in everything.

Slumbering resentment against the high-handed measures of the Regency broke out into armed revolution in the late summer of 1834. A few of the chieftains of the Peloponnesus, still unreconciled to their loss of power, were behind it. The dissatisfaction with the religious establishment of Greece, resented by many monks and a few of the bishops, also played a significant role. This was coupled to the humiliation of the Greek population being ruled and taxed by a government of foreigners. A proclamation of the revolutionists stated, 'they have insulted our churches and our religion, they have destroyed the houses of orphans, in a word, they have ruined us and are continuing to despoil us each day'.[2] The core of the resistance was in the peninsula of Mani, where pro-Russian sentiment was strong and some insurgents were claiming active support would be forthcoming from the tsar. In a short time, the trained Bavarian troops succeeded in pacifying the area and the Regency arrested its leaders. By the end of August the Revolution was over. One of its effects had been to remove Konstantinos Schinas from his post as secretary of the Ministry of Ecclesiastical Affairs. Having been an appointee of Maurer, his going was mourned by none.[3]

In October 1834, Nauplion witnessed the arrival of the Greek

[1] A. de Gise to Count de Bray, Munich, 27 June 1834, MA III, Russland, 2174, no. 36, GS; B. Forth-Rouen to de Rigny, Nauplion, 11 May 1834, Grèce, XVIII, no. 1, MAE. Maurer published his three-volume work *Das griechische Volk in öffentlicher, kirchlicher und privatrechtlicher Beziehung vor und nach dem Freiheitskampfe* as a defense of his actions in Greece in the following year. His subsequent career was that of a legal theoretician and historian, see Karl Dickopf, *Georg Ludwig von Maurer, 1790–1872* (Kallmünz, 1960), pp. 94 ff.

[2] Document enclosed in a dispatch of B. Forth-Rouen to de Broglie, Nauplion, 3 July 1834, Grèce, XVIII, no. 136, MAE.

[3] *The Times*, London, 11 October 1834; B. Forth-Rouen to de Broglie, Nauplion, 14 August 1834, Grèce, XVIII, no. 205, MAE; E. Dawkins to Palmerston, Nauplion, 25 August 1834, F.O. 32, Greece, vol. 45, no. 62, PRO; Dawkins further comments, 'the peasantry had been persuaded by their priests that the Regency and all the Bavarians were Jews, and they had been told that the King was kept a prisoner at Argos by the Regency and that it was the duty of every good subject to deliver him'.

priest, Konstantinos Oekonomos of the Oekonomos, and thus appeared on the scene the second great ecclesiastical figure of the period. Only Theokletos Pharmakidis could favorably compare with Oekonomos—they were men of broad education, deep insight, and both were vigorous writers. Oekonomos was also a brilliant orator, something Pharmakidis was not. Together, these two men could have done much to raise the Greek church to new eminence, but, in fact, they stood on opposite sides. Pharmakidis, with Maurer gone, was left to lead those who supported the Constitution of 1833 and the independent Synod of Greece. In a very short time, Oekonomos took over the forces of opposition to the establishment and hammered away, by pen and voice, at the separation of the church of Greece from the patriarchate.

Like his great adversary, Konstantinos Oekonomos was also born in a village of Thessaly, Tsaritsani. The date was 27 August 1780. His father was a priest and served in the capacity of oeconom, or steward, to the bishop of Elasson. He received a good education, which included French, and was ordained a priest when he was twenty-one years old. Upon the death of his father he succeeded to his position as oeconom, hence his rather unique name, Konstantinos Oekonomos of the Oekonomos. In a short time, his fame as a great churchman and preacher carried all the way to the patriarchate and, in 1808, Gregorios V invited him to come to the capital. He later spent some time at Smyrna, but was in Constantinople, serving at the Phanar in 1821, when the Revolution commenced. He fled the city in the early days of the upheaval, taking a ship to Odessa, and thus when the body of the patriarch was brought to that city he was chosen to preach the eulogy.

In 1822 he received an invitation to come to St Petersburg to continue his studies, eventually joining the Theological Academy there and also acting as an adviser on Greek affairs to the tsar. While in St Petersburg he had published a number of works on religion and philosophy, of which his *Catechism* became very well known. One book, which was dedicated to the tsar, attempted to show the close relationship between the Greek and Russian languages. Philology being at a primitive stage at that time, Oekonomos' study was a noble attempt at a scientific study. Another work set up plans for an ecclesiastical academy which Oekonomos hoped would be established in Greece. In 1834, despite the success he had obtained in St Petersburg, he decided to return to Greece. Before leaving, he was decorated by the Russians with the medal of St Anne and was granted a lifelong pension of 7,000 rubles annually. This was given to him partly as an indemnity, since his valuable library had been lost in a fire while he lived in St Petersburg.

His trip to Greece was through Prussia, where he met the Emperor William I, and then southwards to Italy. In Rome, he was received with great honor by Pope Gregory XVI and the Curial cardinals. Thence he proceeded to Greece, where Pharmakidis noted his arrival carefully. They had never met, but the secretary of the Synod had heard of his impressive reputation in Russia—this was precisely what troubled him, the suspicion that Oekonomos was an agent of the tsar.[1]

The coming of Oekonomos did much to encourage the rather demoralized Russian party of the Greeks. Katakazis already had twelve clerics attached to his residence. A chapel for the Russian mission was commenced whose furnishing arrived from Odessa, courtesy of the Russian navy, bringing ornaments, ikons, music, and even choristers. The extreme conservatives in the Greek church contended that only in this chapel could the Orthodox really worship, since their own church was in schism.[2] Oekonomos now took up his residence in Nauplion and set to work to rally those opposed to Maurer's settlement.[3]

Oekonomos arrived just a few weeks before the government took

[1] Theokletos Pharmakidis, Ἀπολογία [Apologia] (Athens, 1840), pp. 43 ff.

[2] 'Russian Policy in Greece', *Foreign Quarterly Review*, XXXII (January, 1836), p. 374.

[3] On the life of Oekonomos, see D. S. Balanos, '*Κωνσταντῖνος Οἰκονόμος ὁ ἐξ Οἰκονόμων*' [Konstantinos Oekonomos of the Oekonomos], *Ἐκκλησία*, XXXIV (1953), pp. 491–8, as well as the biography by the same author in the *Θρησκευτικὴ καὶ Χριστιανικὴ Ἐγκυκλοπαιδεία* [Religious and Christian Encyclopedia]. See also C. Papadopoulos, *op. cit.* pp. 145–56. Oekonomos' writings were edited by his son Sophokles after his death and published in three volumes, *Τὰ σωζόμενα ἐκκλησιαστικὰ συγγράμματα Κωνσταντίνου Πρεσβυτέρου καὶ Οἰκονόμου τοῦ ἐξ Οἰκονόμων* [The extant ecclesiastical writings of Konstantinos Oekonomos of the Oekonomos] (Athens, 1862–6).

one more step in its program to regulate church affairs, a fact which demonstrated that Maurer's presence was not essential to further legislation in this regard, for, on 1 December 1834, the government established an Ecclesiastical Fund, which was set up to receive the revenues produced from renting the land of the suppressed monasteries, the money gained from the sale of church land, and all legacies and donations made to the church. It also provided that the disbursements of the church be brought under rigid state control. It is of some interest to note that the budget report of the government in 1833 showed the total expenses for the Ministry of Worship as being 114,836 drachmas, while in 1834 they were 360,521. This compares with the costs of the Ministry of War which, in 1833, were 4,630,750 drachmas and in 1834 were 15,177,522. The expenses incurred by the king's court and the Regency were sixteen times greater than the funds spent for church affairs. Only the ministries of Justice and Finance were given less money.[1]

Meanwhile, the Latin Catholics of Greece continued efforts to improve their situation. Pope Gregory XVI named Luigi Blanci, the bishop of Syros, Apostolic Delegate to Greece in August 1834, but the Regency refused to recognize the appointment since it violated their plan to subject all ecclesiastical officials to the government. Weinzierl wrote to Rome complaining about his own position and noting that the Orthodox church had been forced into a system which was '...none other than the territorial system of the Protestants'.[2] The Latin bishops were not in favor with the Regency, as might well be expected—the one gain the Catholics might count in 1834 was the exemption of the Latin monasteries on Syros, Naxos, and Thira from the confiscatory legislation of the government.

[1] Report of 6 April 1835, given in MA I, Griechenland, no. 516, GS. See also Ἐφημερὶς τῆς Κυβερνήσεως, 21 December 1834, no. 41, pp. 285–90; Frederick Strong, *op. cit.* p. 363. When established the ecclesiastical fund received a little less than 190,000 dr. each year.

[2] Matthew Weinzierl to the Congregation for the Propagation of the Faith, Ancona, 8 June 1834, and A. F. de Brimont to Bishop Blanci, Nauplion, 4 June 1834, Rome, Archivio della S. Congregazione di Propaganda, Congressi, 39, Archipeligo; Georg Hofmann, 'Papa Gregorio XVI e la Grecia', in *Gregorio XVI, Miscellanea commemorativa* (Rome, 1949), II, pp. 137–40.

A new aspect of church relations resulted from the increased activity of Protestant missionaries in Greece. The leaders of the Orthodox church have always had a particular suspicion of Catholic and Protestant clergymen in their midst. Soon after independence was declared in Greece, the first Protestant missionaries arrived. The most active were members of the British and Foreign Bible Society who came as early as 1827—a certain Reverend Hartley having settled on Aegina during that year. He was followed by a number of others, but the American John H. Hill became the most famous. Having arrived in 1830, Hill and his wife opened a school for girls in Athens as soon as facilities were available there.[1]

The Bible Society in 1834 published a translation of the Old Testament into modern Greek from the Hebrew text, instead of employing the official Septuagint version, which had always been used previously. The reaction to this was a storm of protest over the Society's activities in Greece. The conservative clerics charged that this was a subtle means by which Protestantism would be introduced into the Greek church. The translator of the work was Neophytos Vamvas, one of the best educated men of all the Greek clergy. He had come from Chios and had studied in many schools including the Patriarchal Academy in Constantinople. Thence he had travelled to Paris where he became a friend of Koraïs while continuing his studies in philosophy. He was active in Greece during the Revolution and after the war made a number of contacts with the recently arrived Protestant missionaries, who discovered him to be one of the outstanding members of the Orthodox church in the country.

Vamvas' critics were from the same group who protested the new ecclesiastical regime in Greece. Their organ, called the *Gospel Trumpet*, was edited by people close to Oekonomos. Another newspaper which shared the *Trumpet's* views was *Savior*; in it appeared an article signed by a priest, Germanos, attacking the Bible Society's

[1] Johann Wenger, *Beiträge zur Kenntniss des gegenwärtigen Geistes und Zustandes der Griechischen Kirche in Griechenland und der Turkei* (Berlin, 1839), pp. 49–72. On this the Russians complained, 'the dominant church of the state is left in abandon while American missionaries freely establish a center of proselytism in Athens...' (Count Nesselrode to Katakazis, St Petersburg, 17 August 1834, in B. Jelavich, *op. cit.* p. 93).

translation as erroneous in many places and a means of proselytism since it was done under Protestant auspices. Germanos claimed, 'the Greeks have no need of a translation, much less any rendering of the Scripture from the Hebrew, because they have the good fortune of possessing the version of the Seventy in their own language'.[1] Vamvas answered the charges in *Athena*, criticizing Germanos for his fussiness over small points in the translation and contending that the Greek people did need a translation in the vernacular.[2]

Alarmed by the appearance of the vernacular Bible, the Holy Synod, on 4 September 1834, forbade its further distribution until its contents might be scrutinized. Until then its use was forbidden.[3]

In a pamphlet published some time later, Vamvas expanded the ideas put forward in his first reply to Germanos—there was no plot save to allow the Greek people to read the Scriptures in the language they could understand. The Society was not out to convert the Greeks—it was altogether from disinterested motives that they provided the translation. Vamvas noted that the Septuagint translation was not a perfect one; in fact, at times, it was even misleading. If the conservatives like Germanos had their way the people will not know the word of God, for he asserted, 'I conclude that all the independent translations of the Holy Scripture into a spoken dialect of Greek are suspect'.[4]

Vamvas was proved right when the Synod ruled, in April 1835, against the use of any translation of the Old Testament other than

[1] Σωτήρ, Nauplion, 21 June 1834, no. 45, p. 187. Germanos may actually have been a pseudonym of Oekonomos.

[2] Ἀθῆνα, Nauplion, 28 July 1834, vol. III, no. 165, pp. 662–4, no. 166, pp. 666, 667.

[3] Konstantinos Oekonomos of the Oekonomos, Τριακονταετηρὶς ἐκκλησιαστικὴ ἤ συνταγμάτιον ἱστορικὸν τῶν ἐν τῷ Βασιλείῳ τῆς Ἑλλάδος [Thirty years of church affairs or the constitutional history of the Kingdom of Greece], vol. II of Τὰ σωζόμενα ἐκκλησιαστικὰ συγγράμματα [The extant ecclesiastical writings], ed. Sophokles of the Oekonomos (Athens, 1862), pp. 301–5; C. Papadopoulos, *op. cit.* pp. 199 ff. The first Bible in modern Greek appeared in Constantinople in 1818 with the approval of the Patriarch Kyrillos.

[4] Neophytos Vamvas, Ἀπάντησις πρὸς τὴν γενομένην διατριβὴν παρὰ τοῦ κ. Γερμανοῦ κατὰ μεταφράσεως τῶν Ἱερῶν Γραφῶν καὶ τῆς Βιβλικῆς Ἑταιρείας [An answer to the article produced by Germanos against the translation of the Holy Scriptures and against the Biblical Society] (Athens, 1836), pp. 3 ff.

the Septuagint for reading in church, or in school, or even for the private use of the clergy, basing its prohibition on the traditions of the Orthodox church. A hint as to what the decision might be was given a month earlier when Vamvas was told by the government that he must reject the Decoration of St Michael and St George which he had been awarded by King William IV of Great Britain for his translation.[1]

The Holy Synod and Vamvas continued to irritate one another for the next few years. Pamphlets, tracts, and letters were exchanged and charges hurled. Vamvas was accused of opening the door to Protestantism because of his allegiance to the Bible Society, while he charged the Synod with obscurantism. A platform for his ideas was provided for Vamvas when he received an appointment to the newly-opened University in Athens as professor of philosophy, where he continued his translating—the four gospels and the Acts of the Apostles being published in 1838.

As might be expected, the most serious opponent of Vamvas was Konstantinos Oekonomos, the leader of the conservative forces in the Greek church. Since Vamvas also supported Pharmakidis and the autocephalous establishment of the Greek church, he was doubly suspect. Vamvas was equal to the task, chiding him in the opening paragraph of a tract entitled *Concerning the Modern Greek Church*, which answered a publication on the question of the sacrament of Orders by Oekonomos:

> The Most Reverend Father Konstantinos Oekonomos of the Oekonomos, who before the struggle for Greek freedom served in Europe as a public teacher and preacher, and who fled to Russia at the beginning of the war, having returned to Greece, but not as a Greek, has put out from his residence in Nauplion a three hundred and sixty-page essay on the Three Sacred Orders.

Vamvas attacked Oekonomos' concern over translations, pointing out that the Septuagint itself was a translation, 'Why this struggle? The Holy Scriptures are the word of God. The word of God is to be given for the salvation of all men...' and for this it is necessary

[1] Ἐφημερὶς τῆς Κυβερνήσεως, 7 March 1835, no. 7, p. 52, and 13 May, no. 17, p. 128.

'that they read and understand the word of God written and taught in the language of their reading and hearing'.[1]

Oekonomos answered Vamvas' charges with a large book of page by page refutation of his rival's opinions. He asked why Vamvas had gone to Cephalonia during the Revolution if he was so concerned with the war record of others. He then made the cruel jab that Vamvas accomplished his translation only with the help of a French-Hebrew dictionary, which demonstrated his own lack of ability. Asserting that the Greek people can read the Scriptures already, Oekonomos charged that Vamvas had simply translated it into a dialect, and to say that the people are starved for the word of God is ridiculous since the Liturgy is full of biblical passages. He quarrelled with Vamvas' translation, claiming it frequently missed the sense, pointing out that this is precisely the problem of human translation. He gives in conclusion a long history of the Septuagint's use in the New Testament and in the Fathers—this he asserts is the word of God, pure and undefiled, which must be the source of teaching in the church.[2]

To this Vamvas replied with a new tract refuting Oekonomos and charging that he had been deliberately misquoted, misunderstood, and falsely accused by his opponent.[3] The debate between the two clerics is conducted in prose filled with righteous indignation, accented by great quantities of exclamation points. In the end, Oekonomos had his way. The present constitution of Greece adopted in 1911 states, 'The text of the Holy Scripture is maintained unchanged, the rendering thereof in another form or language without the previous sanction of the Great Church of Christ in Constantinople is absolutely forbidden'. Vamvas' translation, however, is still on sale at the Athens' office of the British and Foreign Bible Society.[4]

1 Neophytos Vamvas, *Περὶ τῆς Νεοελληνικῆς Ἐκκλησίας* [Concerning the New Greek Church] (Athens, 1838), pp. 5, 6.

2 Konstantinos Oekonomos of the Oekonomos, *Ἐπίκρισις εἰς τὴν Περὶ Νεοελληνικῆς Ἐκκλησίας σύντομον ἀπάντησιν τοῦ...Ν. Βάμβα* [A Criticism of 'Concerning the Modern Greek Church', a concise answer to Neophytos Vamvas] (Athens, 1839).

3 Neophytos Vamvas, *Ἀντεπίκρισις εἰς τὴν ὑπὸ τοῦ Πρεσβυτέρου καὶ Οἰκονόμου Κωνσταντίνου τοῦ ἐξ Οἰκονόμων Ἐπίκρισιν* [An answer to the Criticism of the Priest and Oeconom, Konstantinos of the Oekonomos] (Athens, 1839).

4 A new translation of the Scriptures into demotic Greek caused riots in the streets of Athens in 1909.

The great event of 1835 for the kingdom of Greece was the arrival of King Otho to his majority and the end of the Regency. In preparation, the capital of the country was moved from Nauplion to Athens in January of that year. The problem of the kind of ceremony that would be appropriate immediately presented itself. The Regency wanted it to be a great occasion and to have Otho anointed, but in the Orthodox church this is a sacrament and the Holy Synod told Armansperg they could not allow a Catholic king to be blessed with the Holy Oil. The Russian envoy Katakazis had counselled the Synod on the matter to this effect. Otho himself was warned against the Orthodox ceremony by the Latin bishop of Syros, Luigi Blanci, since it would be a compromise of his own faith.[1] The Synod did send out an order that, in all the churches of Greece, a doxology should be sung for the king on the day of the celebration.

On 20 May, all of Athens was decorated for the event. A crown had come from Munich, but there was no coronation or anointing. Otho attended a service in the church of Ayia Irene where prayers were offered for him. Katakazis and the Russian mission did not attend in protest over Otho's reluctance to convert to Orthodoxy. The king declared, 'In all circumstances I shall prove my profound reverence for the Eastern Church and I will show particular attention to those matters which concern my descendants who shall inherit the throne of Greece.' Thus was handled the important question of Otho's children being raised in the Orthodox faith—the statement was vague enough for anyone to read into it what he wanted, and of course it was not enough for Katakazis. In the evening, the town was illuminated and the celebration was extended for four days. During the festivities Otho made known that he would retain Armansperg as his archchancellor and that the other regents would be dismissed, a bit of news which dismayed the count's enemies.[2]

[1] L. Blanci to the Congregation for the Propagation of the Faith, Syros, 29 May 1835, Rome, Archivio della S. Congregazione di Propaganda, Congressi, 39, Archipeligo. Otho's new Catholic confessor was Father Arneth, who was also strongly opposed to an Orthodox service.

[2] L. Bower and G. Bolitho, *op. cit.* pp. 78–80; Hans Rall, 'Die Anfänge des Konfessionspolitischen Ringens um den Wittelsbacher Thron in Athen', *Bayern: Staat und Kirche, Land und Reich* (Munich, 1961), p. 211. B. Forth-Rouen to Duke de

When informed of Katakazis' action on the day of Otho's coming of age, King Ludwig let it be known he considered it a grave insult. He instructed the Bavarian minister to let it be known in St Petersburg, 'I deplore that in all the affairs which concern Greece, the Imperial Cabinet, by a perspective from which it views its every act, considers the religious belief of King Otho as an affair to which the Russian honor is attached!' Adding his opinion, Baron Gise protested that the demands of Katakazis were out of order, for they 'obviously pass beyond the bounds which agents of foreign powers possess in public law'. His influencing the Synod to refuse to anoint the king was judged altogether improper.[1] Nesselrode replied to the protests that Katakazis had acted on his own judgment, and that he had received no instructions on the matter from the Russian court. The Bavarian minister was assured that the emperor was concerned about Otho's religion only because it meant securing his own throne.[2]

Nesselrode's disarming manner was not consistent with Russian moves later in the summer of 1835. First, there was a dispatch from St Petersburg from Prince Lieven speaking for the tsar, charging Otho with reneging on his promises. The Russian note claimed that, before leaving Munich, Otho had promised that even if he himself did not become Orthodox his children would definitely be raised in that faith. When Otho was shown the communication 'he showed himself personally wounded by the imperative and menacing terms in which it was drafted'.[3] Secondly, there was announced in St Petersburg that the tsar was sending Baron Alexis Stroganov on a special mission to Athens to speak to the king, and to congratulate him on attaining his majority.

No one believed that Stroganov was coming to see Otho to dis-

Broglie, Athens, 2 June 1835, Grèce, XIX, nos. 209, 213, MAE. Forth-Rouen regretted Otho had not spoken with 'more precision and clarity' on the question of succession since it is 'a question to which the highest interest is attached'.

[1] King Ludwig to Lerchenfeld, Munich, 18 June 1835 Baron Gise to Lerchenfeld, Munich, 21 June 1835, MA III, Russland, 2723, GS.

[2] Baron Lerchenfeld to Ludwig, Carlsbad, 12 July 1835, MA III, Russland, 2723, no. 1, GS.

[3] B. Forth-Rouen to Duke de Broglie, Athens, 20 August 1835, Grèce, XX, no. 36, MAE.

cuss pleasantries. His main mission, as it was subsequently revealed, was to pressure Otho on the religious question. If he could not persuade the king himself to become Orthodox, he was to obtain as a minimum an assurance from Otho that his children would be Orthodox. Having arrived in mid-August, the Baron remained in Greece for a month. He had frequent confidential meetings with Otho which caused the king notable anxiety. Apparently, Otho held his ground and Stroganov had to content himself with a half-hearted promise that his heirs would be educated according to Orthodox belief. There was no public announcement of the conclusion of the talks, and Stroganov admitted he found Otho to be as Catholic 'as the King of Spain himself'.[1]

Lest the question of Otho's children remain hypothetical, a search was soon initiated to find someone suitable for the king to marry. The Countess Armansperg had already been forced to console herself with marrying off her daughters to two Greek aristocrats, in the process violating the canons of the Orthodox church which forbade the marriage of two sets of brothers and sisters.[2] It was decided that Otho would return to Germany and circulate among the families with eligible daughters. The trip was a success, Otho was quickly engaged and married to Amalia, the eldest daughter of the grand duke of Oldenburg. Since she was a Protestant, the marriage, held in November 1836, was a quiet one at which the Catholic bishop of Munster officiated. The bishop did not investigate the delicate question of the education of their children.[3]

Upon his return to Greece in February 1837 the king abruptly dismissed Armansperg, and Ignaz von Rudhart was named his successor. The Greeks had hoped the king would choose a native Greek for the position of chancellor and were bitterly disappointed with the announcement of another Bavarian appointee. Already unpopular

[1] Franz Jenison to Gise, Athens, 17 September 1835, quoted in H. Rall, *op. cit.* p. 212; also Lerchenfeld to Ludwig, St Petersburg, 13 August 1835, MA III, Russland, 2723, GS; Forth-Rouen to de Broglie, Athens, 3 and 26 September 1835, Grèce XX, nos. 50, 68, MAE; E. Driault and M. l'Héritier, *op. cit.* II, pp. 141, 142.

[2] The Holy Synod protested but was ignored. Baron Forth-Rouen to Duke de Broglie, Athens, 6 August 1835, Grèce, XX, no. 6, MAE.

[3] L. Bower and G. Bolitho, *op. cit.* p. 92; G. Hofmann, *op. cit.* p. 148.

with the Greek people, von Rudhart did not quite finish a year in office owing to the intrigues of the diplomats and his own incompetence. Thenceforth, Otho took over the duties of the chancellor himself, and presided personally at cabinet meetings. He wanted to rule as an autocrat, but he lacked the ability and the strength of will to do so. It was especially evident that he could not really communicate with others and in the solution of problems which were frequently urgent, Otho simply was unable to reach a decision. While formerly he had been rather well accepted, since the Regency or the chancellor took the blame for government policies which were unpopular, now there was no doubt that, for good or evil, the responsibility was completely the king's.

The representatives of the Powers at Athens were frequently exasperated by Otho. In reality, it was an impossible task to please Russia, France and Britain, since they held such divergent opinions on what the future of Greece must be. Katakazis remained to represent the tsar and to plague King Otho, while Dawkins had been replaced after 1835 by Sir Edmund Lyons to represent British interests in Greece. Lyons had been a great friend of Armansperg—he practically ruled the country while the count was in power—so that after the archchancellor's dismissal he became disenchanted with the Greek government. He wanted Otho to grant a Constitution and opposed his efforts to rule autocratically—in this he was at the opposite pole from Katakazis, who, although he was no friend of Otho, had no sympathy for representational government. The French ministers pursued a policy somewhat in between the liberal British and autocratic Russian course.

The Greek political leaders tended to group themselves around the Power which most represented their views. The 'English party' was headed by Alexandros Mavrokordatos of revolutionary fame and a group of Greeks who looked to Britain for aid in their efforts to influence the government. The 'Russian party' was made up of men like Oekonomos and the conservative churchmen who bitterly resented the church Constitution of 1833. Political chief of the group was Andreas Metaxas, also a revolutionary leader and a former member of the Kapodistrian government. Under the Regency he had served as nomarch in Lakonia, but had been arrested for complicity in the revolutionary movements hatched there and sent into exile. He was later recalled and sent as Greek minister to Spain for a few years. The Russian party had, as its newspaper, *The Century*, while the British view could be found in *Athena*. The third party was really a national party, but was attached loosely to France and led by Ioannis Kolettis. Its major concern was more with the expansion of the Greek border northwards than with any other program. This was 'the Great Idea', the rebirth of the Byzantine Empire which became the dominant note in Greek history for the next hundred years.[1]

Throughout the period covering the next several decades, Greece was forced to suffer from the rivalry of the Great Powers in Europe and especially from their position regarding the Ottoman Empire. The British were intent on propping up the sultan since the Empire had such economic and strategic importance for their interests in the East Mediterranean. Britain was concerned lest independent Greece stir up trouble in an attempt to expand its narrow borders, destroy the delicate balance of power and thus precipitate a general conflict.

The Russians, of course, were also interested in preserving their position in the Ottoman Empire gained after the Treaty of Hunkiar Iskelesi, so that they shared British reluctance to support the aspirations of Greece to broaden its boundaries at the expense of the Turks. The tsar wanted Otho to be a strong king and a successful one—the one complaint against him was his Catholicism. Russia's opposition to Otho was always in the religious area, not the political. The Russian minister, Katakazis, strongly opposed to the king, frequently acted on his own initiative without receiving instructions from St Petersburg. French policy in Greece was to see to it that men favorable to its interests would hold positions in the ministry. For all three powers, events in Constantinople were considered the major area of concern—their policy in Greece was an adjunct to decisions made regarding the Ottoman Empire.

[1] For sketches of the Greek leaders and their parties, see Jules Blancard, *Etudes sur la Grèce contemporaine* (Montpellier, 1886), I, pp. 17–48, 53–68; E. Driault and M. l'Héritier, *op. cit.* II, p. 138.

The changes in the political arena of Greek life had little influence on church affairs during the years. The Synod continued to be dominated by members whose loyalty to the government was the major reason for their appointment. Pharmakidis, as secretary, held an advantageous position from which to combat revisionism. The Synod did legislate further on marriage, on the clerical life, and on preaching.[1] The secretary strongly adhered to the position that marriage legislation was primarily under the jurisdiction of the state, and the synodal decrees reflect that opinion.

An event of great importance for the church occurred when the University of Athens was founded in 1839. Despite the crying need for facilities of higher education, Otho himself, along with his cabinet, delayed implementing the decree passed as early as December 1836 which announced plans for the enterprise. One of the faculties planned for the university was theology. Although the training of clergy should have had the highest priority, up to that time efforts to provide it were limited to impressive bulletins issued by the Ministry of Worship. Thus the Theological School at the university was the first substantial move along these lines when it opened in 1839 after numerous delays. The faculty was composed of only three members, the chairman being Misael Apostolidis, employing as professors Theokletos Pharmakidis and Konstantinos Kontogonis. The next important step towards providing educational facilities for the clergy was the institution founded by the two brothers, Manthos and Georgios Rizaros. When their school opened in January 1843, Georgios had already died but his contribution in planning and financing the institution had been great. Some twenty scholarships were offered by the government the first year of its existence. Such were the feeble efforts provided for clerical training in the church of Greece during its first decade of independence from the patriarchate.[2]

[1] *Αἱ ἀναγκαιότεραι Ἐγκύκλιοι Ἐπιστολαί*, 2 April and 12 November 1835, pp. 59, 64, and 22 August 1838, pp. 106–10.

[2] *Ἐφημερὶς τῆς Κυβερνήσεως*, Athens, 31 December 1836, LXXXVI, p. 446, contains the plans for the university. On education see C. Papadopoulos, *op. cit.* pp. 326 ff. The decree on the Rizaros school is found in *Ἐφημερὶς τῆς Κυβερνήσεως*, Athens, 13 February 1843, no. 4, pp. 11–14.

The literary contest between Oekonomos and Pharmakidis continued over the years. It has already been noted how Neophytos Vamvas sided with Pharmakidis after Oekonomos had attacked his translation of the Scriptures. The conservative party used the pages of the *Trumpet* to hammer away at Pharmakidis' ideas. The publication had moved to Athens from Nauplion in August 1835 so as to be closer to the center of activity in the capital.

One of the celebrated articles in the *Trumpet* attacked the structure of the Synod because it allowed priests as well as bishops to function on it, was therefore uncanonical and, in fact, smacked of presbyterianism. The question had been raised before—what exactly were the degrees of the hierarchy? The Patriarch Gregorios VI had even written a work on the matter. Since this obviously was a weak constitutional point, Oekonomos prepared a book on the subject, entitled *An Epistolary Treatise on the Three Hierarchical Orders of the Church*, published in Nauplion in 1835.[1] In this work, Oekonomos noted how the denial of any division in the sacrament of Holy Orders had begun with Calvin's notion that the church should be governed by ministers rather than priests. That this was obviously heretical he proved from scripture and the tradition of the church. His sources were both the Latin and Greek Fathers as well as the decrees of the Ecumenical Councils, exhibiting a real depth in his scholarship. In the following year, the Patriarch Gregorios VI, well-informed on Greek affairs, issued an encyclical on 'the spreading of so-called presbyterianism' in Greece. The government, under Pharmakidis' influence, chose to ignore the whole issue.[2]

Oekonomos was treading on softer ground when he became involved in a dispute over a number of biblical verses concerning John the Baptist. Here he held the view that the Zachary, killed between the

[1] *Περὶ τῶν τριῶν ἱερατικῶν τῆς Ἐκκλησίας Βαθμῶν ἐπιστολιμαία διατριβή*. A rejoinder to this work appeared in 1841, published by Paulos Kalligas, whose main argument was that all three terms, bishop, priest, and deacon, are different ways of expressing the same reality (*Ἀπάντησις εἰς τὴν ἀπὸ 25 Νοεμβρίου 1835 ἐπιστολιμαίαν διατριβὴν ὡς πρὸς τοὺς τρεῖς ἱερατικοὺς βαθμοὺς τῆς Ἐκκλησίας* [An answer to the epistolary treatise of 25 November 1835 concerning the three hierarchial orders of the church], Athens, 1841).

[2] C. Papadopoulos, *op. cit.* pp. 195 ff.; Theokletos Pharmakidis, *Apologia*, p. 144.

altar and the Holy Place, mentioned by Christ in His talk to the Jews in Luke xxi. 51, is the same Zachary who was the father of John the Baptist.[1] Phamakidis was quick to reply to this, charging that Oekonomos was guilty of a serious misinterpretation of the texts.[2] The encounter was not always kept on polite terms—as when one newspaper suggested in 1837 that 'the great Oekonomos' be named to the Synod, *Athena* asked 'who is this great Oekonomos?' Is he 'great' in the eyes of Constantinople, or in the eyes of the sultan? There are many oeconoms in Greece, the article asserted, so which is the great one? Perhaps it is the oeconom who has just arrived from Russia 'where he fled at the beginning of our sacred struggle from Constantinople'.[3]

This pamphlet war continued on these rather petty matters until a new issue appeared owing to the activities of Theophilos Kairis. This man was a well-known priest of the island of Andros, whose fame rested until 1839 on his charitable activities. As early as 1835 Kairis had begun an orphanage on Andros which had some thirty children at its beginning, but which had had a remarkable growth during the next several years. Not only orphans, but other children were admitted, some of them being well beyond the age when they would have been dependants. The reason for this stemmed from the extraordinary personality of Father Kairis who taught, administered, preached and worked night and day to provide a solid education for his pupils.

Unfortunately, Kairis was such an individualist that his doctrine was not sound. He had spent some time in western universities at Pisa and Paris, as had Pharmakidis and Vamvas, and like them he had come under the influence of Koraïs during the heady days of Napoleonic France. His philosophical thought was molded according to the ideas of Auguste Comte, his theological speculation followed the deism of the Enlightenment—the result was an original philo-

[1] Περὶ Ζαχαρίου τοῦ Πατρὸς τοῦ Προδρόμου [Concerning Zacharias, the Father of the Precursor] (Athens, 1838), in Τὰ σωζόμενα ἐκκλησιαστικὰ συγγράμματα [The extant ecclesiastical writings], ed. Sophocles of the Oeconomos (Athens, 1862), I, pp. 326–48.

[2] Περὶ Ζαχαρίου υἱοῦ Βαραχίου [Concerning Zachary son of Barachias] (Athens, 1838).

[3] Ἀθῆνα, Athens, 31 July 1837, vol. VI, no. 458, p. 1875.

sophical system which he called Pietism. He published a work containing his ideas entitled *A Summary of Pietistic Teaching*, which enunciated his elaborate thought and which went so far even as to suggest a reformed calendar with new names for the months.[1]

Due to Kairis' highly respected qualities, Pietism was not only found in his school but began to win adherents throughout Andros and beyond, as his three hundred or more students carried the enthusiasm for their professor's doctrine into all parts of Greece and the Ottoman Empire. In February and March of 1839 reports began reaching the patriarchate, while other rumors came to Athens, speaking of Kairis' heterodox teaching. Inquiries were commenced, but all the letters from the civil authorities supported Kairis. Since the Holy Synod in Athens was left unsatisfied, it first sent the protosynkellos of the bishop of Cyclades to Andros and eventually addressed a personal letter to Kairis to ascertain his views. Pharmakidis, who was a friend, drew up the letter which centered on the report that Kairis denied the existence of the Trinity.

The letter was sent on 10 July 1839 and the answer was received shortly afterwards. Kairis avoided a direct response, stating that he was a philosopher, not a theologian, hence the question of the Trinity was not a topic about which he was concerned. He went on to give a résumé of his philosophy but hardly in a manner to satisfy the Holy Synod. A new letter was dispatched for further clarification on 25 August—did he believe all that was a part of the Orthodox faith and did he accept the Trinity as taught by that church? To this Kairis replied in general terms, adding that he intended to leave Greece the following March. Pharmakidis, who thought him the victim of some of his enemies, was content, 'here we have the easy solution to the scandalous drama'.[2]

The matter was not allowed to rest there, however, because of the intervention of the patriarch, Gregorios VI. In late September he issued an encyclical which condemned Pietism, charging it with heretical doctrine and blasphemies against God, the Orthodox church,

[1] Ἐπιτομὴ θεοσεβικῆς διδασκαλίας (Athens, 1839).

[2] K. Oekonomos, *Thirty Years of Church Affairs*, pp. 399–407; T. Pharmakidis, *Apologia*, pp. 181–6; C. Papadopoulos, *op. cit.* pp. 224–65.

and Holy Scripture. Gregorios demanded that the parents of students in Kairis' school remove them.[1] Not to be outdone by the patriarch, the Holy Synod in Athens flew into activity. On their request, the government sent a naval vessel to arrest Kairis and bring him to Athens. On 21 October the accused cleric appeared before the Synod to answer the charges of heresy placed against him.

Kairis responded to the questions of the Synod just as he had replied to its letters. He reiterated that his subject was philosophy not religion, and to say Pietism was a form of religion was to misunderstand the whole point of it. Pharmakidis apparently was willing to accept this defense, the Synodal members were not.[2] A few days later, a decision was given by the Synod suspending Kairis from the priesthood, accusing him of apostasy and heresy, and ordering him exiled to a monastery on Skiathos.[3]

Although *The Century* supported the Synodal decision, Kairis was defended in *Athena* and *Friend of the People*. The latter publication called him a 'new Socrates' and a 'martyr of goodness' while the former likened the sending of a warship to arrest him to tactics more in accord with the Turks or the pope than the Orthodox church. It claimed that his real crime was that he tried to educate the youth of Greece, something not wanted by the reactionary churchmen who condemned him.[4] A final salvo was fired by the patriarch in a further condemnation of Kairis in December. This incident of Kairis and his Pietism marks the one great dogmatic issue during the period of the autocephalous church of Greece. Kairis was later freed from his exile, but remained an unrepentant Pietist until his death in 1866.

The condemnation of Kairis provided the opportunity which the enemies of Pharmakidis had long been awaiting. They claimed that,

[1] Manuel Gedeon, *Πατριαρχικαὶ Ἐφημερίδες* [Patriarchal papers] (Athens, 1936), p. 410; Tryphonos Evangelidis, *Ἱστορία τοῦ Ὄθωνος, Βασιλέως τῆς Ἑλλάδος* [History of Otho, King of Greece] (Athens, 1893), p. 246.

[2] Pharmakidis states, 'I was of the opinion that the matter should have been handled quietly and calmly...' (*Apologia*, p. 190).

[3] *Ἐφημερὶς τῆς Κυβερνήσεως*, Athens, 18 November 1839, no. 24, p. 110; Sartiges to Marechal, Athens, 8 November 1839, Grèce, xxx, no. 83, MAE.

[4] *Αἰών*, Athens, 12 November 1839, no. 110, p. 1; *Ἀθῆνα*, Athens, 28 October and 15 November 1839, nos. 664 and 669, pp. 3614, 3634; C. Papadopoulos, *op. cit.* p. 269.

by supporting Kairis in the beginning, he had shown sympathy for heresy. Agitation to get him out of the Synod was nothing new to the secretary, but this time he was unable to weather the storm. The Minister of Worship, Glarakis, announced his dismissal as of 20 November 1839. He received, as compensation, an appointment to the university as professor of Greek philology—a subject about which, he complained, he had very little knowledge or training.[1]

Pharmakidis' dismissal was applauded by the Russian party, who looked upon him as their worst enemy; Katakazis had long worked for his removal as a stumbling block to harmonious relations between the Greek people and the government. The news was also cause for celebration at the patriarchate in Constantinople, where Pharmakidis was considered the arch-foe of the church, since it was he who had co-operated with Maurer in drawing up the Church Constitution of 1833. The representatives of the western Powers, on the other hand, were not pleased with the turn of events, looking upon it as a Russian ploy to restore communication between the Greek church and the patriarchate. According to the French minister in Athens, Sartiges, the rejection of Pharmakidis:

...has produced here an astonishing and general discontent; for it has been known that efforts were being made by the Greek church of Constantinople to place once more the Greek national church under it. It was also known that the Holy Synod, supported by the sympathies of Russia and the active zeal of its legation in Athens, has been working to return the Greek church to the jurisdiction of the patriarch of Constantinople. This has made it evident, all at once, that the reunion of the two churches has, in fact, been morally accomplished.[2]

[1] T. Pharmakidis, *Apologia*, pp. 1–4, 203–6. He describes his getting this dismissal, 'I opened the letter with great care and read it not only once, but two or three times, for I could not convince myself that it was really true. It appeared to me to be so unbelievable and outlandish!'

[2] Sartiges to Marechal, Athens, 9 December 1839, Grèce, XXXIX, no. 103, MAE. The position of the Paris government had been outlined in a dispatch of 25 April 1839: 'Perhaps we feared in 1833 that the separation of the two churches would be imprudent and premature, but the experience has been successful...now we can only consider any modification of this independence as the result of projects due to political influence which it is in our right and interest, within Greece, to strongly oppose' (Count Molé to Lagrenée, Paris, 25 April 1839, quoted in E. Driault and M. l'Héritier, *op. cit.* II, p. 139).

Not many weeks passed before Pharmakidis was at work writing a defense of his activities in the Greek church which was published in 1840. In it he claimed that he was the victim of political intrigue, launched by Oekonomos, because of his contribution in separating the church of Greece from the patriarchate in 1833. He reviewed his past activities, claiming that what he had done was simply an attempt to give to the church the same autonomy and independence the state enjoyed after the Revolution. In fact, he claimed, the church had been independent since the death of Patriarch Gregorios V, and the Constitution of 1833 did nothing more than ratify the existing situation. He defended the Synod of Nauplion as one which had legitimately acted in the name of the Greek church and people, and whose decision had been freely reached. This the bishops were empowered to do by the new political situation existing in the nation, and the Greek church was no less Orthodox than the churches of Alexandria, Antioch and Cyprus, which were outside the jurisdiction of Constantinople. An independent church, Pharmakidis asserted over and over, was essential to a sovereign state.[1]

The appearance of the *Apologia* was cheered by the friends of the ousted secretary and ridiculed by his enemies. A public attack on it was made in *The Century*, while Oekonomos spoke of it as that 'most apologetic Apologia'.[2]

In the summer of 1840, Pharmakidis made a move to discredit his opposition by accusing Oekonomos of heresy before the Holy Synod. In a sermon which the leader of the conservative churchmen had delivered at the monastery of Megaspelaion, Oekonomos had used a phrase concerning Mary, the mother of Christ, which the former secretary of the Synod judged to be contrary to the orthodox teaching on the Trinity. Oekonomos had addressed Mary as 'the unmarried Spouse of God the Father, the excellent dwelling place of the consubstantial and eternal Trinity'. The letter of complaint

[1] *Apologia*, pp. 1–6; 14–17; 24–35.

[2] *Αἰών*, Athens, 21 July 1840, no. 180, p. 3; D. S. Balanos, ''*Ἀνέκδοτοι ἐπιστολαὶ Κωνσταντίνου Οἰκονόμου τοῦ 'ἐξ Οἰκονόμων*' [Unpublished letters of Konstantinos Oekonomos of the Oekonomos], *Πραγματεῖαι τῆς Ἀκαδημίας Ἀθηνῶν* [Acts of the Athenian Academy], v, no. 1 (1936), p. 15.

was sent to the Synod in early July and, in a matter of days, a response was given absolving Oekonomos of any heretical teaching since the Fathers of the church had used similar phrases.[1]

The membership of the Synod, as Pharmakidis was well aware, after the appointments of July 1839, had, for the first time since the separation from Constantinople, fallen into the hands of bishops opposed to the Constitution of 1833. At its head was Dionysios of Kynourias, who had held the position before, but the two new members added that month were Joseph of Messenia and Ignatios of Gortyna, prelates who were known as advocates of reunion with Constantinople.[2] They owed their appointment to the increased militancy of the conservatives grouped around Oekonomos, who had succeeded in winning over the Secretary of Ecclesiastical Affairs Glarakis, to his point of view.

Evidence of increased hostility towards the government party in the Greek church had been mounting. The Synod had refused to welcome the metropolitan of Rhodes with recognition after he had been ousted by the patriarch; then, in a decision of April 1839, it had absolutly forbidden marriages between Orthodox and members of another faith. This had been suggested as a move which was meant to stop Bavarian inroads into Greece, while increasing the possibility of contacts with Russia. A further action meant to show the government that the Synod was at odds with the present situation was the unanimous decision—when there was a question of consecrating new bishops for Greece—that this could only be done validly if approval came from the church of Constantinople.[3]

The conservative members of the Greek church had been sufficiently drawn together by the events of 1839 that their strength was now formidable. Supported by the Russian embassy, they also

[1] Oekonomos, *Thirty Years of Church Affairs*, pp. 443–54; D. S. Balanos, *Θεόκλητος Φαρμακίδης* [Theokletos Pharmakidis] (Athens, 1933), p. 39.

[2] *'Εφημερὶς τῆς Κυβερνήσεως*, Athens, 29 July 1839, no. 15, p. 76. The other two members were Gerasimos of Idhra and Theodoritos of Sellasias.

[3] Panayotis Pipinelis, 'Η *Μοναρχία ἐν* 'Ελλάδι, *1833–1843* [The Monarchy in Greece] (Athens, 1932), pp. 295 ff.; K. Oekonomos, *Thirty Years of Church Affairs* p. 375; Sartiges to Marechal, Athens, 9 and 19 August, Grèce, XXXIX, nos. 186 and 212, MAE.

received leadership from Andreas Metaxas and Michael Vodas and others associated with *The Century*. Their program was also the beneficiary of a work entitled *East and West*, which appeared the same year. Attributed to the Russian Prince Wolkonsky, the theme of the work was the great solidarity existing between all Orthodox peoples, while emphasizing the differences which separated the Eastern churches from the West. It deplored the situation of the church of Greece since it was no longer united with the patriarch of Constantinople and urged Otho to become Orthodox and reunite the two churches.[1]

The more extreme of the conservatives were not content with the overthrow of Pharmakidis and therefore began to plan further moves. A secret group was formed in 1839, known as the Philorthodox Society, which was headed by Colonel Nikitas Stamatelopoulos. The society planned to incite an insurrection against the Turks in Epirus, Thessaly and Macedonia, while, at the same time, putting an Orthodox prince on the Greek throne. In a letter to Georgios Kapodistrias, younger brother of the late president, Stamatelopoulos sketched his plans to carry out the coup, but the letter fell into the hands of the police and its author was arrested. Besides this incriminating document, the police also turned up a sort of 'catechism' of the Society which asked the question 'By whom shall we be supported?', and the answer was given 'N.A.R.'—standing for Nicholas, Autocrat of Russia. Thus the Russian party got its name 'N.A.R.'

The conspirators were rapidly rounded up by the government, and the Holy Synod was quick to issue a warning to the Greek faithful not to join any society which sought to disturb the peace. In fact, it seems that the Philorthodox Society numbered only a few people, but the emotions and fears of the moment tended to exaggerate its importance. It did have one important effect. Colonel Stamatelopoulos had been a great friend of Katakazis, even standing as godfather to one of his children. The Russian envoy's closeness to the conspiracy resulted in his recall for a time to St Petersburg,

[1] Lagrenée to Duke of Montebello, Athens, 17 May 1839, Grèce, XXXIX, no. 21, MAE; E. Driault and M. l'Héritier, *op. cit.* p. 194.

but he returned to his post in Athens after satisfying the tsar concerning his conduct.[1]

Now it was the turn of the conservatives to be put on the defensive. *The Century* cried foul, claiming that the country was being devastated by foreigners intent on bringing a 'western spirit' to Greece, and demanded that something be done to stop the fanatics who were waging a compaign against the Orthodox church.[2] But the protests were in vain. When the annual appointments to the Synod were announced in the summer of 1840 the more avid pro-Russian bishops were dismissed, while in Constantinople itself British pressure put on the Porte resulted in a change at the patriarchate, Gregorios VI being forced to resign his post.[3]

With the Russian influence at a low point for the time being, the life of the Greek Orthodox church over the next few years was rather placid. Major complaints were still being articulated concerning the system—the scarcity of efficient bishops was especially noted, as older men died and no younger ones were able to replace them.

The Latin community in Greece during the years from 1835 to 1843 saw some gains come its way. The long-sought recognition of Luigi Blanci, bishop of Syros, as Apostolic Delegate to Greece was at last obtained, after a conversation between Blanci and Otho in May 1838. Otho had been unaware of the Regency's efforts to stop Blanci's appointment in 1834.[4] Various statistics show that the number of Latin Catholics was on the increase, but the hostility shown by their Orthodox countrymen did not abate.[5] When the British

[1] E. Driault and M. l'Héritier, *op. cit.* pp. 195–7; Ἀθῆνα, Athens, 27 December 1839, no. 681, p. 3681; Αἰών, Athens, 3 January 1840, no. 123, p. 2; P. Pipinelis, *op. cit.* p. 295.

[2] Αἰών, Athens, 1 January 1840, no. 120, p. 1; 28 January, no. 131, p. 1; 2 June, no. 167, p. 1.

[3] The immediate occasion for Gregorios' dismissal had been his condemnation of the British and Foreign Bible Society's translation of the scripture into modern Greek, an act considered inexcusable by the British minister at Constantinople. Gregorios returned as patriarch in 1867 for another term.

[4] Ἐφημερὶς τῆς Κυβερνήσεως, Athens, 8 January 1838, no. 22, p. 116; G. Hofmann, 'Papa Gregorio XVI', II, p. 143.

[5] A statistical survey in 1835 put the total number of Catholics in Greece at that

traveller, William Mure, was at Levadhia in 1838 he visited a school where the reading text consisted of a polemical work against the Catholic church, causing him to comment, 'from the tenor of the doctrines it inculcated, it would appear that the Roman Pontiff and his Eternal City are considered by the Greek theologians, as they have been by a large portion of our own for some centuries past, as the Babylonian beast, and the great source of heresy and corruption to the universal Christian Church'.[1] Mure's experience was hardly unique.

The year 1843 marks a turning point in Greek history, since it is a year of revolution. The authority of Otho was successfully challenged and resulted in the drawing up of a Constitution for the country. Greece had fought in 1821 for freedom from despotic rule, and while it is true that their Bavarian monarch can hardly be equated with the sultan, still Otho's insistence on making all the decisions, which often enough meant interminable delays, resulted in a great clamor for change. Many felt that to have stopped short of a Constitution meant that the first revolution was left incomplete —others were simply exasperated at the king's inefficient adminstration. The British had always wanted Otho to grant a constitution; it was his own father, King Ludwig, and the Russians who warned Otho not to do it. Moreover Otho had no real confidence in his people. Over the years, the king's insistence on remaining a Catholic, his distrust of the Russian party, and his failure to state definitely that his children would be raised Orthodox brought Russian good will to an end. There would be no tears shed for Otho in either London or St Petersburg in 1843.

The year began with a steadily rising clamor of complaint against the government. Otho was no intellectual nor an efficient organizer —he did not understand the complexities of finance and successful administration. The representatives of the Powers at Athens made every effort to convince him of the need for reform, but the king

time at 17,648, of whom 1850 were Bavarians, Rome, Archivio della S. Congregazione di Propaganda, Congressi, 39, Archipeligo. In 1840, Strong counted nearly 25,000 of whom 11,200 were inhabitants of Tinos and 5,700 were on Syros (F. Strong, *op. cit.* p. 365).

[1] William Mure, *op. cit.* I, p. 244.

hesitated. He had lost the confidence of his own ministers. Sir Edmund Lyons reports a conversation with Iakovos Rizo-Neroulos, 'that minister told me in strict confidence that King Otho had become so deceptive, indecisive, and presumptuous that it was almost impossible to transact any business with His Majesty'.[1] The feeling grew throughout the country that either reforms must come or the king must go.

The church issue played its part in contributing to the discontent. The greatest source of complaint, as has been mentioned, was the lack of capable bishops and the government's unwillingness to resolve the situation. Failure in the hierarchy was paralleled by the lack of parish clergy to care for the spiritual needs of the people. Petitions were addressed to the king stating that 'we do not even have a preacher to declare the word of God to our people', but Otho did not reply except by having the officials arrest those who were the most outspoken.[2] Only after the pressure became irresistible did the king consent to the possibility of permitting the number of bishoprics to be increased in July of 1843—however, this did not solve the major problem of providing new bishops for the kingdom of Greece. Among public officials there was a growing sentiment that sooner or later relations must be restored with Constantinople if the church in Greece was going to survive.

The demands for political change and the need for financial assistance in a situation approaching national bankruptcy brought action at last on the night of 2 September 1843, when Colonel Demetrios Kallergis led his troops before the royal palace and demanded that Otho dismiss his German advisers and summon a National Assembly to draft a Constitution. Again Otho hesitated. The representatives of the Powers, especially Lyons and Katakazis, arrived to counsel him and he was finally brought around to see that either he admit the changes suggested or give up his throne. Otho agreed to Kallergis'

[1] Edmund Lyons to Lord Aberdeen, Athens, 5 April 1843, F.O. 32, Greece, vol. 121, no. 39. Previous dispatches contain the same information, 1 February 1843, 19 February and 11 March, vol. 120, nos. 10, 12, and 20, PRO.

[2] Extract from an assembly held at Messenia and enclosed in a dispatch from E. Lyons to Aberdeen, Athens, 30 December 1842, F.O. 32, Greece, vol. 120, no. 12, and 4 March 1842, no. 26, PRO.

demands—he dismissed his Bavarian aides, appointed a ministry of Greek nationals and summoned a National Assembly to draw up a Constitution for the country.[1]

The coup had been completely bloodless and orderly, neither lives nor property having been damaged. Among the idealistic participants hopes were high that the Constitution might bring a new era to Greece, others regarded it as a move by Britain and Russia and their partisans in Greece to gain power within the state. Tsar Nicholas I, however, when informed of the revolt, was not at all pleased. He was strongly opposed to any and all revolutions. Katakazis had acted on his own in supporting the Constitutionalists, and his efforts were rewarded by his recall to St Petersburg. In the palace, however, Otho and Amalia saw the event in a different light, and sought to fix the blame for their present discomfort. In general, the royal couple tended to blame the ill will of Tsar Nicholas; still Otho had to admit that nearly everyone in Greece favored a constitutional monarchy. He wrote in a letter to his father that he did not believe the new situation would last, 'anarchy and the oppression of the people by irregular soldiers will probably result. May God come quickly to the aid of the country.' He also stated, 'I knew that my abdication would throw the people into anarchy, although this course would have been more agreeable to me personally'.[2]

Another problem, which Otho and Amalia both felt deeply, was the fact that their marriage was childless. Physicians assured them that there was no physical reason for their sterility. Queen Amalia wrote her father-in-law praising Otho's demeanor during the time of the revolt, adding at the conclusion, 'the only thing lacking

[1] C. Papadopoulos, *op. cit.* p. 303; G. Finlay, *A History of Greece*, ed. H. F. Tozer (Oxford, 1877), VII, p. 130; Αἰών, Athens, 21 December 1842, no. 318, p. 1; Ἀθηνᾶ, Athens, 26 September 1842, no. 954, p. 4071.

[2] Otho to Ludwig, Athens, 15 September 1843, quoted in L. Bower and G. Bolitho, *op. cit.* pp. 123, 124; A. Chroust, *op. cit.* V, pp. 11–13; E. Lyons to Aberdeen, Athens, 16 September 1843, F.O. 32, Greece, vol. 122, no. 107, PRO. 'Russia saw that by continuing to support King Otho's anti-national system of government, she was bringing herself into discredit with the Greeks; in order therefore to recover herself she found it necessary to join England in manifesting an opposition to that system...' (Lyons to Aberdeen, Athens, 21 September 1843, F.O. 32, Greece, vol. 122, no. 112, PRO).

is children, and I know that God will send them to me in His own time'.[1]

The National Assembly would not convene until November, so the intervening weeks were filled with proposals and suggestions as to what should be included in the new Constitution. As far as church affairs were concerned, the conservative faction argued that now was the time to re-establish relations with the patriarch of Constantinople. Oekonomos visited Constantinople in October to sound out the feelings of the patriarch, to ascertain if the same arrangement by which the Russian church was independent, yet in union with Constantinople, might also be possible for Greece. In Athens, *The Century* editorialized that the Constitution should set up the church in accordance 'with the Great Church of Christ, which is the center of all the Orthodox churches, in full dogmatic and canonical union and harmony, along the lines of the other independent and autocephalous Orthodox churches'.[2]

Otho confided to the British and French representatives that he feared being offered the choice of becoming Orthodox or abdicating the throne. He asked the representatives of the western Powers if Britain and France would support him in such a dilemma even to the extent of sending in troops. Neither Lyons nor Piscatory, the French minister, would give him much encouragement.[3]

The National Assembly opened in Athens on 8 November 1843. It was a remarkable scene in many ways if for no other reason than that its president, Panoutsos Notaris, was 106 years old. The delegates, dressed in the various local costumes whence they came, sat cross-legged in circles on the floor. The furniture of their hall had come from Otho's palace and included a portrait of King Ludwig and other Wittelsbach monarchs. After the first meeting, Colonel Kallergis asked that all the king's furniture be returned to the palace along with the pictures. The Assembly cheered the suggestion.

[1] Amalia to Ludwig, Athens, 1 January 1844, quoted in L. Bower and G. Bolitho, *op. cit.* p. 132. In November 1844, Ludwig wrote to Otho, 'it is most important that you have sons' (*ibid.* p. 133).

[2] Αἰών, Athens, 8 September 1843, no. 491, p. 1; C. Papadopoulos, *op. cit.* p. 304.

[3] E. Lyons to Aberdeen, Athens, 27 September 1843, F.O. 32, Greece, vol. 122, no. 113, PRO.

Two men tended to dominate the Assembly and their voices were the ones most heeded in the discussions. These were Alexandros Mavrokordatos and Ioannis Kolettis, the leaders of the English and French parties respectively. The Russian party was unable to produce a leader of equal stature, but its strength was evident in the discussions. It would be a mistake to think of these groups, however, as being dominated by affairs outside the country—rather these labels are simply ways to express the tendencies and influences of the combinations within the Assembly. The Constitution makers were altogether concerned with domestic affairs, with establishing a government in Greece which would be managed by themselves rather than by bureaucrats from Bavaria or by an inept monarch.

The meeting of this constitutional assembly offered an excellent opportunity to the revisionists in the church of Greece. Two particular goals were to be achieved, the first was the re-establishment of relations with the patriarchate and the second was the modification of the legislation of 1833. As a corollary to the latter, there was also an almost universal sentiment that the Constitution should make a clear statement on the religion of the Greek monarch, namely, that he must be Orthodox.

As soon as discussions were opened, various petitions were addressed to the delegates. The Holy Synod of Greece sent a petition to the Assembly which asked for the following changes in the ecclesiastical establishment. First, it was suggested that the king name the president of the Synod only on the proposal of the other synodal members; secondly, that all the laws contrary to the church canons be repealed; thirdly, that in the internal matters of the church, the state limit itself to acting only as a mediator. Other proposals included the manner of directing seminaries; the exemption of clergy from testifying in court, and releasing them from taking oaths. The Holy Synod also asked that every effort be made to renew the contact between the patriarch of Constantinople and the church of Greece, with the latter freely recognizing his spiritual authority.[1] The thinking in the petition was heavily influenced by Oekonomos.

[1] T. Piscatory to Guizot, Athens, 30 November 1843, Grèce, XII, no. 52, MAE.

In December, the Synod was ready with a ten-point schema which included most of the measures already proposed with some modifications. It made the Synod, as might be expected, more powerful and practically autonomous of the civil authority. The king was to be the 'protector' of the church and was to see to it that synodal regulations were executed, but his power to influence decisions through the procurator's veto was abrogated. The Synod suggested, moreover, that the number of episcopal sees in Greece be raised to twenty-six and outlined the duties and privileges of the bishop's office. The final article of the schema professed that the church of Greece now desired to work out, in common deliberations between the hierarchy and government officials, 'an ecclesiastical formula which would recognize the Great Church of Christ of Constantinople as the center of all like-believing Orthodox churches'.[1]

Almost immediately, in November, discussions had opened on the question of King Otho's religion. The king was highly sensitive on the matter; informally he had mentioned that his children would be raised Orthodox, but there was no definite commitment on the matter. The fact that his marriage had been childless so far made this question academic. According to the Treaty of London, the succession would pass to his brother Luitpold if Otho had no children and this seemed to be quite likely now. Luitpold, of course, was Catholic and had already married an Italian princess, a factor which made the Greeks feel that the chances of the continuation of a Catholic dynasty were very great. This they wanted to prevent. The British and French representatives in Athens, as well as the Bavarian minister, were insistent that to insert a clause requiring Otho or any future monarch to be Orthodox violated the Treaty of 1832, but such remonstrances carried little weight with the members of the Assembly. Nearly all were agreed that the Constitution should see to it that at least the future kings of Greece should be Orthodox.

[1] C. Papadopoulos, *op. cit.* p. 305. *Athena* commented that the suggestions were fairly good, but it hoped the delegates 'would protect the rights of the people and of the King from the inroads of clerical power by a religious establishment which would set up general boundaries for it, according to the arrangement of constitutions found in other advanced nations' (*'Αθῆνα*, Athens, 29 December 1843, no. 1080, p. 9026).

Already in November one of the churches in Athens had dropped Otho's name from the Liturgy, as a kind of spiritual dethronement.[1]

It was at the twenty-third session of the Assembly, on 3 January 1844, that the official business of that body turned to ecclesiastical affairs. The debate lasted for three days, during which time a whole range of church matters were brought up, from the separation from the patriarchate to the reform of marriage legislation. The opening speech was made by Michael Schinas, deputy of Koroni and a close personal friend of Konstantinos Oekonomos. He proposed nine articles for the Constitution:

Article One. The dominant religion of Greece is the Holy Eastern Orthodox Church of Christ. All other recognized religions are tolerated and enjoy the protection of the law. Any proselytism or any other activity against the dominant religion is forbidden.

Article Two. The Orthodox Church of Greece, recognizing as its head, Our Savior Jesus Christ, is dogmatically and canonically united by an indissoluble bond with the Great Church of Constantinople and with all other Orthodox churches. Politically it is independent and administered, according to the Apostolic and Conciliar Canons and the Holy Traditions, by a Synod of Bishops, of which the President is chosen by the bishops of the country and confirmed by the King, the members of which are called to sit according to the date of their consecration in episcopal orders.

Article Three stated that the king is the defender and protector of the church in external matters; Article Four raised the number of dioceses to twenty-six. Articles Five and Six spoke of the establishment of seminaries and monasteries, and called for a better administration of the money in the Ecclesiastical Fund. Article Seven required a limitation on questions about which clergy might be called upon to testify in court; Article Eight forbade the participation of clerics

[1] T. Piscatory to Guizot, Athens, 10 November 1843, Grèce, XLI, no. 14; Guizot to Piscatory, Paris, 16 December 1843, Grèce, XLI, no. 73, MAE; Edmund Lyons to Aberdeen, Athens, 30 November 1843, F.O. 32, Greece, vol. 122, no. 144, PRO. It did not help Otho's position that King Ludwig in Munich was affirming that none of his grandchildren would be raised in the Greek religion (Burgoing to Guizot, Munich, 4 January 1844, quoted in A. Chroust, *op. cit.* V, p. 33).

in political matters and in elections, or taking oaths, while the final article set up the machinery by which the civil and religious authorities might regulate their relations.[1]

In explaining the articles which he proposed, Schinas assured the delegates that Article Two did not set up a state within a state, nor did it subordinate political power to church authority, but simply asserted that the church, as the guide of the religious life of the people, was in union with all the other Orthodox churches. This unity required that the Greek church be based upon the same canons that the other churches used as their foundation. He also pointed out that the present independence of the Greek church was not valid, since 'it can never be demonstrated that an independent church exists without its autonomy being recognized by that church with which it was formerly joined'.[2] The examples of Cyprus and Russia were cited as examples of lawful independent churches.

The discussion that followed revolved around the use of the word 'canonically' in Article Two. One of the delegates complained that its meaning was already included in 'dogmatically', another saw it as a possible threat to the independence of the church.

The second day of discussion, 4 January, saw the arguments continue over the use of 'canonically' in Article Two. One delegate argued that it was obvious that the church was based on the canons, but another said it should be spelled out since, in fact, the present arrangement based on the 1833 Constitution was not canonical. Several speakers stated their belief that church matters were not in the competence of the National Assembly and any statements had better refrain from specifics. Schinas replied to this by asserting that the delegates had the right and even the duty to speak on these subjects.

The third day of discussion saw several new attempts at rewording and then the matter was put to a vote. In a slightly amended form the first two articles were accepted, but only after 'canonically' had been removed from Article Two. The other seven articles were not

[1] The Athenian National Assembly of the Third of September, *Πρακτικά* [Acts] (Athens, 1844), pp. 114–16.

[2] *Ibid.* p. 116.

accepted. The opposition to Schinas' plans had been led by Spyridon Trikoupis who had made a major contribution to the 1833 Church Constitution and had participated both in its drafting and in the Nauplion Synod which accepted it. In a long speech he claimed that the setting up of the independent Synod was done in complete conformity with the wishes of the people and the clergy. He argued that the Ecclesiastical Commission had enjoyed full freedom and that the government had decided nothing 'before it heard the opinion of all the hierarchy'. His efforts at last succeeded in watering down the proposals of Schinas on a plea that they meant a diminution of the power of the civil authorities.[1]

The controversy in the Assembly was mirrored in the press between the newspapers representing the liberal viewpoint, *Athena*, and the conservative side, *The Century*. The latter had hailed Schinas' propositions as repairing the damage done by the foreigners who were the authors of the establishment of 1833. This had resulted in schism and fragmentation in the Orthodox world and the editors were sure that the adoption of Schinas' measures for the Constitution would be of great benefit to Greece. *The Century* also was vigorous in support of the proposal to insert a religious condition for the occupant of the throne.[2] *Athena* took the view that most of Schinas' proposals were unnecessary. It objected to 'canonically' and was careful to report the remark of the delegate, A. Paikos, 'it is impossible to set up an independent state with a church subject to another foreign power'.[3]

Attention in the Assembly during February centered on the article defining the religion of the sovereign. The British government urged Lyons to resist such a move since it was a unilateral revision of the agreements made by the protecting Powers in 1832 and 1833, and

[1] *Ibid.* pp. 124–32, 136–7. Trikoupis' speech is given in Ἀθῆνα, Athens, 15 January 1844, no. 1088, p. 9055. For a discussion of the Assembly's work, see C. Papadopoulos, *op. cit.* pp. 309 ff.; Paul Karolidis, *Σύγχρονος Ἱστορία τῶν Ἑλλήνων καὶ Λοιπῶν Λαῶν τῆς Ἀνατολῆς ἀπὸ 1821 μέχρι 1921* [Contemporary History of the Greeks and the Other Peoples of the East from 1821 until 1921] (Athens, 1922), III, pp. 21–3; Tryphonos Evangelides, *op. cit.* pp. 220–67.

[2] Αἰών, Athens, 12 January 1844, no. 498, pp. 1–5; 2 February 1844, no. 503, p. 1.

[3] Ἀθῆνα, Athens, 19 January 1844, no. 1086, pp. 9055, 9056.

such a move, the foreign minister claimed, could not be tolerated. Lord Aberdeen wrote to the Russians that he believed both governments should work to prevent the contemplated move. He said that his government believed that it would be a good thing for the king to become Orthodox, but it did not want it written into the Constitution that Otho or his brothers must change their faith if they expected to inherit the throne in Athens.[1] The French minister, Piscatory, wrote to his government that he was working with Mavrokordatos and Kolettis, but popular sentiment was against them, and in February they began to 'show themselves less disposed to fight against public opinion'.[2]

It was public opinion which carried the day and an article was inserted into the Constitution which read as follows: 'The crown of Greece pertains to the dynasty of King Otho. His successor shall profess the Greek Orthodox religion.' The final draft of the Constitution, approved 10 March 1844, contained this succinct statement on the church: 'The dominant faith in the kingdom of Greece is the Greek Orthodox religion. United by an indissoluble bond to the Great Church of Constantinople, the church of Greece is, however, autonomous and exercises independently of any other church its rights of sovereignty, and is administered by a Holy Synod of bishops.'[3]

It is evident that the hopes of the traditionalist opinion in the church of Greece were frustrated with the Constitution. Too little had been said to make any significant change in the church arrangement of 1833. The delegates of the Assembly wanted to have it both ways—to be united with Constantinople and thus be legitimate while at the same time keeping the church of Greece autonomous so that, in fact, it would remain subservient to the civil power in Greece. In other words, the Constitution of 1844 was a victory

[1] Aberdeen to Lyons, London, 6 and 14 February 1844, F.O. 32, Greece, vol. 126, nos. 9, 12, PRO. The Foreign Minister noted in a letter to Brunnow, 20 February 1844: 'In this respect I fully share the conviction of the Imperial Cabinet, and I think it would be most unfortunate to perpetuate a Catholic dynasty.' This communication is found enclosed in Grèce, XLI, no. 212, MAE.

[2] T. Piscatory to Guizot, Athens, 10 February 1844, Grèce, XLI, no. 167, MAE.

[3] E. Driault and M. l'Héritier, *op. cit.* II, pp. 255–6; G. Finlay, *op. cit.* VII, p. 197.

for Greek nationalism, it was not a victory for the churchmen who shared the thought of Konstantinos Oekonomos.[1]

Contributing to the final decision had been a number of literary works issued before or during the meeting of the Assembly. Neophytos Vamvas, famous for his Scriptural translations and currently at the University of Athens, authored *A Timely Treatise Concerning the Origin and the Authority of the Patriarchs and the Relation between Church Authority and Civil Power.*[2] In it, Vamvas stressed that the growth of patriarchal power had been the result of historical circumstances and did not have any special significance other than what had come to it, as it were, accidentally. Common faith and charity were the important elements of church life and gave unity to it, not patriarchal authority. This pamphlet was quickly answered by Oekonomos from arguments supporting a contrary position. The main literary work of Oekonomos over the next few years, however, was an excellent four-volume work on the Septuagint, which far surpassed all critical studies of that version of the Bible made previously. It is, without doubt, the most scholarly work produced by a Greek theologian in the first half of the nineteenth century.[3]

The Latin Catholics of Greece noted that the Constitution omitted mention of their past guarantees and was, on the whole, a document which seemed to presume that all Greeks were Orthodox. Protests of the Catholic bishops were sent to France, while Pope Gregory XVI wrote to the Habsburg Emperor, Ferdinand, to use his good offices to intercede for the Catholics in Greece. Bishop Blanci even requested a decision from Rome as to whether a conscientious Catholic might take an oath of allegiance to the new Constitution since it was

[1] For a discussion of the religious aspects of the Constitution, see Konstantinos Duovouniotis, *Σχέσεις Ἐκκλησίας καὶ Πολιτείας ἐν τῇ Ἐλευθέρᾳ Ἑλλάδι* [Church and state relations in independent Greece] (Athens, 1916), pp. 32–6; Christos Androutsos, *Ἐκκλησία καὶ Πολιτεία ἐξ Ἐπόψεως Ὀρθοδόξου* [Church and state from the Orthodox view] (Athens, 1920), pp. 58–64.

[2] *Διατριβὴ αὐτοσχέδιος περὶ τῆς Ἀρχῆς καὶ Ἐξουσίας τῶν Πατριαρχῶν καὶ περὶ τῆς Σχέσεως τῆς Ἐκκλησιαστικῆς Ἀρχῆς πρὸς τὴν Πολιτικὴν Ἐξουσίαν* (Athens, 1843).

[3] *Περὶ τῶν Ο' Ἑρμηνευτῶν τῆς Παλαιᾶς Γραφῆς* [Concerning the Seventy Translators of the Old Testament] (Athens, 1844–9). Even his critic Vamvas was quoted, 'when Oekonomos speaks, other preachers must be silent' (*Αἰών*, Athens, 25 February 1843, no. 421, p. 1).

prejudicial to Catholics. The French and Austrians did intervene on behalf of the Greek Catholics and the issue was solved by allowing Catholics to swear to the Constitution, adding a clause 'provided the rights of the Catholic church are preserved'.[1]

The first ministry under the Constitution was formed by Alexandros Mavrokordatos. It lasted only a few months, however, and was succeeded in August 1844 by a cabinet headed by Ioannis Kolettis. For the next three years, Kolettis adroitly manoeuvred successfully between the demands of Otho and those of the Greek parties with their various opinions on the direction of the affairs of state. He was able to win over the Orthodox party by urging 'the Great Idea' of Greek expansion to the north. This appeal to nationalism had the effect of taking some of their pressure off Otho. The French were Kolettis' major supporters (he was serving as Greek ambassador in Paris when the Revolution of 1843 occurred) and for a while Great Britain was content with him. However, Russia was disenchanted with Kolettis precisely because of his attitude towards the church question. Much to its chagrin and to the dismay of the Orthodox friends of Oekonomos, the list of Synodal appointments in 1844 contained the name of Theokletos Pharmakidis. After five years of disfavor, he was named to his old position as secretary to the Holy Synod and restored to the theological faculty of the University of Athens.[2]

On 7 September 1844 the now constitutional monarch of Greece, Otho, addressed the National Assembly elected to represent the Greek people according to the provisions of the Constitution. Among the points he mentioned which he deemed important for the Assembly to consider were those dealing with religion. A few months later, in January 1845, Kolettis appointed a commission of clergy and laity to make suggestions on what legislation was needed. The prime minister did not appoint Pharmakidis to this commission,

[1] Bishop of Syros to Piscatory, Syros, February, n.d., 1844, Grèce, XLI, no. 156, MAE; Georg Hofmann, 'Papa Gregorio XVI', II, pp. 145–54. The pope's letter to Ferdinand is in *Acta Gregorii Papae XVI*, ed. Antonio M. Bernasconi (Rome, 1901), III, p. 369.

[2] Jules Blancard, *op. cit.* I, p. 112; D. S. Balanos, *op. cit.* p. 40. Pharmakidis had issued a translation of the New Testament during the years 1842–5.

although one of the Synod's subordinates, Theophanes Siatistios, was among those chosen. The committee was charged with drawing up two bills—one was to outline the proper method of church administration and its relations to the government, the other was to consider how many bishops were needed in Greece and how they might be supported.

The Commission reported a month later, urging that the church be given greater autonomy and that the Synod's membership be broadened. The suggestion was made that the Synod's name be changed to the 'Synod of the Church of the Kingdom of Greece' rather than the 'Synod of the Kingdom of Greece' in order to emphasize its increased independence from state control. There were some on the commission who favored a complete separation of church and state, but a more moderate measure was suggested by the realistic members of the group.[1]

The prime minister was not ready to submit the proposed legislation to the Assembly until 18 May 1845. Kolettis introduced the measures, which he had modified to some degree from the proposals of the Commission, with the suggestion that greater clarification was needed, especially on the relationship between the Holy Synod and the Government's Ministry of Worship. He stressed that the proposed legislation would give greater importance to the Synod and that it would reserve positions on the Synod for bishops only. The text of the measure contained twenty-seven articles. Among other changes, besides those previously mentioned, Article Three extended the terms of the synodal members to three years. Another clause set up machinery for solving questions which would concern the political authorities. The Synod was given strong powers regarding the internal affairs of the church, but these were still limited to matters 'which do not in any way interfere with civil authority'. The Synod was still forbidden to correspond directly with any spiritual or secular power outside of Greece—an obvious move to limit possible contacts with Constantinople or St Petersburg. Members of the clergy were not released from testifying in courts, a

[1] C. Papadopoulos, *op. cit.* pp. 338, 339; W. Brunet de Presle and Alexandre Blanchet, *Grèce depuis la conquête romaine jusqu'à nos jours* (Paris, 1860), p. 584.

particular point of agitation between the followers of Oekonomos and the government.[1]

The Russian party's organ, *The Century*, claimed that the proposed legislation was still dominated by 'a spirit foreign to the Eastern Orthodox Church'. It claimed the measure violated a number of canons, and while apparently giving additional power to the Synod, in fact it remained 'the servant of the government'. It called on the members of the Assembly to bring out a truly satisfactory bill.[2]

The bill was sent to a committee of the Assembly which proceeded to make a number of changes, but they were such that the civil power still retained the upper hand. The revised version appeared on 27 June and debate was opened. Michael Schinas, the head of the Orthodox party in the Assembly, rose to the occasion, attacking the measure on many accounts. Neophytos Doukas also made a long speech scoring those provisions which he interpreted as a Catholic plot to take over Greece. To agree to such a measure, he proposed, would be a great mistake; in fact, he prophesied, 'the anger of the Lord is rising to its measure'.[3] However, the various sections of the bill were proposed individually and passed, then a final draft was voted on favorably by the Assembly, 16 July, despite the objections of the Orthodox party. According to the Constitution, the bill then had to be introduced into the Gerousia, or Senate, for its approval. For reasons not altogether evident, Kolettis did not introduce the ecclesiastical bill to that body.[4] The obvious inference is that Kolettis was never really serious about changing the church settlement of 1833.

[1] *Πρακτικὰ τῶν Συνεδριάσεων τῆς Βουλῆς ἐν τῇ Πρώτῃ Βουλευτικῇ Συνόδῳ τοῦ Ἔτους 1844–1845* [Acts of the meetings of the Assembly in the first parliamentary session of the year 1844–1845] (Athens, 1846), III, pp. 1233–58.

[2] *Αἰών*, Athens, 26 May 1845, no. 625, p. 1; 13 and 16 June, nos. 630 and 631, p. 1.

[3] Neophytos Doukas, *Λόγος πρὸς τοὺς Βουλευτὰς καὶ Γερουσιαστὰς ὑπὲρ τοῦ Ἐκκλησιαστικοῦ Νομοσχεδίου* [A Speech to the Members of the Assembly and Senate concerning the ecclesiastical bill] (Athens, 1845), p. 5.

[4] *Πρακτικά*, III, pp. 1625, 1656, 1692, 1693 and 1853; C. Papadopoulos, *op. cit.* pp. 340–3; Report of B. Forth-Rouen, 30 April 1852, Grèce, LVII, no. 316, MAE, noted that 'the grand principles which guarantee the rights of temporal sovereigns were maintained'. He does not know why Kolettis never submitted the bill to the Senate.

In January of 1847, church matters came up for discussion again when Schinas introduced a bill into the Assembly concerning the bishops of the church. He proposed that the number of sees be raised to forty-eight, that the bishops be selected by the Synod and confirmed by the king. This legislation suffered the same fate as the previous measure, since it did not come before the Senate before the death of Kolettis in September 1847. Thus Maurer's Constitution remained in force.[1]

The relations between the Latin and Orthodox churches were troubled anew in 1848 when Pope Pius IX issued an encyclical to the Greeks urging that they—the lost sheep of Christ—should 'return at last to the flock of Christ'. The Orthodox need have no fear, the pope assured them, for 'no burden will be imposed that is not a necessary one'.[2] Such an address only served to exasperate the Orthodox both in Greece and in the Ottoman Empire. The then reigning Patriarch Anthimos and the Synod of Constantinople blasted the document as a fraud and a plague, stating, 'Of those heresies, which the Lord knows, have spread over a great part of the world, at one time was Arianism, today it is Papism. But this, too (as the former has already disappeared), although successful for the moment, will not last to the end, but will disappear and be cast down, and a great voice shall cry out, It is destroyed!'[3] In opposition to Rome, there was a united Orthodox front, no matter how divided the Eastern church may have been on other points.

The following year, 1849, is of interest because of a new or rather revived argument between Oekonomos and Pharmakidis over the issue of whether clerics should take oaths. The pages of *Athena* and *The Century* were filled with the acrimonious exchange. Pharmakidis published a book of over two hundred pages entitled *Oekonomos of the Oekonomos, or Concerning an Oath*, which discussed almost every conceivable aspect of the problem. The patriarch assisted Oekonomos

[1] *Αἰών*, Athens, 18 January 1847, no. 752, p. 1; *Ἀθῆνα*, Athens, 16 January 1847, no. 1381, p. 2; C. Papadopoulos, *op. cit.* p. 344.

[2] Pius IX, *Acta* (Rome, 1854), I, pp. 84, 89.

[3] *Ἐγκύκλιος τῆς μιᾶς, ἁγίας, καθολικῆς, καὶ ἀποστολικῆς ἐκκλησίας ἐπιστολὴ πρὸς τοὺς ἁπανταχοῦ Ὀρθοδόξους* [An Encyclical letter of the one, holy, catholic, and apostolic church to the Orthodox everywhere] (Constantinople, 1848).

with an encyclical upholding his position in October 1849, which called Pharmakidis' work 'a rotten little book'.[1]

While this debate went on, stirrings in Athens and Constantinople were felt which made this issue seem unimportant in comparison. At last, the bitterness of the separation of the church of Greece from Constantinople had been somewhat sweetened by the passage of time in the minds of the churchmen in the Phanar. In Athens, the number of bishops capable of exercising their office was reduced to a handful. Reluctantly Otho and his ministers realized something had to be done. The time was ripe on both sides for negotiation. Both in Athens and the Phanar people were anxious to seek an end to the painful schism if only an occasion would present itself so that each might retain its proper dignity. They did not have too long to wait.

[1] *'Αθῆνα*, Athens, 4 July 1849, no. 1605, p. 3; *Αἰών*, 25 September 1848, no. 905, p. 12; 29 June and 9 July 1849, nos. 976 and 979, p. 1; D. S. Balanos, *op. cit.* pp. 41–7; T. Pharmakidis, *Οἰκονόμος ὁ ἐξ Οἰκονόμων ἤ περὶ Ὅρκου* (Athens, 1849).

CHAPTER 8

THE SYNODAL TOMOS AND ITS RECEPTION IN GREECE

It had become increasingly obvious as the years passed that no one was really satisfied with the state of tension existing between the church of Greece and the patriarch of Constantinople. By 1849 Georg von Maurer's Church Constitution had been in effect for sixteen years. In some ways it had served its purpose well, but everyone was aware of its limitations. The fact that it could never provide for the continuation of the episcopate in Greece was evident. The only hope for regularized church life rested in a reunion between the Athens Synod and the patriarchate. From the point of view of the Greek prelates in the Phanar, the continuation of the schism was a painful reality. It was to the advantage of both parties to find a means of reconciliation.

The occasion which served to thaw the relations between the church of Greece and the patriarchate of Constantinople happened upon the death of the Greek statesman, Iakovos Rizo-Neroulos, 17 December 1849. At the time of his death he was serving as Greek minister to the Porte, after a long career in both foreign and domestic affairs with the government of independent Greece. Much to the surprise of the Athenian delegation in Constantinople, it received word from the Phanar that the Patriarch Anthimos IV would be pleased to assist at the funeral. On the day of the burial, the patriarch along with twelve other bishops officiated at the service. Such an event marked a dramatic change in the policy of the patriarchal church, which up to that time had persisted in ignoring the independent position of the Greek church and anyone closely connected with the government which had created the Church Constitution of 1833. Rizo-Neroulos had been not only a willing servant of King Otho, but also the author of a Greek history containing strong criticism of the church previous to 1821.[1] The patriarch was now obviously content to forget about the past in his desire to show respect to the memory of a distinguished Greek Christian.

This gesture by the patriarch and Synod was well received in Athens by a few highly placed Greek nationals in the government, who wanted to see the situation of the church of Greece rectified. Some of them, among whom was Alexandros Mavrokordatos, therefore suggested to King Otho that the moment had arrived for negotiations with the patriarch. Mavrokordatos volunteered to go to Constantinople as the emissary of the king, but Otho rejected him—he was too liberal for the monarch's taste—and instead appointed Petros Deligiannis then serving as an official in the Greek Foreign Office. Deligiannis was named Greek ambassador to the Porte, which gave him an official position from which he might contact the church officials in Constantinople. The king also selected the priest and professor of theology, Misael Apostolidis, to go to Constantinople and award the partiarch the Order of the Savior in gratitude for his service at the funeral of Rizo-Neroulos. Along with Apostolidis went letters from the Greek foreign minister, Anastasios Londos, and the president of the Holy Synod of Greece, Bishop Neophytos of Attica, bearing their felicitations and at the same time stating the wish of both the government of Greece and the Holy Synod for a rapid restoration of brotherly relations between the churches.

Anthimos accepted the decoration and expressed his gratitude to the Greek government, but returned unopened the letter from the president of the Synod in Athens, stating that he knew of no president of a Synod in Athens—the only Synod he was aware of had its seat in Constantinople and was directed by the patriarch of that city.[2]

[1] Iakovos Rizo-Neroulos, *Histoire moderne de la Grèce depuis la chute de l'empire d'orient* (Geneva, 1828).

[2] Chrysostomos Papadopoulos, *Ἱστορία τῆς Ἐκκλησίας τῆς Ἑλλάδος* [History of the church of Greece] (Athens, 1920), pp. 351 ff.; Thomas Wyse to Lord Palmerston, Athens, 28 July 1850, F.O. 32, Greece, vol. 182, no. 113, London, Public Record Office, hereafter PRO; Baron M. Pergler von Perglas to King Ludwig, Athens, 15 January 1850, MA III, Griechenland, 2192, no. 3, Munich, Geheimes Staatsarchiv, hereafter GS.

Despite this rebuff, the ice had been broken between the Greek government and the patriarchate for the first time since 1833, in so far as Anthimos had accepted its decoration.

During the next few months a number of circumstances created the proper atmosphere for the start of a dialogue between Athens and Constantinople. First, the popularity of King Otho in Athens rose significantly in the early months of the year 1850 when Greece was faced with a crisis due to a blockade of the Piraeus by the British navy. Known as the Don Pacifico affair, this action was the result of British insistence that the Greek government settle the claims it owed to a number of English citizens in Greece. When Otho declined, the British ambassador to Athens, Sir Thomas Wyse, with Palmerston's consent, summoned the fleet and blockaded the port. Otho's refusal to back down fanned the flames of Greek nationalism; not only were his own people strongly supporting him, but the French and Russian ministers in Athens rallied behind him to resist Britain. During the first few months of 1850, the diplomatic front in Athens was kept very busy as a result of this move. The Russians, who had been traditionally cool to Otho because of the religious question, now were especially eager to capitalize on the wave of anti-British sentiment in official circles; their ambassador, Persiany, gave his full support to Otho at the time.

The Russians at the Porte were also brought into the picture. Here they urged the Synod and patriarch to soften their position towards Greece in its moment of crisis. The patriarch was well aware of his need for Russian support for the Orthodox in the Ottoman Empire; he also knew how the tsar had resisted the schism of the Greek church from the very beginning. Anthimos himself appreciated the complexities of the situation since practically his whole career had been spent at the Phanar—he was in fact now serving his second term as patriarch.[1]

Otho kept the Russians informed of the crisis in Greece by sending Konstantinos Zographos to St Petersburg as his special envoy, and

[1] On Anthimos IV, see Manuel Gedeon, Πατριαρχικοὶ Πίνακες [Patriarchal Lists] (Constantinople, 1890), pp. 694–8. He had begun his second term as patriarch in October 1848.

while there is no doubt that his first task was to gather support for Greece against the British blockade, there is little doubt that it was also an opportune moment to discuss church affairs.[1] Eventually, the British settled their differences with the Greek government and the blockade was lifted after France had arbitrated the dispute. The incident had served its purpose as far as improving relations between Otho and Tsar Nicholas, thus enabling the Greek monarch to consider a new move toward reunion with Constantinople. He could now be assured of Russian support in his attempt to rescue the church of Greece from its precarious position of soon becoming a church without bishops.

Towards the end of May, on a report from Apostolidis that his dealings with the Phanar over the past months had made him certain that a letter from Greece would now be acceptable, the Holy Synod of Greece was encouraged to address a new appeal through the government to ascertain the feelings of the patriarchate concerning recognition of the church of Greece. Otho was pleased to entertain their request, and once again commissioned Apostolidis with a long letter signed by the Council of Ministers outlining the position of the church in Greece, which the latter was to present to the patriarch.

Once Apostolidis had received his instruction from Athens in early June, Deligiannis wrote to the patriarch asking for an audience and informing Anthimos of King Otho's letter and the mission of the emissary from Athens:

... the purely religious purpose that the government of the King proposes in this communication, consists, Holy Father, in rendering clear and manifest the indissoluble spiritual unity that the Orthodox Church of Greece shares with the universal church of the Orthodox, and that the Great

[1] Lord Bloomfield to Palmerston, St Petersburg, 23 and 26 February 1850, F.O. 65, Russia, vol. 376, nos. 53, 59, PRO. In another dispatch the British ambassador reported a conversation between Zographos and Nicholas in which the tsar spoke with great bitterness about Britain but cautioned, 'notwithstanding all that I have said to you, I must not go to war with England, because the material interests of Russia do not require that I should have recourse to this extreme measure, but I shall give the Greek government every other support in my power' (Bloomfield to Palmerston, St Petersburg, 10 March 1850, vol. 376, no. 81). In June 1850, Tsar Nicholas wrote a letter 'of the most affectionate character' to Otho, assuring him of Russian sympathy. Bloomfield to Palmerston, St Petersburg, 26 June 1850, F.O. 65, Russia, vol. 378, no. 208, PRO.

Church of Jesus Christ might by recognizing and approving the form instituted for its spiritual administration, fortify and consolidate by its benediction this unity founded and taught by God.[1]

The letter which Apostolidis carried to the patriarch traced the history of the establishment of the kingdom of Greece as an independent state in 1821, noting that, owing to political circumstances and upheavals in Greece at the time, 'it was impossible to establish an ecclesiastical authority to govern the church according to the precise sense of the Holy Canons...' It then went on to speak of the Synod of Nauplion in 1833, where unanimous consent of the hierarchy was given to set up a permanent Synod in Greece, 'as it exists in the Orthodox Church of Russia'.

The letter continued to stress how all was done legally and in the proper order and how the Synod had scrupulously guarded the dogma of the church, noting that, at the Constitutional Assembly of 1843, Article 2 professed the indissoluble unity of the Greek church with Constantinople. Now, the ministers write, they are seeking the recognition and approval of the patriarch and his Synod for the church of Greece, so that full communion and co-operation for the good of the Orthodox church might be obtained.[2] Accompanying this letter was one from the Holy Synod of Greece confirming the sentiments of the communication sent by the Council of Ministers. Once again, Anthimos was reluctant to accept the letter from the Synod, but others were inclined to do so and he relented.[3]

In the intervening days, before the Synod should meet, negotiations continued between the parties involved. The Russian minister, Titov, was active in the discussions, letting it be known that the tsar supported the request for recognition. Even the Ottoman

[1] P. Deligiannis to Patriarch Anthimos, Constantinople, 4 June 1850. This letter and the subsequent communications are found in *Documents publiés sur l'affaire de l'indépendance de l'Eglise de Grèce* contained in a dispatch of Thomas Wyse to the Foreign Office, Athens, 8 September 1850, F.O. 32, Greece, vol. 183, no. 135, PRO.

[2] President of the Council, A. Kriesis, *et al.* to the Patriarch, Athens, 30 May 1850, in *Documents publiés*, vol. 183, no. 135, PRO.

[3] Paulos Karolidis, *Σύγχρονος Ἱστορία τῶν Ἑλλήνων καὶ τῶν Λοιπῶν Λαῶν τῆς Ἀνατολῆς ἀπὸ 1821 μέχρι 1921* [Contemporary history of the Greeks and the other peoples of the East from 1821 until 1921] (Athens, 1922–4), II, pp. 6–20. C. Papadopoulos, *op. cit.* pp. 354 ff.

ministers, Reshid Pasha and Ali Pasha, followed the discussions with interest and approbation.[1]

On 16 June, the Synod of Constantinople met and reviewed the position of the church of Greece. With little difficulty it was decided that Constantinople should accede to the request for recognition of the church of Greece, provided that certain conditions were met. A number of other sessions of the Synod were held in order to satisfy everyone concerned. At the same time the officials at the Phanar were at work on the necessary documents to be sent to Greece. When they were ready, on 29 June, after the celebration of the Liturgy of Saints Peter and Paul, in the Great Hall of the patriarchate, the Synodal Tomos was read which re-established relations between the churches of Constantinople and the other eastern patriarchates with the church of independent Greece.

The Tomos was preceded by an introduction given by the Patriarch Anthimos. In it, he took notice of the communications sent to the Synod and testified to the doctrinal purity which the church of Greece had retained. He addressed himself primarily to the letter received from the Holy Synod of Greece rather than the communication from the government officials. No doubt, this was an effort to emphasize that what was happening was the concern of the church, not the civil authorities. The patriarch went on to say with what joy the two churches are now reunited, like a lost child to its mother. He has informed all of the Orthodox churches of the decision so that they too may recognize the status of the church of Greece, which is now entitled to call itself 'autocephalous' and to look to its Synod as its authority in brotherly love.

The Synodal Tomos opened with a tribute to the unity with which Christ had endowed His church. It went on to speak of the necessity of a visible hierarchy within the church to preserve the

[1] Otho conferred the Grand Cross of the Order of the Savior upon these Turkish officials and Fuad Effendi. Reshid Pasha acted as though he was not aware of the reason, telling Stratford Canning he supposed 'that the Court of Athens entertained a general wish to obtain his good will, though he observed to me at the same time that a gift of half the Kingdom would not alter his sentiments respecting Greece' (S. Canning to Palmerston, Constantinople, 18 June 1850, F.O. 78, Turkey, vol. 820, no. 199, PRO).

faith and assure harmony among the faithful, and then noted the request of the church of Greece, that of its hierarchy, its people, as well as its government, for a restoration of its bonds with Constantinople. Guided by the Holy Spirit, the patriarch and Synod of the Great Church had now decided to grant this appeal.

The church of Greece, henceforward, was to be considered autocephalous, with its supreme religious authority vested 'in a permanent Synod composed of bishops, called to serve successively according to the date of their consecration, having for president the metropolitan of Athens. It shall direct the affairs of the church according to the Sacred Canons in all liberty and without any hindrance or temporal intervention.' It was further recommended that the Synod be known as 'The Holy Synod of the Church of Greece'.

The church was ordered to place the name of the ecumenical patriarch into the Liturgy along with that of the other eastern patriarchs. It was promised 'that at any time when there is need, it shall receive the Sacred Chrism from the Holy and Great Church of Jesus Christ'. The president of the Synod in Athens was required to send a synodal letter to the other churches, once he had taken office, to inform them of his position and, in case of need for deliberation among the heads of Orthodoxy, he should join them in Constantinople.

The document continued:

> As for those things which concern the internal affairs of the church, that is to say, the election and consecration of bishops, the number and the rank of their sees, the ordination of priests and deacons, marriage and divorce, the administration of monasteries, the discipline and education of the clergy, the preaching of the divine word, the censorship of books contrary to religion, all these matters and others which are similar, are to be regulated by the Holy Synod by means of a synodal decree, which must not in any way circumvent the Sacred Canons of the holy councils, nor the traditional customs and procedures followed by the Eastern Orthodox Church.[1]

Such were the conditions established for the reconciliation of the churches. Needless to say, they presented a point of view which

[1] The text of the Synodal Tomos may be found in C. Papadopoulos, *op. cit.* pp. 356–60, and in *Sacrorum Conciliorum nova et amplissima collectio*, ed. Joannes D. Mansi (Graz, 1961), XL, cols. 450–8.

significantly contrasted with the internal situation of the church of Greece. Recognition by Constantinople, according to the Tomos, also meant an internal revolution within Greece itself which would remove the church from its subservient position to the state. Deligiannis had not been authorized to agree to any conditions—in accepting these he went far beyond his or Apostolidis' instructions.

Along with the Tomos, the patriarch and Synod addressed a pastoral letter to the people of Greece announcing the reunion of the two churches and assuring them that their church was now canonically recognized as autocephalous. It urged them to preserve their faith intact and to look to their Synod, now established according to proper procedure, for their supreme ecclesiastical authority and 'possessing all the rights which previously pertained to the apostolic and ecumenical patriarchal throne'. They were to submit to its orders and decisions and to recognize its ordinations and the bishops consecrated under its authority. A personal letter of congratulations from the patriarch of Jerusalem, Kyrillos, was also included in the documents forwarded to Greece.[1]

Athens was filled with the news (both true and false) of the negotiations. The press carried as much information as was available, but since all was done in secret, there was not too much to say. When the government in Athens first received the news that the Tomos contained a long list of suggestions concerning the internal order of the church, it was not at all to its liking. Deligiannis had reported on 3 July, 'all had perfectly succeeded in the sense of the propositions of the Greek government'. In a later dispatch, reaching Athens four days later, he was forced to admit, 'some things are written which would have been better not written'. The government had heard one report that the patriarch insisted on naming the members of the Synod, but this, of course, was not substantiated.[2]

While awaiting the delegates' return to Athens with the docu-

[1] The patriarchal letter is in *Documents publiés*; the letter from the patriarch of Jerusalem was not included, but only mentioned, vol. 183, no. 135, PRO.

[2] Karl von Gasser to King Ludwig, Athens, 30 July 1850, MA III, Griechenland, 2192, no. 140, GS; Edouard Thouvenel to Général Witte, Athens, 8 June 1850, Grèce, LIV, no. 69, Correspondance politique, Ministère des Affaires Etrangères, Paris, hereafter MAE.

ments, Sir Thomas Wyse wrote to London that verbal reports of the Tomos and its contents had come as a great shock to Athens, since the negotiators had been instructed that recognition must be granted 'without any conditions or qualifications whatever' and in conformity with Article 2 of the Constitution which forbade the church to be put under any foreign ecclesiastical power. Now, he reported, upon hearing of the result, the Greek government felt that although recognition has been obtained, it was 'in a manner the very reverse of what was intended and expected by His Majesty'. As a consequence of the proceedings, 'the Ministry and Court have been thrown into the greatest confusion. The *Αἰών* and the Russian organs and agents generally are in exultation and the Constitutional Party (British), divided as to causes and consequence, seem for the most part disposed, until the arrival of official information and the government shall proceed to action, to hold back.' Some saw it as a 'stratagem of Russian policy' to draw the church of Greece, and through the church the nation, under its control.

Government officials told Wyse that they proposed delaying the arrival of the documents and the negotiators until a new Synod should be nominated. This would give the government time to work out a policy as to the next step. Apostolidis had been quoted as saying the Greek government should not worry about the contents of the documents; the British ambassador could not explain why the government's own negotiator should have accepted the conditions in the Tomos, 'Mr Delgannis' [sic] conduct is considered more inexplicable, some believe him to have been deceived, others to have deceived his colleagues and the Government under the auspices of Russian agency and intrigue'. He expects that Otho will pursue 'the usual temporizing policy...If so, both faults—acceding reluctantly to the proposition and acceding too late for any benefit it may produce to himself and to the country—will be committed.'[1]

The French view was similar to that of the British according to the report sent to Paris by its minister, Sabatier:

It is certain today that M. de Titov was the grand agitator of this affair at Constantinople and that Russian influence has dictated the Patriarchal

[1] T. Wyse to Lord Palmerston, 28 July 1850, F.O. 32, Greece, vol. 182, no. 113, PRO.

Bull. M. Deliany was fooled or seduced; the Greek Government, pressed by circumstances has accepted everything to gain time, but the process is not finished and must be judged in the last resort by the next assembly.

Sabatier felt that the Russians would probably exercise strong influence in Greece once the Synod was set up according to the conditions of the Tomos.[1]

Apostolidis and Deligiannis arrived on 16 July at the Piraeus bringing the Tomos and the other documents. For two days they were in quarantine, but the Minister of Worship and other officials went to see them at once. The government officially welcomed them as great heroes although the members of the Council had their misgivings—still popular opinion was such that everyone had to appear enthusiastic. Otho talked with Deligiannis for over two hours as to what had happened at the Phanar—then, to the amazement of all, Otho announced he was going to leave Greece for two months and Queen Amalia would take over his position as regent.[2]

Before leaving, Otho saw to it that a decree was issued on 23 July concerning the Synod. It announced that a number of bishops already in Athens would make up a provisional Synod until the Assembly had an opportunity to pass the necessary legislation setting up the new church organization in conformity with the Tomos. The bishops were supposed to sit according to their seniority under the presidency of Neophytos, bishop of Attica. It was rumored that some of the appointees would not accept their places on the provisional Synod, but they all appeared.

Upon the close of the Assembly session, which occurred five days later, Otho reviewed the year and thanked the members for their support during the difficult times when the British blockade was in force. Otho also made this announcement:

[1] Sabatier to Général Witte, Athens, 18 September 1850, Grèce, LIV, no. 156, MAE. See also 'Αθῆνα, Athens, 10 July 1850, no. 1697, p. 2; Αἰών, Athens, 17 June 1850, no. 1073, p. 1, 28 June, no. 1076, and 12 July, no. 1080.

[2] Gasser to King Ludwig, Athens, 30 July 1850, MA III, Griechenland, 2192, no. 140, GS; Sabatier to Général Witte, Athens, 28 July 1850, Grèce, LIV, no. 145, MAE; T. Wyse to Lord Palmerston, Athens, 6 August 1850, F.O. 32, Greece, vol. 183, no. 155, and 8 August, no. 117, PRO.

That which adds still more to the satisfaction I feel on this occasion is the canonical recognition, so long desired by the Nation, of the independence of the Greek church, and consequently the re-establishment of relations with the Great Church of Constantinople. In the short space of time which elapsed between the achievement of this important work and the end of the session, my Government has not been permitted to submit to you, Sirs, projects of the necessary laws concerning the administration of the Church of the Kingdom. I wanted, nevertheless, to announce this memorable event to the members of this legislative body in its last meeting.[1]

As a matter of fact, Otho did not really want any legislation to come too soon. The conditions placed into the heart of the Tomos were unacceptable to him, yet he could not turn these down overtly without causing a storm of protest within Greece. He resorted to his old pattern of delay—the church had its recognition and the government might now approach internal change in a leisurely manner. It was not to Otho's advantage to have Maurer's Constitution of 1833 overturned completely.

A few days after the close of the Assembly, Otho left the country according to plan, and Queen Amalia was left in charge. She consulted the Synod, read the Tomos to its members, but omitted the sections dealing with the conditions laid down by the patriarch.[2] Only Theokletos Pharmakidis, secretary of the Synod, spoke in opposition to the patriarchal document. Under her signature a decree was issued announcing that the church of Greece had received canonical recognition of its autocephalous nature from Constantinople and that, although the Assembly had as yet not acted, still she was constrained to announce the good news and order a day of celebration for the event.[3] On Sunday 20 August, the churches of the whole nation were filled with prayers of thanksgiving and doxologies because of the restoration of their bonds with the patriarch. In Athens, the queen and the court, a number of the diplomatic

[1] Quoted in a dispatch from T. Wyse to Lord Palmerston, Athens, 6 August 1850, F.O. 32, Greece, vol. 183, no. 115, PRO.

[2] Ἐφημερὶς τῆς Κυβερνήσεως [The Government Newspaper], Athens, 16 August 1850, no. 26, p. 271.

[3] Konstantinos Dyovouniotis, Σχέσεις Ἐκκλησίας καὶ Πολιτείας ἐν τῇ Ἐλευθέρᾳ Ἑλλάδι [Church and state relations in independent Greece] (Athens, 1916), p. 43.

corps, and the clergy of the city gathered at Ayia Irene. Following a service of prayer, the bishop of Kynourias proclaimed the Tomos, which was then followed by a reading of the patriarch's letter to the people of Greece by Apostolidis. The ceremony, which included a short talk by Apostolidis crediting the king with the opening of negotiations, consumed over an hour and ended with cheers for Otho and Amalia.[1]

As a reward for his activities Apostolidis was named secretary to the provisional Synod while Pharmakidis was dismissed. Obviously to retain this arch-foe of patriarchal authority in Greece was an impossibility. For a second time, he had been ousted by a change in fortune, and just as he had done after his dismissal in 1840, he commenced the writing of a book to justify his position. Apostolidis was loaded with other positions—such as that of rector of the University of Athens—and was then commissioned by the queen to go to St Petersburg and inform the Russian church of the new relationship between the church of Greece and the patriarchate.

Apostolidis had a triumphant journey on his way to bear the glad tidings to the Russians. He journeyed via Constantinople where he was fêted by the patriarch and the Synod as the hero of the hour. While there he requested that some vessels of Holy Chrism be sent to Athens, and this was done. Thence he made his way to the Russian capital where there was a glittering reception arranged for him. The tsar and his family spoke to him in a personal audience, but the Russian Synod was a bit skeptical, announcing that they should come into communion with the church of Greece only after the terms of the Tomos were executed by the Greek government. Apostolidis spent the winter in St Petersburg, then left to visit King Ludwig in Munich, where another warm reception awaited him before his return to Greece.[2]

[1] Sabatier to Général Witte, Athens, 8 September 1850, Grèce, LIV, no. 221, MAE; Gasser to King Ludwig, Athens, 3 September 1850, MA III, Griechenland, 2192, no. 157, GS. On the evening of the celebration the Minister of Worship, Korphitakis, was assassinated at the door of his home. The murderers were not concerned with the Tomos, however, but with a personal grudge—nevertheless it seemed to have a certain symbolism about it.

[2] K. Gasser to King Ludwig, Athens, 31 October 1850, MA III, Griechenland, 2192, no. 185, GS; B. Forth-Rouen to Turgot, Athens, 10 June 1852, Grèce, LVIII, no. 135, MAE.

The fall and winter of that same year saw Greece elect new members to the Assembly. Since many of the candidates of the opposition along with their supporters suffered from intimidation the government party emerged triumphant. Presumably one of the first and most important tasks of the new Assembly would be a discussion of the Tomos and the passage of the necessary legislation to make it operable in the state. This was not, however, the plan of King Otho, although many a government-sponsored candidate basked in the king's popularity because of his success with Constantinople. The king's enthusiasm for meeting the terms of the Tomos was cool indeed—the Tomos had been proclaimed, the people were happy, and as far as Otho was concerned that was enough for the present.

There were, after all, other distractions for the Orthodox party in Greece in 1851. First was the dispute over the Holy Places in Palestine which arose out of renewed French interest in that part of the world and hence a vigorous defense of the 'rights' of the Latin Catholics in that area. It started in 1850 almost at the same time that the discussions on recognition of the Greek church in Constantinople were in progress. A French envoy from Louis Napoleon demanded that the Holy Places, which had slowly fallen into the hands of the Greek monks during the last centuries, be returned to Latin clergy. The Russians, of course, were the great defenders of Orthodoxy in the Holy Land as elsewhere in the Ottoman domain and strongly resisted French intervention at the Porte. The negotiations between the French and the Turkish officials were carefully watched by all Orthodox, who once again saw Rome bearing down on them.

The sympathy of the Greek church was all on the side of the Russians in trying to prevent any change in the *status quo*, for it was Greek monks who served as the custodians of the shrines. After long negotiations, in 1852 the Porte ruled that the French had made their point—therefore a number of the Holy Places were to be returned to the Latins, and the keys of the church at Bethlehem were to be in their custody. The settlement came at a time when Louis Napoleon was no longer interested in the affair (since he had consolidated his position in France, his Catholic support was no longer so important) and he was now seeking to open talks directly with the tsar to find a satisfactory arrangement. But by this time the issue had fanned Orthodoxy all over the world into a rage. The French minister, Forth-Rouen, wrote to Paris that the conflict over the Holy Places had brought the Russian party in Greece real strength. He noted further, 'the flag of religion, which has often been used in Greece, is brought out again. Religion is in danger and its children are called once more to run to its defense...Religion is in Greece a powerful element for intrigue, and in representing Catholicism as invading, as menacing Orthodoxy...one is sure to move the spirits profoundly.'[1]

Another source of agitation in Greece concerned the work of Protestant missioners, especially that of the Reverend Jonas King, an American minister who had opened a school in Athens. Many conservative churchmen in the city looked upon his educational work as a great danger to Orthodoxy in Greece and therefore sought a way to have his school closed. Eventually, King was put under arrest and found guilty on charges of reviling the Greek religion in March 1851. He was given a short jail sentence and ordered to leave Greece, but was saved from this through the intervention of the American minister at Constantinople, George P. Marsh, who acted on his behalf.[2]

Otho did not return to Greece from his trip to the west until May 1851. He was still cheered over the recognition of the church of Greece and began to think of what should come next. To keep everyone aware that ecclesiastical affairs were still very much on his mind, one of the first official acts after his return was to receive the Synod and confer the Grand Cross of the Order of St Michael upon its president, Bishop Neophytos of Attica. Having accomplished this

[1] Baron Forth-Rouen to Baroche, Athens, 8 October 1851, Grèce, LVII, no. 14, MAE. On the Holy Land dispute and its effect on Greece, see Edouard Driault and M. l'Héritier, *Histoire diplomatique de la Grèce* (Paris, 1925), II, pp. 370ff. Other dispatches from Forth-Rouen speak of the difficulties France was having in Greece at the time, 7 and 28 October, 27 November and 6 December, LVII, nos. 4, 52, 165, and 182, MAE.

[2] K. Gasser to King Ludwig, Athens, 1 April 1851, MA III, Griechenland, 2193, no. 34, GS; T. Wyse to Palmerston, Athens, 17 March 1852, F.O. 32, Greece, vol. 198, no. 38, PRO.

much, Otho sat back and waited. *The Century* saw through Otho's policy and voiced its complaint, 'the Ecclesiastical Bill sleeps in its usual deep slumber, never to be roused. And what man, thinking about it a little bit, ever hopes to see it voted upon and put into action?'[1] The Bavarian envoy Maximilian Pergler von Perglas also understood Otho's policies and informed Ludwig '...it will be disastrous for Greece if it is obliged to execute it (the Tomos) to the letter as the Napist party, the organ of Russia, wants'.[2]

A bit of humor was added to the situation in January 1852. The government had requested a copy of the regulations by which the Russian synod was governed. The request was granted and a Latin copy of the *Kanonismos*, as it was called, was sent to Athens from St Petersburg, where it was given to some university professors for translating into Greek. The translation was then left at the house of the minister Damianos without any explanation. Damianos read it and thought it the work of a secret plot to overthrow the king and interpreted the Oath of the Holy Synod of Russia as the plotters' initiation ceremony. Otho was informed, authorities began a search, until Otho himself in reading over the documents noted the mistake, and the police were called off the hunt.[3]

In late January, Otho dismissed the Minister of Worship, Varvoglu, and appointed in his stead Stavros Vlachos. This man was one of the most prominent members of the Russian party in Greece. He had formerly been a tailor and had had no background in government service. His zeal for Orthodoxy followed along the lines set down by the leader of the conservatives, Konstantinos Oekonomos. Otho knew that such a move would be welcomed by Russia; possibly he felt that he would be able to control his new minister rather easily. On his appointment, Forth-Rouen was quoted as saying, 'the king has raised the Russian flag in Greece', while Wyse was moved to

[1] *Αἰών*, Athens, 29 September 1851, no. 1196, p. 1.

[2] P. von Perglas to King Ludwig, Athens, 18 November 1851, MA III, Griechenland, 2193, no. 126, GS. Because the Greek letter 'Rho' is written like the Latin letter 'P', westerners frequently called the Russian party 'Napist', instead of 'Narist'.

[3] P. von Perglas to King Ludwig, Athens, 12 January 1852, MA III, Griechenland, 2194, no. 9, GS; T. Wyse to Lord Palmerston, Athens, 17 January 1852, F.O. 32, Greece, vol. 198, no. 8, PRO.

comment that Vlachos 'is little qualified by his want of religious moderation and superior education for the onerous duties of an office become lately of peculiar responsibility'. The Russians, for their part, applauded the nomination as 'a guarantee of a prompt execution of the Tomos'.[1]

Otho's campaign to curry favor with the tsar included the extension of an invitation to Prince Constantine of Russia to visit Athens on his travels, but the prince did not accept. It was not in Russia's plans at the moment, while the issue of the Holy Land was still undecided, to disturb the Turks.[2]

Meanwhile, Vlachos was at work on the important bills which must be submitted to the Assembly. He did not consult the other ministers who were close to the king, but reported all of his work directly to Otho and the progress of the measures was kept secret. Vlachos was intent upon freeing the Synod completely from the secular power, and on this point a great deal of discussion was forthcoming.[3] Otho persisted in delaying a final decision on any matter, a characteristic which drew a comment from the Bavarian minister, 'I know of no other reasons for the delay in the decisions of the king, than the general difficulty which His Majesty has shown for some time to occupy himself seriously with his ministers concerning the important affairs of state'.[4]

Otho's neglect extended to financial matters and administrative decisions as well; much of his time he spent brooding over the succession to his throne. Throughout the country brigandage was rampant and plots and counterplots to overthrow the king were a part of everyday existence. The extreme Orthodox partisans were quite

[1] P. von Perglas to King Ludwig, Athens, 10 February 1852, MA III, Griechenland, 2194, no. 26, GS; T. Wyse to Palmerston, Athens, 7 February 1852, F.O. 32, Greece, vol. 198, no. 16, PRO; B. Forth-Rouen to Turgot, Athens, 17 February 1852, LVII, no. 77, MAE.

[2] P. von Perglas to King Ludwig, Athens, 3 February and 15 March 1852, MA III, Griechenland, 2194, nos. 22 and 34.

[3] Baron Forth-Rouen to Turgot, Athens, 17 and 27 March, Grèce, LVII, nos. 163 and 179, MAE; T. Wyse to Granville, Athens, 6 April 1852, F.O. 32, Greece, vol. 199, no. 41, PRO.

[4] P. von Perglas to King Ludwig, Athens, 27 April, MA III, Griechenland, 2194, no. 58, GS. His dispatches during these weeks are full of pessimism about Otho.

restive; a monk by the name of Christophoros had for months been preaching throughout the country of the evils of the western church and all who belonged to it. Everywhere he drew great crowds who fought to touch him. The Holy Synod tried to get him into a monastery, but he refused, announcing that 'he recognizes no sovereign but the Emperor of Russia', and urged the people to overthrow the present foreign establishment in Greece. In Athens itself, at Easter, the name of Otho was omitted from the prayers for the monarch in the Liturgy.

During March, Sir Thomas Wyse wrote a long memoir to London attempting to explain the situation as he saw it at that time. He noted that while the French policy was difficult to explain in Greece, he was well aware of what Russia wanted; its policy shows, he said, that it is 'indifferent apparently to Constitutions, which it regards as ephemeral, but inexorable, enduring, indefatigable for the securing and extension of the Religious Union, in which it sees the Union of all things else. Constitutions could never collect the forces of Greek systems and races scattered through the vast extent of the Turkish Empire, much less animate them; Religion can!' In Greece the Russians were active all over the country in pushing religious affairs and supporting monasteries and churches, which explained the popularity they enjoyed among the ordinary people.[1]

At this juncture, in late April, while religious issues were uppermost in the minds of many, an old voice was heard once more—Theokletos Pharmakidis published anonymously his new book *The Synodal Tomos or concerning Truth*, a strong attack on the Tomos and what it represented. The work is 605 pages in length and reviews practically every possible facet of the church problem in Greece. His message was no different from his previous stand—only a bit more bitter. He wondered how the heroes of independence who had shed 'martyrs' blood' would look upon restoring the church to a foreign power. The church, he asserted, had been independent since March 1821 due to the will of the Greek people—to have relations restored with Constantinople meant subservience, a step into darkness.

Pharmakidis claimed that Apostolidis had made a great mistake

[1] T. Wyse to Granville, Athens, 6 March 1852, F.O. 32, Greece, vol. 198, no. 28, PRO.

when he accepted the conditions found in the Tomos. He had no authority, either on his own or because of his office as emissary, to flaunt clearly the law of the country and the Constitution. There was nothing uncanonical about the establishment set up in 1833, 'the Eastern Church is everywhere joined to the state, never being separated from it, never divided from the sovereigns since Byzantine times, and always subordinate to them'. What the Tomos was doing was to set up two powers, 'a state within a state' inside Greece. The author analyses every statement within the Tomos and finds that each is either contrary to history or to law. He rightfully asserts that there never was any canonical union between Greece and Constantinople until after the eighth century—if now the patriarchate is faithful to the ancient traditions, it should not be concerned with canonical union with Athens and independent Greece. If Greece needs the Holy Chrism from Constantinople, Pharmakidis asks, why not baptismal water and bread and wine for the Eucharist? The church of Greece has been consecrating bishops for nineteen centuries, it needs no new instructions on this matter. The book ends with a ringing call to resist the conditions required by the Tomos and to keep the church of Greece independent.[1]

As might be expected *Athena*, which represented the liberal secular view, was enthusiastic about Pharmakidis' work, claiming that it fulfilled a real need in setting the matter straight while the legislation concerning the Tomos was pending. *The Century*, the protagonist of the conservative orthodox party, was just as anxious to take the opposite view and offered its readers a daily diet of attacks upon the book. Eventually, Konstantinos Oekonomos, the standard-bearer of the conservatives, brought out a pamphlet which refuted Pharmakidis' statements sentence by sentence.[2] In May of 1852, the Holy Synod

[1] Theokletos Pharmakidis, Ὁ Συνοδικὸς Τόμος ἢ Περὶ Ἀληθείας [The synodal Tomos or concerning truth] (Athens, 1852), pp. 2–18, 57–80, 124–31, 161–7, 250, 468–72. The Russian minister Persiany was quite upset, announcing that if the Greek government followed the opinions here, 'the relations between Greece and Russia would be absolutely changed' (P. von Perglas to King Ludwig, Athens, 13 July 1852, MA III, Griechenland, 2194, no. 100, GS).

[2] *Ἀθῆνα*, Athens, 8 and 11 May 1852, nos. 1864, 1865, p. 1; *Αἰών*, Athens, 3, 7, 10 May, 8 June, nos. 1254, 1255, 1256, and 1264; Konstantinos Oekonomos of the

of Greece labeled Pharmakidis' book a 'scandalous and blasphemous book against the Church'.

After waiting for Otho and Vlachos to reach some sort of agreement on the legislation to be proposed, the Council of Ministers at last had the measure put before them in early May. The Minister of Worship said that his intentions were to please both the clergy of Greece and the government. The proposals were altogether in line with the conditions imposed by the Tomos.

The more liberal members of the Council strongly protested Vlachos' measures. At least one threatened to resign if certain modifications were not made. For some reason, King Otho did not object to Vlachos' proposals and was even willing to have the Synod practically independent of the royal power. But Christiades, Minister of Foreign Affairs, let it be known that Vlachos' work would be revised—there was no danger that the bill would take away the royal prerogative.[1]

While the discussions continued, the Russians were active, supporting the churchmen who wanted the Tomos accepted. Their minister to Athens, Persiany, announced that he expected to see 'the full and entire execution of the Tomos' and threatened the tsar would take strong action if the measure was amended. According to Perglas, 'Mr Persiany claims to have the best sentiments, but he is more faithless than a cat'. Otho told Persiany he was sure a solution agreeable to both the clergy and the government would be reached.[2]

At the same time, the movement of Christophoros was mounting in intensity. Not only did he attack the king as 'anti-Christ' but he claimed the Synod was made up of Jews engaged in an attempt to separate the church from the patriarchate of Constantinople. An

Oekonomos, *Παράρτημα εἰς τὸ τρίτον τμῆμα*... [An answer in three parts to 'Concerning Truth'] (Athens, 1852), in Τὰ *σωζόμενα ἐκκλησιαστικὰ συγγράμματα* [The extant ecclesiastical writings], ed. Sophokles of the Oekonomos (Athens, 1862–6).

[1] Baron Forth-Rouen to Turgot, Athens, 19 and 26 May 1852, Grèce, LVII, nos. 46 and 62, MAE; P. von Perglas to Ludwig, Athens, 11 and 18 May, MA III, Griechenland, 2194, nos. 76 and 75, GS.

[2] P. von Perglas to King Ludwig, Athens, 30 May 1852, MA III, Griechenland, 2194, no. 85, GS. In St Petersburg the Bavarian minister was told by Count Nesselrode that the Russian court not only expected the Tomos to be accepted but that Otho should become Orthodox (Baron de Bray to King Ludwig, St Petersburg, 31 March 1852, MA III, Russland, 2736, no. 26, GS).

army of a thousand men followed him. By now, the government considered his preaching a sufficient threat to warrant his arrest. Accordingly he and other monks who were stirring up the people were ordered to be taken into custody, lest at the critical moment, when legislation concerning the Tomos was being introduced into the Assembly, the government should find itself embarrassed by a popular uprising.[1] The Holy Synod also condemned Christophoros, excommunicating him by a decree of 15 May 1852.

Meanwhile, the discussion in the Council continued. Not only was Otho concerned, but even Queen Amalia sat in on the discussions and made some 'grave modifications'.[2] Vlachos reported that some members of the Synod insisted on the original draft of his bills or they would resign and go to Aegina. This threat had served to harden the opposition in the Council against letting the bishops have their way.

The discussions centered on how to merge the ideas of the Tomos and still keep the church under the surveillance of the state. One suggestion had been to make the Synod the head of the church, adding 'under the sovereignty of the king'. The Synod's one strong point was the fact that no bishops had yet been nominated, nor would they be, unless a minimum of the conditions of the Tomos would be guaranteed by the proposed legislation. By June 1852, only eight bishops were left in all of independent Greece. The cabinet meetings were stormy; Vlachos fought off any attempt to amend his proposals or any concession to the secular power. He was especially concerned that the Synod's authority should not be subject to the phrase 'under the sovereignty of the king'. Both Wyse, the British minister, and Forth-Rouen, the French ambassador, urged Otho and the liberals in the Cabinet to amend Vlachos' measures; Wyse counselled, 'spiritual weapons are not easily met by temporal and once let out of the hands of authority they are not to be regained'.[3]

[1] P. von Perglas to King Ludwig, Athens, 8 June 1852, MA III, Griechenland, 2194, no. 87, GS; T. Wyse to Earl of Malmesbury, Athens, 26 May and 5 June 1852, F.O. 32, Greece, vol. 199, nos. 63 and 65, PRO.

[2] Baron Forth-Rouen to Turgot, Athens, 15 and 17 June, Grèce, LVII, nos. 167 and 169, MAE.

[3] T. Wyse to Earl of Malmesbury, Athens, 7 June 1852, F.O. 32, Greece, vol. 199, no. 66, PRO; Baron Forth-Rouen to Turgot, Athens, 17 June 1852, Grèce, LVIII,

After some time, the Council of Ministers and the king finally reached agreement on the measure to be submitted to the legislature. All were convinced that the delicacy of the matter required a decision to be reached as quickly as possible and with the least amount of difficulty. This would best be done by seeking a unanimous vote of approval. So it then fell to the ministers of the Council to convince the members of the Assembly that any debate or discussion of the measure in the chamber might endanger the whole affair. At the house of Mr Zaimis was held a meeting of the deputies while the senators gathered at General Church's residence. Only with difficulty was agreement reached that there should be no debate, but at last this was achieved and the bill was therefore assured of success. Some delegates of the extreme Orthodox party threatened at first to walk out of the meeting, but they were so few that they were persuaded to stay and eventually even these reluctantly concurred with the majority.[1]

The text of Law Two Hundred and One, as the measure was called, omitted any mention of the Tomos but followed many of its principles. Article One defined membership in the church and noted that the head of the church was Christ Himself. 'It is spiritually governed by canonical prelates, conserving in their integrity, as all the other Orthodox churches of Christ, the holy Apostolic and Conciliar Canons and the Sacred Traditions.' The second article established that the supreme ecclesiastical power would rest in a permanent Synod, bearing the name 'The Holy Synod of the Church of Greece'. In neither article was there any mention of the role of the king, nor did it say, as some of the liberals had hoped, that the Synod acted under the sovereignty of the king. This was not really necessary, since other articles in the law gave the king and the government many opportunities to interfere in church affairs.

no. 181, MAE. Wyse believed that the Phanariote families in Athens were really anxious for the settlement, since already 'these families are rich, intelligent, experienced and for the most part unscrupulous. They have a direct interest in becoming the managers of this new instrument, being excluded by decree (one of the results of the Constitution) respecting Heterochthonism, from participation in the Government and the honors of state.'

[1] T. Wyse to Malmesbury, Athens, 6 July 1852, F.O. 32; Greece, vol. 199, no. 79, PRO.

Article Three concerned the membership of the Synod. It was to consist of five members, all bishops having sees within Greece and each having an equal voice in its deliberations. These prelates would serve on the invitation of the government, according to the date of their consecration, while the president of the Synod would always be the metropolitan of Athens. Article Four required a long loyalty oath to the king which was strong on the Synod's attachment to the throne, and in the sixth provision the law established a Royal Commissioner to serve in almost the same capacity as that of procurator. His duties were to countersign all of the synodal acts and no action could be taken without his signature. He represented royal power in the Synod, as was his duty, since 'the surveillance of all that happens in the kingdom is inherent in the supreme power of the king, in whom resides the sovereignty of the state'. Other articles divided the external activities of the church from those which were considered internal. Their outlook was such that the area of the latter was quite limited, while external matters, in which the state might interfere, received a very broad interpretation. Article Twenty renewed the prohibition of any correspondence between the Synod and any external ecclesiastical or political authority without prior censorship by the Minister of Worship. The law also still required clerics to take oaths and to give testimony in courts, but a number of safeguards were agreed to in order that no one's conscience be offended.[1]

The bill obviously fell far short of the conditions put forward by the Tomos and was repugnant on that score to the conservative Orthodox in the Assembly. The liberal members also were unhappy over some of its provisions, yet there was no debate and no amendments offered according to the agreement reached beforehand. The Russian minister Persiany tried desperately to get the law amended; he 'supplicated and menaced at the home of the foreign minister, to obtain the retraction of the law or at least its modification'. The

[1] The text is in Αἱ *ἀναγκαιότεραι* Ἐγκύκλιοι Ἐπιστολαί, *Διάταξεις καὶ* Ὁδηγίαι *τῆς* Ἱερᾶς *Συνόδου τῆς* Ἐκκλησίας *τῆς* Ἑλλάδος [The most important encyclical letters, decrees and directives of the Holy Synod of the church of Greece from the years 1834–1854] (Athens, 1854), pp. 242–54.

Russians were obviously right in charging that Law Two Hundred and One omitted a great deal of the Tomos and modified some of the points it included.

When a final vote was called for, the measure passed unanimously, 7 June 1852, only two days after it had been introduced. It then went to the Senate where it received another unanimous vote. Thus Law Two Hundred and One, although far from perfect, was a sufficiently satisfactory compromise that members on all sides felt they could support it. This effect was surely unexpected by the conservative Orthodox party, and especially by the Russian mission in Athens. According to Forth-Rouen, they had overplayed their hand, 'the Emperor of Russia will probably discover that his agents were too precipitous and they put too much pressure on Greece, not taking into enough consideration the national sympathies...According to the bishop of Syros, "Never forget this, we are Greek before we are Russian".'[1]

That the law was passed was surely a great relief to the king, although his ability to have his way in the Assembly and the Senate had practically guaranteed eventual success. The great majority of legislators were there because of their subservience to the royal will. Elections for lawmakers were carried out in Greece in such a way that there was little chance of an effective opposition developing in either the Assembly or the Senate. This explains the ease with which the law was passed. Edmund About, a French visitor to Greece in the 1850s, surmized, 'all the offices, without exception, are for sale, and if the king wanted an assembly of deaf-mutes elected, he could have it, if he paid the price'.[2]

Despite the acceptance of the law by the two houses of the legislature, Otho delayed signing the measure, giving rise to new rumors and speculation. Some thought the Russian ambassador Persiany was

[1] Baron Forth-Rouen to Turgot, Athens, 26 June 1852, Grèce, LVIII, no. 275, MAE. Wyse rejoiced, 'It is the most serious check which Russian propagandism has for many years received, and is a very remarkable and significant expression, especially after recent events in Constantinople and the Peloponnesus, of public opinion on the subject' (Wyse to Earl of Malmesbury, Athens, 26 June 1852, F.O. 32, Greece, vol. 199, no. 76, PRO).

[2] Edmond About, *La Grèce contemporaine*, 3rd ed. (Paris, 1858), p. 218.

behind the delay, others believed it simply to be due to Otho's usual procrastination. Action, however, came in still another area on 28 June, when a law concerning bishops and their sees was introduced.

This law, known eventually as Law Two Hundred, established twenty-four bishops for Greece. Athens was to be a metropolitanate, ten of the more important sees were to become archbishoprics and there would be ten other dioceses. The law determined how bishops should be selected—the Synod would nominate three men and the king would then choose who would receive the appointments. While giving the church a certain latitude, there was no doubt that the king and the Ministry of Worship retained their authority.[1]

A Committee in the Assembly, appointed to examine the law, was ready to report a few days later. Like the previous bill, it was recommended by the Committee that it be passed without amendment. There was some discussion and explanation of the measure—then on 5 July a vote was taken which carried the measure through the Assembly by a large majority. The bill had an equally easy time of it in the Senate—thus assuring that the acute need of the church of Greece for new bishops would soon be answered.[2] On 9 July, Otho signed Law Two Hundred as well as Law Two Hundred and One, inverting the order in which they had been introduced and passed in the legislature.[3] The first new bishop to be appointed was Misael Apostolidis, who had played such a significant role in the negotiations between the patriarchate and the church of Greece. His consecration took place in September, and by the end of 1852 eleven other bishops had been named, restoring new life to the church of Greece.

Despite the fact that the two laws hardly measured up to the terms of the Tomos for the recognition of the autocephalous church of Greece, the patriarch did not deny it recognition, although he would surely have had a right to do so. Neither piece of legislation over-

[1] The text of the law is in Αἱ *ἀναγκαιότεραι* 'Εγκύκλιοι 'Επιστολαί, pp. 230–41.

[2] *Πρακτικὰ τῶν Συνεδριάσεων τῆς* Βουλῆς *κατὰ τὴν Δευτέραν Σύνοδον τῆς* Τρίτης Περιόδου, *1852* [Acts of the meetings of the Assembly in the second session of the third period, 1852] (Athens, 1852), II, pp. 205–16, 220–1, 249–51.

[3] Law Two Hundred was published in the 'Εφημερὶς *τῆς* Κυβερνήσεως, 10 July 1852, pp. 183–6; Law Two Hundred and One appeared on 24 July 1852, pp. 195–8.

turned Maurer's Constitution of 1833—it was simply modified. Possibly not even this would have occurred had it not been for the desperate episcopal situation of Greece. The state, at that time represented by King Otho, was in no mood to relinquish its control over the church, which was, in fact, already too weak to put up much opposition. Although the situation was such that any concerned Orthodox cleric or layman could hardly be satisfied, still the church of Greece was in communion with Constantinople again and for this one could be thankful.

CONCLUSION

THE preceding chapters have briefly covered the political history of the Greek Orthodox church under the sultans from 1453, and subsequently and, in more detail, its status under the various revolutionary governments during the war, the presidency of Ioannis Kapodistrias, and finally the monarchical rule of the Bavarian King Otho and his ministers. There can be no doubt that the church under the sultans preserved the Hellenistic heritage of language, culture and faith, but at the same time it became a church corrupted by the decadent Ottoman system under which it lived. The tragedy of this account is that the position of the church, which should have been bright in independent Greece, was, in fact, not substantially improved under later Christian rulers.

The four hundred years of Turkish suzerainty allowed simony and ignorance to flourish—in 1852 these conditions were still not eradicated. The sultans had reduced the bishops of the church to the status of extensions of their own regime; in 1833 the Constitution of the church of Greece performed the same function. The laws of 1852 did not change the situation, even though this had been a condition of the recognition of the autocephalous nature of the church of Greece by the Tomos of 1850.

The great weakness of the church during these years was its subservience to state power and the consequent interference by civil authority in its internal affairs. Tied so closely to autocratic rulers and corrupt administrators it was impossible that the church should have been able to progress. The patriarchate had been so much at the mercy of venal officials at the Porte that it was exceedingly difficult for it to exercise any sort of enlightened leadership. The situation of the Synod of independent Greece in this regard was not a significant improvement over Ottoman times.

One of the great disasters for the Greek church was its lack of intellectual life and vigorous leadership during this period. The few names that stand out in this work were trained in the west or at the Great School of the patriarchate, but, by far, the calibre of bishops in the Orthodox church was low. This same condition persisted, of course, in independent Greece. It was not the fault of the church so much as it was that of the system under which only monks were chosen as bishops for reasons other than their intellectual ability or administrative skill. The names of Konstantinos Oekonomos and Theokletos Pharmakidis deserve special mention. These men, so different in their points of view, were men of real ability and intellectual competence. No one has equalled their accomplishments since they passed from the scene.

The role that Russia played during these years was significant. The Greeks believed the tsar and his church to be a model of the perfect Orthodox nation. The myth was much more important than the fact. Time after time, beginning with Peter the Great, the Russians called upon their fellow Orthodox to resist the sultan in the name of religion, but at the heart of Russian policy were its own interests in the Mediterranean area. Russia continuously objected to Otho, a Catholic, serving as the head of an Orthodox state where the church was so closely tied to the government. This, at least, was a legitimate complaint.

Nationalism is another factor which played a significant role during these years. To be Greek was to be Orthodox in 1821 and the clergy played a leading role in the Hetairia and the beginning of the Revolution. Slowly, however, the church lost its influence owing to the loss of personnel and the confused conditions of the war, so that by the time of Kapodistrias the position of the church was already quite weak. From 1828 until 1852 this decline continued since the ranks of capable bishops were not replenished. One could still find extreme devotion to Orthodoxy in 1852, but it could not compare to the enthusiasm engendered by 'The Great Idea' of Greek expansion against the Turks. Secular nationalism had begun to replace religious fervor. Great fury could be raised by the fact that King Otho was not Orthodox, but it was anger born of political as much as religious motivation. When the real issues of church-state relations appeared in 1833 or 1852, the number of those willing to witness to the rights of the church proved to be remarkably small.

BIBLIOGRAPHY

PRIMARY SOURCES

London: British Museum
  Department of Manuscripts
    Stratford Canning MSS.
    Richard Church MSS.
    William Huskisson MSS.
    Robert Peel MSS.
    Lord Strangford (Percy C. Smythe) MSS.
    Richard Wellesley MSS.
  Public Record Office: Foreign Office
    Greece F.O. 32, vols. 3–26, 35–40, 42, 177–84, 198–9.
    Turkey F.O. 78, vols. 98–102, 221–4, 817–20, 846–7.
    Bavaria F.O. 9, vols. 64–7.
    Russia F.O. 65, vols. 376–8.

Munich: Geheimes Staatsarchiv
    MA I Politisches Archiv.
    MA III Die Diplomatischen Berichte, 1799–1918.
    Bayer Gesandtschaft, St Petersbourg.

Paris: Archives du Ministère des Affaires Etrangères
    Correspondance Politque, Grèce, vols. 1–20, 28–30, 41, 50–8, 119, 126, 232, 250, 251.

Rome: Archivio Segreto Vaticano, Segretario di Stato
    Sezione Esteri, 1822–31.
    Sezione Interno, 1822–5.
  Archivio della S. Congregazione di Propaganda
    Scritture riferite, Congressi, Archipeligo (1821–35).
    Lettere della S. Congregazione (1822–4).

SECONDARY SOURCES

About, Edmond. *La Grèce Contemporaine*. 3rd. ed., Paris, 1858.

Αἱ *ἀναγκαιότεραι Ἐγκύκλιοι Ἐπιστολαί, Διατάξεις, καὶ Ὁδηγίαι τῆς Ἱερᾶς Συνόδου τῆς Ἐκκλησίας τῆς Ἑλλάδος (1834–1854)* [The most important encyclical letters, decrees and directives of the Holy Synod of the church of Greece]. Athens, 1854.

Amantos, Konstantinos. 'Οἱ προνομιακοὶ ὁρισμοὶ τοῦ Μουσουλμανισμοῦ ὑπὲρ τῶν Χριστιανῶν' [The Moslem decrees of privileges concerning Christians]. 'Ελληνικά, IX (1936), pp. 103–66.
Androutsos, Christos. 'Εκκλησία καὶ Πολιτεία ἐξ ἐπόψεως ὀρθοδόξου [Church and State from the Orthodox view]. Athens, 1920.
Argyropoulos, P. A. 'Les Grecs au service de l'empire ottoman', *L'Hellénisme Contemporain*. Ser. 2, VII (1953) in *Le Cinq-Centième Anniversaire de la Prise de Constantinople*, pp. 151–78.
Aristoklis, Theodoros. Κωνσταντίνου Α' τοῦ ἀπὸ Σιναίου Πατριάρχου Κωνσταντινουπόλεως [Konstantinos I of Sinai, Patriarch of Constantinople]. Constantinople, 1866.
Arnakis, George G. 'Byzantium and Greece', *Balkan Studies IV*, II (1963), pp. 379–400.
'The Greek Church of Constantinople and the Ottoman Empire', *Journal of Modern History*, XXIV (Sept. 1952), pp. 235–50.
'The Role of Religion in the Development of Balkan Nationalism', in *The Balkans in Transition*, Charles and Barbara Jelavich, eds., pp. 115–44. Berkeley, 1963.
Atesis, Vasileios. 'Επίτομος ἐπισκοπικὴ 'Ιστορία τῆς 'Εκκλησίας τῆς 'Ελλάδος [An abridged episcopal history of the church of Greece]. Athens, 1948.
'Η 'Εκκλησία τῶν 'Αθηνῶν ἀπὸ τοῦ *1833* μέχρι σήμερον [The church of Athens from 1833 to the present]. Athens, 1957.
Αὐτοβιογραφία τοῦ 'Ιωάννου Καποδίστρια [Autobiography of Ioannis Kapodistrias]. Michael Laskaris, ed. Athens, 1940.
Bacopoulos, George T. *Outline of the Greek Constitution*. Athens, 1950.
Balanos, D. S. Πολιτεία καὶ 'Εκκλησία [State and Church]. Athens, 1920.
'Αἱ θρησκευτικαὶ ἰδέαι τοῦ 'Αδαμαντίου Κοραῆ' [The religious ideas of Adamantios Koraïs], 'Αθῆναι, 1920.
''Ανέκδοτοι ἐπιστολαὶ Κωνσταντίνου Οἰκονόμου τοῦ ἐξ Οἰκονόμων' [Unpublished letters of Konstantinos Oekonomos of the Oekonomos], Πραγματεῖαι τῆς 'Ακαδημίας 'Αθηνῶν, V. Athens, 1936.
'Κωνσταντίνος Οἰκονόμος ὁ ἐξ Οἰκονόμων' [Konstantinos Oekonomos of the Oekonomos], 'Εκκλησία, XXXIV, no. 24 (1957), pp. 491–8.
Θεόκλητος Θαρμακίδης, *1784–1860* [Theokletos Pharmakidis]. Athens, 1933.
Benz, Ernst. *Die Ostkirche im Lichte der Protestantischen Geschichtsschreibung von der Reformation bis zur Gegenwart*. Munich, 1952.

Bernasconi, Antonio M. (ed.). *Acta Gregorii Papae XVI*, vol. III. Rome, 1901.

Bétant, E. A. (ed.). *Correspondance du Comte J. Capodistrias, Président de la Grèce*. 4 vols. Geneva, 1839.

Bikelas, Demetrios. *La Grèce avant la Révolution de 1821*. Paris, 1884.

Le Rôle et les Aspirations de la Grèce dans la Question d'Orient. Paris, 1885.

Blancard, Jules. *Etudes sur la Grèce contemporaine*. 2 vols. Montpellier, 1886.

Blancard, Théodore. *Les Mavroyeni*. 2 vols. Paris, 1909.

Bonis, K. G. 'Gennadius Scholarius, der erste Partriarch von Konstantinopel nach der Eroberung (1454) und sein Politik Rom gegenüber', *Kyrios*, I (1960–1), pp. 83–108.

Botzaris, Notis. *Visions Balkaniques dans la préparation de la Révolution Grecque, 1789–1821*. Paris, 1962.

Bower, Leonard, and Gordon Bolitho. *Otho I, King of Greece*. London, 1939.

Brunet de Presle, W., and Alexandre Blanchet. *Grèce depuis la conquête romaine jusqu'à nos jours*. Paris, 1860.

Cantemir, Demetrios. *The History of the Growth and Decay of the Ottoman Empire*. N. Tindal, trans. London, 1734.

Carayon Auguste. *Les relations inédites des Missions de la Compagnie de Jésus à Constantinople et dans le Levant*. Paris, 1864.

Chroust, Anton. *Gesandtschaftsberichte aus München, 1814–1848*, Abteilung I. *Die Berichte der französischen Gesandten*. 5 vols. Munich, 1935.

Clugnet, Léon. 'Les offices et les dignités ecclésiastiques dans l'Eglise grecque', *Revue de l'Orient chrétien*, III (1898), pp. 452–8, IV (1899), pp. 116–28.

Cobham, Claude D. *The Patriarchs of Constantinople*. London, 1911.

Crawley, C. W. *The Question of Greek Independence*. Cambridge, 1930.

Crusius, Martinus (ed.). *Turcograeciae: Liber I*, Ἱστορία Πολιτικὴ Κωνσταντινουπόλεως. Manuel Malaxos, *Liber II*, Πατριαρχικὴ Κωνσταντινουπόλεως Ἱστορία [Book I, The Political History of Constantinople; Book II, The Patriarchal History of Constantinople]. Basel, 1584.

Dakin, Douglas. *British and American Philhellenes during the War of Greek Independence, 1821–1833*. Thessaloniki, 1955.

d'Avril, Adolphe. *Documents relatifs aux Eglises de l'Orient et à leur rapports avec Rome*. Paris, 1885.

de Barenton, Hilaire. *La France Catholique en Orient*. Paris, 1902.

de la Croix, (Sieur). *Etat présent des nations et églises Grècque, Arménienne et Maronite en Turquie*. Paris, 1695.

de Martens, George F. *Recueil de Traités d'Alliance...des puissances et états de l'Europe depuis 1761 jusqu'à présent*. 2nd ed., vol. II (1771–1779). Göttingen, 1817.

Dimitrakopoulos, Andronikos. *Ὀρθόδοξος Ἑλλάς, ἤτοι περὶ τῶν Ἑλλήνων τῶν γραψάντων κατὰ Λατίνων καὶ περὶ τῶν συγγραμμάτων αὐτῶν* [Orthodox Greece, being the writings of the Greeks against the Latins and their literature]. Leipzig, 1872.

de Tott, Francis. *Mémoires du baron de Tott sur les Turcs et les Tartares*. 2 vols. Paris, 1785.

Dickopf, Karl. *Georg Ludwig von Maurer, 1790–1872*. Kallmünz, 1960.

Diehl, Charles. 'The Greek Church and Hellenism' in *Greece in Evolution*, ed. G. F. Abbott, pp. 43–68. London, 1919.

d'Ohsson, Mouragea. *Tableau général de l'Empire ottoman*. 8 vols. Paris, 1824.

Doukas, Neophytos. *Ἐπιστολὴ πρὸς τὸν Παναγιώτατον Πατριάρχην Κύριον Κύριλλον περὶ ἐκκλησιαστικῆς εὐταξίας* [Letter to His Holiness, Patriarch Kyrillos, concerning the Ecclesiastical Order]. Vienna, 1815.

Λόγος πρὸς τοὺς Βουλευτὰς καὶ Γερουσιαστὰς ὑπὲρ τοῦ ἐκκλησιαστικοῦ νομοσχεδίου [Speech to the members of the Assembly and the Senate concerning the ecclesiastical bill]. Athens, 1845.

Driault, Edouard, and Michel l'Héritier. *Histoire diplomatique de la Grèce*. 5 vols. Paris, 1925.

Dyovouniotis, Konstantinos. ''Ἡ *κατὰ τὸ* 1834 *Διάλυσις τῶν Μοναστηρίων ἐν τῇ* Ἐλευθέρᾳ Ἑλλάδι' [The 1834 dissolution of the monasteries in independent Greece], *Ἱερὸς Σύνδεσμος*, XII (1908).

Σχέσις Ἐκκλησίας καὶ Πολιτείας ἐν τῇ Ἐλευθέρα Ἑλλάδι [Church-state relations in independent Greece]. Athens, 1916.

Ἐγκύκλιος τῆς Μιᾶς, Ἁγίας, Καθολικῆς, καὶ Ἀποστολικῆς Ἐκκλησίας Ἐπιστολὴ πρὸς τοὺς ἁπανταχοῦ Ὀρθοδόξους [Encyclical letter of the one, holy, catholic and apostolic church to the Orthodox everywhere]. Constantinople, 1848.

Eliot, Sir Charles (Odysseus). *Turkey in Europe*. London, 1906.

Emerson, James, Count Pecchio and W. H. Humphreys. *A Picture of Greece in 1825*. 2 vols. London, 1826.

Emerson, James. *The History of Modern Greece*, vol. II. London, 1830.

Evangelidis, Tryphonos F. Ἱστορία τοῦ Ὄθωνος, Βασιλέως τῆς Ἑλλάδος [History of Otho, King of Greece]. Athens, 1893.

Finlay, George. *History of Greece*, ed. H. F. Tozer, vols. v, vi and vii. Oxford, 1877.

Gedeon, Manuel I. Χρονικὰ τῆς Πατριαρχικῆς Ἀκαδημίας· ἱστορικαὶ εἰδήσεις περὶ τῆς Μεγάλης τοῦ Γένους Σχολῆς, *1454–1830* [Chronicle of the Patriarchal Academy: historical information concerning the Great School of the People]. Constantinople, 1883.

Ἐπίσημα Γράμματα Τουρκικὰ ἀναφερόμενα εἰς τὰ ἐκκλησιαστικὰ ἡμῶν δίκαια [Official Turkish documents dealing with our ecclesiastical laws]. Constantinople, 1910.

Πατριαρχικαὶ Ἐφημερίδες [Patriarchal Newspapers]. Athens, 1936.

Πατριαρχικοὶ Πίνακες [Patriarchal Lists]. Constantinople, 1890.

Gelzer, Heinrich. *Geistliches und weltliches aus dem Turkisch-griechischen Orient*. Leipzig, 1900.

Germanos, Metropolitan of Old Patras. Ὑπομνήματα περὶ τῆς Ἐπαναστάσεως τῆς Ἑλλάδος [Recollections of the Greek Revolution]. Athens, 1837.

Germanos, Metropolitan of Sardis. 'Πίναξ τῶν Ἐπισκόπων καὶ Πατριαρχῶν Κωνσταντινουπόλεως, ἀλφαβητικὸς καὶ χρονολογικός' [List of the bishops and patriarchs of Constantinople, alphabetically and chronologically arranged], Ὀρθοδοξία, iii (1928), pp. 29–37.

Gibb, H. A. R. and Harold Bowen. *Islamic Society and the West*. New York, 1950.

Gill, Joseph. *The Council of Florence*. Cambridge, 1959.

Gobineau, Joseph A. *Deux études sur la Grèce moderne*. Paris, 1905.

Gordon, Thomas. *History of the Greek Revolution*. 2 vols. London, 1832.

Green, Philip J. *Sketches of the War in Greece*. London, 1827.

Gregoriou, Paulos. Σχέσεις Καθολικῶν καὶ Ὀρθοδόξων [Relations between Catholics and Orthodox]. Athens, 1958.

Greg, William R. *Sketches in Greece and Turkey*. London, 1833.

Hammer, Joseph von. *Geschichte des Osmanischen Reiches*, vols. i–iv. Pest, 1834–6.

Haralambides, Theodor. 'Die Kirchenpolitik Griechenlands', *Zeitschrift für Kirchengeschichte*, vi (1935), pp. 158–92.

Hasluck, Frederick W. *Christianity and Islam under the Sultans*, ed. Margaret Hasluck. 2 vols. Oxford, 1929.

Hertzberg, Gustav. *Geschichte Griechenlands seit dem Absterben des antiken Lebens bis zur Gegenwart*, vol. iii. Gotha, 1878.

Hofmann, Georg. *Das Papsttum und der Griechische Freiheitskampf.* Vol. 136, *Orientalia Christiana Analecta.* Rome, 1952.

'I Cattolici di Fronte all'Insurrezione Greca (1821–1829)', *La Civiltà Cattolica,* 21 June, 1950.

Il Vicario Apostolico di Costantinopoli, 1453–1830. Vol. 103, *Orientalia Christiana Analecta.* Rome, 1935.

'La Chiesa Cattolica in Grecia, 1600–1830', *Orientalia Christiana Periodica,* II, 1–2. Rome, 1936.

'Papa Gregorio XVI e la Grecia', *Gregorio XVI, Miscellanea commemorativa,* vol. II. Rome, 1949.

Hore, A. H. *Eighteen Centuries of the Orthodox Greek Church.* London, 1899.

Hurewitz, Jacob. *Diplomacy in the Near and Middle East: a documentary record,* vol. I. Princeton, 1956.

Iorga, Nicola. *Byzance après Byzance.* Bucharest, 1935.

Geschichte des Osmanischen Reiches, vol. V. Gotha, 1913.

Histoire des Roumains et de leur civilisation, 2nd ed., Bucharest, 1922.

'Quelques données nouvelles au sujet des relations entre les principautés Roumaines et l'Eglise Constantinopolitaine dans la seconde moitié du XVIIe siècle', *Académie Roumaine, Bulletin de la section historique,* II (1915), pp. 134–63.

Janin, R. *Constantinople Byzantine.* Paris, 1950.

'Constantinople, le Patriarcat Grec' in *Dictionnaire d'Histoire et de Géographie Ecclésiastique* (1956), XIII, pp. 629–739.

La Géographie ecclésiastique de l'Empire Byzantin. 3 vols. Paris, 1953.

Jelavich, Barbara. *Russia and Greece during the Regency of King Othon, 1832–1835.* Thessaloniki, 1962.

A Century of Russian Foreign Policy. New York, 1964.

Jelavich, Charles. 'Some Aspects of Serbian Religious Development in the Eighteenth Century', *Church History,* XXIII (1954), pp. 144–52.

Jourdain, Philippe. *Mémoires historiques et militaires sur les événements de la Grèce.* 2 vols. Paris, 1828.

Juchereau de St Denys. *Histoire de l'Empire ottoman depuis 1792 jusqu'en 1844.* 2 vols. Paris, 1844.

Kaldis, William P. *John Capodistrias and the Modern Greek State.* Madison, Wisconsin, 1963.

Kalligas, Paulos. *Ἀπάντησις εἰς τὴν ἀπὸ 25 Νοεμβρίου 1835 ἐπιστολιμαίαν διατριβὴν ὡς πρὸς τοὺς τρεῖς ἱερατικοὺς βαθμοὺς τῆς Ἐκκλησίας* [A response to the literary treatise of 25 November, 1835 concerning the three hierarchical orders of the church]. Athens, 1841.

Οἱ τρεῖς ἱερατικοὶ βαθμοὶ τῆς Ἐκκλησίας κατὰ τὸν Πρεσβύτερον καὶ Οἰκονόμον Κωνσταντίνον τὸυ ἐξ Οἰκονόμων [The three hierarchical orders of the church according to the priest and oeconom, Konstantinos of the Oekonomos]. Athens, 1841.

Kabouroglos, Demetrios. *Μελέτη περὶ τοῦ βίου καὶ τῆς δράσεως τοῦ Παλαιῶν Πατρῶν Γερμανοῦ* [A study of the life and work of Germanos of Old Patras]. Athens, 1912.

Kandiloros, Takis. *Ἱστορία τοῦ ἐθνομάρτυρος Γρηγορίου τοῦ Ε′* [History of the national martyr, Gregorios V]. Athens, 1909.

Karolidis, Paulos. *Ἱστορία τῆς Ἑλλάδος ἀπὸ τῆς ὑπὸ τῶν Ὀθωμανῶν ἁλώσεως τῆς Κωνσταντινουπόλεως μέχρι βασιλείας Γεωργίου τοῦ Α′* [History of Greece from the Ottoman conquest of Constantinople until the reign of George I]. Athens, 1925.

Σύγχρονος Ἱστορία τῶν Ἑλλήνων καὶ τῶν Λοιπῶν Λαῶν τῆς Ἀνατολῆς ἀπὸ 1821 μέχρι 1921 [Contemporary history of the Greeks and the other peoples of the East from 1821 until 1921]. 4 vols. Athens, 1922–4.

Kimmel, Ernest J. *Monumenta Fidei Ecclesiae Orientalis*. Jena, 1850.

Konidaris, Gerasimos. "Ἑλλάς" [Greece], *Θρησκευτικὴ καὶ Χριστιανικὴ Ἐγκυκλοπαιδεία* [Religious and Christian Encyclopedia], III (1940), pp. 315–99.

Ἐκκλησιαστικὴ Ἱστορία τῆς Ἑλλάδος [Ecclesiastical History of Greece], vol. I. Athens, 1954–60.

Ἡ Ἑλληνικὴ Ἐκκλησία ὡς πολιτιστικὴ δύναμις ἐν τῇ ἱστορίᾳ τῆς Χερσονήσου τοῦ Αἵμου [The Greek church as a civilizing force in the history of the Balkans]. Athens, 1948.

Συμβολὴ εἰς τὴν εἰσαγωγὴν τῆς ἐκκλησιαστικῆς ἱστορίας τῆς Ἑλλάδος [A contribution to the introduction to the ecclesiastical history of Greece]. Athens, 1938.

Koraïs, Adamantios. *Ἀριστοτέλους πολιτικῶν τὰ σωζόμενα* [The extant work of Aristotle's *Politics*]. Paris, 1821.

Kritovoulos. *History of Mehmed the Conqueror*, trans. Chas. T. Riggs. Princeton, 1954.

Kyriakos, Anastasios. *Ἐκκλησιαστικὴ Ἱστορία* [Church History]. 2 vols. Athens, 1881.

Geschichte der Orientalischen Kirchen von 1453–1898, trans. Erwin Rausch. Leipzig, 1902.

LaJonquière, A. de. *Histoire de l'Empire ottoman*. 2 vols. 2nd ed., Paris, 1914.

Laskaris, Stamatios T. *Διπλωματικὴ Ἱστορία τῆς Ἑλλάδος, 1821–1914* [Diplomatic history of Greece]. Athens, 1947.

Ἡ Καθολικὴ Ἐκκλησία ἐν Ἑλλάδι [The Catholic Church in Greece]. Athens, 1924.

Laurent, V. 'Chrétiens sous les Sultans', *Echos d'Orient*, XXVIII (1929), pp. 398–412.

Lavriotis, Kurillos. Πατριαρχικὸν Χρονικόν [Patriarchal chronicle], ed. Manuel Gedeon, Ἀθηναῖον, VI (1877), pp. 3–53.

Leake, William B. *An Historical Outline of the Greek Revolution*. London, 1826.

Researches in Greece. London, 1814.

Travels in Northern Greece. 4 vols. London, 1835.

Legrand, Emile. *Relations de l'établissement des P.P. de la Compagnie de Jésus en Levant*. Paris, 1869.

Le Quien, Michael. *Oriens Christianus*. 3 vols. Paris, 1740.

Lesur, Charles-Louis (ed.). *Annuaire historique universel pour 1821*. Paris, 1822.

Malaxos, Manuel. *Historia politica et patriarchica Constantinopoleos*. Bonn, 1849.

Mamoukas, Andreas Z. Τὰ *κατὰ τὴν* Ἀναγέννησιν τῆς Ἑλλάδος [The events concerning the rebirth of Greece]. 11 vols. in 3. Athens, 1839–52.

Τὰ Μοναστηριακά [Monastic Affairs]. Athens, 1859.

Mansi, Joannes D. (ed.). *Sacrorum Conciliorum nova et amplissima collectio*, vol. XL, pp. 419–31. Graz, 1961.

Martens, Feodor F. *Etude historique sur la Politique Russe dans la question d'Orient*. Paris, 1877.

Mathas, Zacharios. Κατάλογος ἱστορικὸς τῶν πρώτων ἐπισκόπων... [Historical list of the first bishops]. Nauplion, 1837.

Maurer, George Ludwig von. *Das griechische Volk in öffentlicher, kirchlicher und privatrechtlicher Beziehung vor und nach dem Freiheitskampfe*. 3 vols. Heidelberg, 1835.

Mavrokordatos, Georgios. Περὶ τῆς Ἐκκλησίας τῆς Ἑλλάδος [Concerning the church of Greece]. Athens, 1852.

Mendelssohn-Bartholdy, Karl. *Geschichte Griechenlands von der Eroberung Konstantinopels durch die Türken im Jahre 1452 bis auf unsere Tage*. 2 vols. Leipzig, 1870.

Graf Johann Kapodistrias. Berlin, 1864.

Metternich, Richard (ed.). *Memoirs of Prince Metternich*, trans. A. Napier, vol. IV. New York, 1881.

Mexas, Valerios G. Οἱ Φιλικοί [The Friendly Society]. Athens, 1937.

Mikhailowitch, Nicholas. *Empereur Alexandre I.* Paris, 1931.

Mousset, Jean. *La Serbie et son Eglise, 1834–1900.* Paris, 1938.

Mure, William of Caldwell. *Journey of a Tour in Greece.* 2 vols. London, 1850–1.

Neale, John M. *A History of the Holy Eastern Church.* 2 vols. London, 1850–1.

Nesselrode, Alexandre de (ed.). *Lettres et Papiers du Comte de Nesselrode,* vols. VI and VII. Paris, 1908.

Oekonomos of the Oekonomos, Konstantinos. *Κατήχησις, ἤ 'Ορθόδοξος διδασκαλία τῆς Χριστιανικῆς πίστεως* [A Catechism, or the Orthodox teaching of the Christian faith]. Vienna, 1813.

Discours prononcé en Grec, à Odessa, le 29 juin, 1821 pour les funérailles du Patriarche Grégoire. Paris, 1821.

'Επίκρισις εἰς τὴν Περὶ Νεοελληνικῆς 'Εκκλησίας σύντομον ἀπάντησιν τοῦ... Νεοφύτου Βάμβα [A criticism of 'Concerning the Modern Greek Church', a concise answer to Neophytos Vamvas]. Athens, 1839.

Περὶ τῶν Ο' 'Ερμηνευτῶν τῆς Παλαιᾶς Θείας Γραφῆς [Concerning the Seventy translators of the Old Testament]. 4 vols. Athens, 1844–9.

Περὶ τῶν τριῶν ἱερατικῶν τῆς 'Εκκλησίας Βαθμῶν ἐπιστολιμαία διατριβή [An epistolary treatise on the three hierarchical orders of the church]. Nauplion, 1835.

Τὰ σωζόμενα ἐκκλησιαστικὰ συγγράμματα Κωνσταντίνου Πρεσβυτέρου καὶ Οἰκονόμου τοῦ ἐξ Οἰκονόμων [The extant ecclesiastical writings of the priest and oeconom, Konstantinos of the Oekonomos], ed. Sophokles of the Oekonomos, 3 vols. Athens, 1862–6.

Otetea, A. 'L'Hétairie d'il y a cent cinquante ans', *Balkan Studies,* VI, 2 (1965), pp. 249–64.

Palmieri, Aurelio. 'La chiesa ellenica nel secolo XIX', *Bessarione,* ser. II, III (1902), pp. 281–6; IV, pp. 70–87, 205–16, 347–54.

Panayotakos, Panayotis. *'Εκκλησία καὶ Πολιτεία ἀνὰ τοὺς αἰῶνας* [Church and State through the Centuries]. Athens, 1939.

'Ο Οἰκουμενικὸς Πατριαρχικὸς Θρόνος τῆς Κωνσταντινουπόλεως, ἐκκλησιαστικὴ καὶ πολιτικὴ θέσις [The Ecumenical Patriarchal throne of Constantinople, its ecclesiastical and political position]. Athens, 1948.

Papadopoullos, Theodore H. *Studies and Documents relating to the History of the Greek Church and People under Turkish Domination.* Brussels, 1952.

Papadopoulos, Chrysostomos. *'Εκκλησία 'Αθηνῶν* [The Church of Athens]. Athens, 1928.

Ἱστορία τῆς Ἐκκλησίας τῆς Ἑλλάδος [A History of the Church of Greece]. Athens, 1920.

'*Ἡ Ἐκκλησία Κωνσταντινουπόλεως καὶ ἡ Μεγάλη Ἐπανάστασις τοῦ* 1821' [The church of Constantinople and the great revolution of 1821], *Θεολογία*, XXI (1950), pp. 477–503.

Ἡ Θέσις τῆς Ἐκκλησίας καὶ τοῦ Ἑλληνικοῦ Ἔθνους ἐν τῷ Τουρκικῷ Κράτει [The status of the church and the Greek people during the Turkish rule]. Athens, 1935.

Papadopoulos, Constantin G. *Les privilèges du Patriarcat oecuménique dans l'Empire ottoman*. Paris, 1924.

Papadopoulo-Vrétos, André. *Mémoires sur le Président Jean Capo d'Istria*. 2 vols. Paris, 1837–8.

Paparrigopoulos, Konstantinos. *Ἱστορία τοῦ Ἑλληνικοῦ Ἔθνους* [A History of the Greek People], vols. VI and VII. Athens, 1932.

Parish, Henry H. *Diplomatic History of the Monarchy of Greece*. London, 1838.

Pellion, General. *La Grèce et les Capodistrias pendant l'occupation française de 1828 à 1834*. Paris, 1855.

Petit, L. 'Règlements généraux de l'Eglise Orthodoxe en Turquie', *Revue de l'Orient Chrétien*, III (1898), pp. 393–425, IV (1899), pp. 227–47.

Petrakakos, Demetrios. '*Ἐκκλησία καὶ δίκαιον κατὰ τὴν Ἑλληνικὴν Ἐπανάστασιν*' [Church and law during the Greek revolution], *Ἐκκλησιαστικὸς Φάρος*, XXXV (1936), pp. 425–64, XXXVI (1937), pp. 37–76, 145–75, 300–31, 408–40, XXXVII (1938), pp. 98–128, 172–200, 272–304, 417–44.

Pfeilschifter, Georg. *Die Balkanfrage in der Kirchengeschichte*. Munich, 1913.

Pharmakidis, Theokletos. *Ἀπολογία* [Apologia]. Athens, 1840.

Οἰκονόμος ὁ ἐξ Οἰκονόμων ἢ περὶ ὅρκου [Oekonomos of the Oekonomos, or concerning an oath]. Athens, 1849.

Ὁ Συνοδικὸς Τόμος ἢ περὶ Ἀληθείας [The synodal Tomos, or concerning truth]. Athens, 1852.

Philimon, Ioannis. *Δοκίμιον Ἱστορικὸν περὶ τῆς Φιλικῆς Ἑταιρείας* [Historical treatise on the Philike Hetairia]. Nauplion, 1834.

Phillips, W. Alison. *Greek War of Independence*. London, 1897.

Phrantzes, Amvrosios. *Ἐπιτομὴ τῆς Ἱστορίας τῆς Ἀναγεννηθείσης Ἑλλάδος, 1715–1835* [A summary of the history of Greece reborn]. 3 vols. Athens, 1839–41.

Phrantzes, Georgios. *Χρονικόν* [Chronicle], ed. Immanuel Bekker. Bonn, 1838.

Pichler, Aloysius. *Geschichte der Kirchlichen Trennung zwischen dem Orient und Occident*. 2 vols. Munich, 1864–5.

Pipinelis, Panayotis. 'Η Μοναρχία ἐν 'Ελλάδι [The monarchy in Greece]. Athens, 1932.

Pirri, Pietro. 'Lo statto della chiesa ortodossa di Costantinopoli...', *Miscellanea Pietro Fumasioni-Biondi*, pp. 79–103. Rome, 1947.

Pitzipios, Jacques G. *L'Eglise Orientale*. Rome, 1855.

La Question d'Orient, Mémoire sur la Politique Russe en Orient. Malta, 1852.

Pius IX. *Acta*, vol. I. Rome, 1854.

Pouqueville, François-C. *Histoire de la régénération de la Grèce*. 2nd ed., 4 vols. Paris, 1825.

Voyage de la Grèce. 2nd ed., 6 vols. Paris, 1826–7.

Prokesch-Osten, Anton F., von. *Geschichte des Abfalls der Griechen vom Türkischen Reiche in Jahre 1821 und der Gründung des Hellenischen Königreiches*. 6 vols. Vienna, 1867.

Rall, Hans. 'Die Anfänge des Konfessionspolitischen Ringens um den Wittelsbacher Thron in Athen', *Bayern: Staat und Kirche, Land und Reich*, pp. 181–216. Munich, 1961.

Raybaud, Maxime. *Mémoires sur la Grèce*. 2 vols. Paris, 1824–5.

Renseignemens sur la Grèce et sur l'administration du Comte Capodistrias (par un Grec Témoin oculaire). Paris, 1833.

Returns to an Address of the Honorable House of Commons by Sir Thomas Maitland of the Senate. London, 1822.

Rizo-Neroulos, Iakovos. *Histoire moderne de la Grèce depuis la chute de l'empire d'orient*. Geneva, 1828.

Romano, Gaetano. *Cenni Storici della Missione della Compagnia di Gesu in Grecia*. Palermo, 1912.

Runciman, Steven. *The Fall of Constantinople, 1453*. Cambridge, 1965.

'Russian Policy in Greece', *Foreign Quarterly Review*, XXXII (1836), pp. 361–85.

Rycaut, Paul. *The Present State of the Greek and Armenian Churches*. London, 1679.

Sathas, Konstantinos. Βιογραφικὸν Σχεδίασμα περὶ τοῦ Πατριάρχου 'Ιερεμίου Β' [Biographical Sketch of Patriarch Jeremias II]. Athens, 1870.

Schmitt, Herrmann J. *Kritische Geschichte der neugriechischen und der russischen Kirche*. Mainz, 1854.

Silbernagl, Isidor. *Verfassung und gegenwärtiger Bestand sämmtlicher Kirchen des Orients*. Landshut, 1865.

Skandamis, Andreas. Ἡ Τριακονταετία τῆς Βασιλείας τοῦ Ὄθονος, *1832–1862* [The thirty years of the monarchy of Otho]. Athens, 1961.

Smith, Thomas. *An Account of the Greek Church*. London, 1680.

Spiliadis, Nickolaos. Ἀπομνημονεύματα διὰ νὰ χρησιμεύσωσιν εἰς τὴν νέαν ἱστορίαν τῆς Ἑλλάδος [Memoirs to serve for a modern history of Greece]. 2 vols. Athens, 1851.

Stephanides, Vasileios. 'Die geschichtliche Entwicklung der Synoden des Patriarchats von Konstantinopel', *Zeitschrift für Kirchengeschichte*, LV (1936), nos. 1 and 2, pp. 127–58.

Ἐκκλησιαστικὴ Ἱστορία ἀπ' ἀρχῆς μέχρι σήμερον [Ecclesiastical History from the beginning until the present]. Athens, 1948.

'Οἱ πρῶτοι μετὰ τὴν Ἅλωσιν χρόνοι τοῦ Οἰκουμενικοῦ Πατριαρχείου καὶ ἡ γένεσις τοῦ Γεροντισμοῦ' [The first years of the Ecumenical Patriarchate after the Conquest and the beginning of the Senate], Ἐκκλησιαστικὴ Ἀλήθεια, XXXV (1915).

Συμβολαὶ εἰς τὴν ἐκκλησιαστικὴν ἱστορίαν καὶ τὸ ἐκκλησιαστικὸν δίκαιον [Contributions to church history and law]. Constantinople, 1921.

Strong, Frederick. *Greece as a Kingdom; or a Statistical Description of that country from the arrival of King Otho in 1833 to the Present Time*. London, 1842.

Temperley, Harold. *England and the Near East, the Crimea*. London, 1936.

Thiersch, Frédéric. *De l'Etat actuel de la Grèce*. 2 vols. Leipzig, 1833.

Thouvenel, L. *La Grèce du roi Othon*. Paris, 1890.

Topping, Peter. 'Greek Historical Writing on the Period, 1453–1914', *Journal of Modern History*, XXXIII, no. 2 (June, 1961), pp. 157–73.

Tournefort, Joseph P. *Relation d'un voyage du Levant*. 2 vols. Paris, 1717.

Trikoupis, Spyridon. Ἱστορία τῆς Ἑλληνικῆς Ἐπαναστάσεως [A History of the Greek Revolution]. 4 vols. London, 1853–7.

Ubicini, Jean Henri. *Lettres sur la Turquie*. 2 vols. Paris, 1853.

Vailhé, S. 'Eglise de Constantinople', *Dictionnaire de Théologie Catholique* (1910), III, pp. 1307–1519.

Vakalopoulos, Apostolos. Ἱστορία τοῦ Νέου Ἑλληνισμοῦ [History of New Hellenism], vol. I. Thessaloniki, 1961.

Vamvas, Neophytos. Ἀντεπίκρισις εἰς τὴν ὑπὸ Πρεσβυτέρου καὶ Οἰκονόμου Κωνσταντίνου τοῦ ἐξ Οἰκονόμων ἐπίκρισιν [A counter criticism of the critique by the priest and oekonom, Konstantinos of the Oekonomos]. Athens, 1839.

Ἀπάντησις πρὸς τὴν γενομένην διατριβὴν παρὰ τοῦ κ. Γερμανοῦ κατὰ μεταφράσεως τῶν Ἱερῶν Γραφῶν καὶ τῆς Βιβλικῆς Ἑταιρείας [An answer to the treatise by Germanos against the translation of Holy Scripture and the Biblical Society]. Athens, 1835.

Διατριβὴ αὐτοσχέδιος καὶ περὶ τῆς Ἀρχῆς τῆς Ἐξουσίας τῶν Πατριαρχῶν καὶ περὶ τῆς Σχέσεως τῆς Ἐκκλησιαστικῆς Ἀρχῆς πρὸς τὴν Πολιτικὴν Ἐξουσίαν [A timely treatise concerning the origin and the authority of the patriarchs and the relation between church authority and civil power]. Athens, 1843.

Περὶ τῆς Νεοελληνικῆς Ἐκκλησίας [Concerning the new Greek church]. Athens, 1838.

Vapheides, Philaretos. *Ἐκκλησιαστικὴ Ἱστορία ἀπὸ τοῦ Κυρίου Ἡμῶν Ἰησοῦ Χριστοῦ μέχρι τῶν καθ' ἡμᾶς χρόνων* [Church History from Our Lord Jesus Christ until our own times], vol. III. Constantinople, 1912.

Velandiotis, Ezekiel. *Ἰωσὴφ ὁ Ἀνδρούσης, ὅμηρος δεσμοφόρος ἐν Τριπολιτζᾷ, μινίστρος τῆς Θρησκείας καὶ Δικαίου κατὰ τὸν Ἀγῶνα* [Joseph of Androusa, imprisoned hostage in Tripolitza, Minister of Religion and of Justice during the war]. Athens, 1906.

Villemain, Abel. *Lascaris, ou les Grecs du quinzième siècle*. Paris, 1825.

Vourazelis, Helen. *Ὁ Βίος τοῦ Ἑλληνικοῦ Λαοῦ κατὰ τὴν Τουρκοκρατίαν ἐπὶ τῇ βάσει ξένων περιηγητῶν* [The life of the Greek people under Turkish rule from the descriptions of travellers]. Athens, 1939.

Vovolinis, Konstantinos. *Ἡ Ἐκκλησία εἰς τὸν Ἀγῶνα τῆς Ἐλευθερίας* [The church in the struggle for freedom]. Athens, 1952.

Waddington, George. *The Conditions and Prospects of the Greek or Oriental Church*. 2nd ed. London, 1854.

Walsh, Robert. *A Residence in Constantinople*. 2 vols. London, 1836.

Ware, Timothy. *Eustratios Argenti: A Study of the Greek Church under Turkish Rule*. Oxford, 1964.

Webster, Charles. *The Foreign Policy of Castlereagh, 1815–1822*. London, 1925.

Wenger, J. *Beiträge zur Kenntniss des gegenwärtigen Geistes und Zustandes der Griechischen Kirche in Griechenland und der Türkei*. Berlin, 1839.

Woodhouse, C. M. *The Greek War of Independence*. London, 1952.

Ypsilantis, Athanasios. *Τὰ μετὰ τὴν Ἅλωσιν* [Events after the Conquest]. Constantinople, 1870.

Zakythinos, Dionysios. *Ἡ Πολιτικὴ Ἱστορία τῆς Νεωτέρας Ἑλλάδος* [The Political History of Recent Greece]. Athens, 1962.

Ἡ Τουρκοκρατία: Εἰσαγωγὴ εἰς τὴν Νεωτέραν Ἱστορίαν τοῦ Ἑλληνισμοῦ [The Turkish rule: an introduction into the recent history of Hellenism]. Athens, 1957.

Zallonis, Marc-Philippe. *Essai sur les Fanariotes*. Marseilles, 1824.

NEWSPAPERS

Athens	*Αἰών* [Century], 1832–52.
Nauplion and Athens	*Ἀθῆνα* [Athens], 1835–52.
Nauplion and Athens	*Σωτήρ* [Savior], 1834–8.
Nauplion	*Εὐαγγελικὴ Σάλπιγξ* [The Gospel Trumpet], 1834–5.
Smyrna	*Courrier de Smyrne*, 1829–31.
Idhra	*Ὁ Φίλος τοῦ Νόμου* [Friend of the Law], 1825–6.
London	*The Times*, 1830–5.

GOVERNMENT PUBLICATIONS

Ἐφημερὶς τῆς Κυβερνήσεως [The Government Newspaper]. Nauplion, 1833–4; Athens, 1834–52.

Γενικὴ Ἐφημερὶς τῆς Ἑλλάδος [General newspaper of Greece]. Aegina, 1827–9; Nauplion, 1829–31.

Πρακτικά, Ἡ τῆς Τρίτης Σεπτεμβρίου ἐν Ἀθήναις Ἐθνικὴ Συνέλευσις [Acts. The National Assembly of the Third of September in Athens]. Athens, 1844.

Πρακτικὰ τῶν Συνεδριάσεων τῆς Βουλῆς ἐν τῇ Πρώτῃ Βουλευτικῇ Συνόδῳ τοῦ ἔτους 1844–1845 [Acts of the meetings of the Assembly in the first parliamentary session of the year 1844–1845], vol. III. Athens, 1846.

Πρακτικὰ τῶν Συνεδριάσεων τῆς Βουλῆς κατὰ τὴν Δευτέραν Σύνοδον τῆς τρίτης περιόδου, 1852 [Acts of the meetings of the Assembly in the second session of the third period, 1852], vol. II. Athens, 1852.

INDEX